PRACTICAL SHOP MATHEMATICS

Thomas C. Power

Gregg Division
McGraw-Hill Book Company

New York   St. Louis   Dallas   San Francisco   Auckland
Bogotá   Düsseldorf   Johannesburg   London   Madrid
Mexico   Montreal   New Delhi   Panama   Paris
São Paulo   Singapore   Sydney   Tokyo   Toronto

Related McGraw-Hill Books

Breneman: Mathematics, second edition
Cooke, Adams: Arithmetic Review for Electronics
Cooke, Adams: Basic Mathematics for Electronics, fourth edition
Calter: Problem Solving with Computers
Dow: Basic Industrial Mathematics: A Text Workbook
Hemmerling: Elementary Mathematics for the Technician
Jamison: Introduction to Computer Science Mathematics
Kuehn: Mathematics for Electricians, third edition
Palmer, Bibb, Jarvis, & Mrachek: Practical Mathematics, sixth edition
Rice, Knight: Matematicas Technicas, second edition
Rice, Knight: Technical Mathematics, third edition
Rice, Knight: Technical Mathematics with Calculus, third edition
Richmond: Calculus for Electronics, second edition
Schachter: Calculus and Analytic Geometry
Singer: Basic Mathematics for Electricity & Electronics, fourth edition
Singer: Mathematics at Work: Fractions
Singer: Mathematics at Work: Decimals
Singer: Mathematics at Work: Algebra
Zurflieh: Basic Technical Mathematics Explained

To my wife Starene.

Library of Congress Cataloging in Publication Data

Power, Thomas C
  Practical shop mathematics.

  Includes index.
  1. Shop mathematics. I. Title.
TJ1165.P69   512'.1   78-8943
ISBN 0-07-050591-8

1234567890 WCWC 7865432109

The editor for this book was Gerald O. Stoner, the art and design coordinator was Tracy Glasner, the designer was Blaise Zito Associates, Inc., the art supervisor was George T. Resch, the cover designer was Barbara Soll, and the production supervisor was May Konopka. It was set in Melior and Helvetica by A Graphic Method Inc.
Printed and bound by Webcrafters Inc.

CONTENTS

Expressing ratios
finding the value of x in a poopootion

PREFACE

This text has been prepared for students in entry-level occupational programs, and is suitable for the community college and secondary levels. Students involved in class-testing this material were from automotive mechanics, agriculture, drafting, forestry, machine shop, welding, and a variety of other trade programs.

The title *Practical Shop Mathematics* accurately describes this text. For instance, the fact that the small gear travels faster than the larger gear is a result of mathematical computation. Because a student can relate this to a practical concept, the understanding of both basic mathematics and shop concepts are enhanced. A workbook approach was chosen over a conventional format for two reasons. A workbook helps most students who have a difficult time in organizing mathematical solutions, and it provides the instructor with a convenient procedure.

The contents are organized into units which begin with basic fractions and progress to right-angle trigonometry. Within each unit, topics are introduced with worked-out examples and ample problems that can be used for teaching the topic or for homework assignment. Student evaluation problems test the students' progress periodically within each unit, and a set of comprehensive review questions test comprehension of the entire unit. Metrics are introduced in the fourth unit and then used interchangeably throughout the text.

This text provides numerous worked-out examples, but does *not* contain pages of explanations and rules—*Practical Shop Mathematics* does not rely on rote learning. Instead, it supplies many illustrated problems and allows instructors to use their own individual teaching skills.

Thomas C. Power

CHAPTER ONE
FRACTIONS

Although the use of calculators and the metric system would seem to make fractions obsolete, they are vital in measurement and exist in everyday experiences. This unit will provide a review of basic fraction skills and applications.

1-1
Numerators and Denominators

The most important rule to remember when working with any fraction is that the numerator and denominator ($\frac{N}{D}$) may be multiplied or divided by the same number and the value of the fraction is not changed.

Example

$\frac{1}{2}$ may be changed to $\frac{5}{16}$ by multiplying the numerator and denominator by 5 or multiplying by $\frac{5}{5}$.

$$\frac{1}{2} \times \frac{5}{5} = \frac{5}{10}$$

Example

$\frac{6}{18}$ may be divided by 6 provided both numerator and denominator are divided by 6 or divided by $\frac{6}{6}$.

$$\frac{6}{18} \div \frac{6}{6} = \frac{1}{3}$$

Exercises   Perform the indicated multiplication and division

1. $\frac{2}{3} \times \frac{4}{4} = \frac{8}{12}$ 2. $\frac{3}{4} \times \frac{6}{6} =$

3. $\frac{5}{8} \times \frac{5}{5} =$ 4. $\frac{3}{16} \times \frac{3}{3} =$

5. $\frac{3}{32} \times \frac{7}{7} =$ 6. $\frac{11}{16} \times \frac{4}{4} =$

7. $\dfrac{9}{64} \times \dfrac{5}{5} =$ 8. $\dfrac{7}{32} \times \dfrac{6}{6} =$

9. $\dfrac{10}{32} \div \dfrac{2}{2} =$ 10. $\dfrac{12}{16} \div \dfrac{4}{4} =$

11. $\dfrac{8}{32} \div \dfrac{8}{8} =$ 12. $\dfrac{14}{32} \div \dfrac{2}{2} =$

13. $\dfrac{24}{64} \div \dfrac{8}{8} =$ 14. $\dfrac{8}{16} \div \dfrac{8}{8} =$

15. $\dfrac{12}{32} \div \dfrac{4}{4} =$ 16. $\dfrac{11}{33} \div \dfrac{11}{11} =$

Reduce to lowest terms:

17. $\dfrac{8}{16} \div \dfrac{\mathbf{8}}{\mathbf{8}} = \dfrac{\mathbf{1}}{\mathbf{2}}$ 18. $\dfrac{12}{32}$

19. $\dfrac{14}{16}$ 20. $\dfrac{6}{8}$

21. $\dfrac{48}{64}$ 22. $\dfrac{24}{32}$

1-2 Common Denominators

In working with fractions, it is often necessary to change all fractions so that they will have a common denominator. For instance, in order to add $\frac{1}{2}$, $\frac{1}{5}$, and $\frac{3}{4}$, the fractions would be changed to fractions with the same denominator, preferably the smallest number. By inspection or trial and error it would appear that a denominator of 20 would work.

Example

$$\dfrac{1}{2} \times \dfrac{\mathbf{10}}{\mathbf{10}} = \dfrac{\mathbf{10}}{\mathbf{20}}$$

$$\dfrac{1}{5} \times \dfrac{\mathbf{4}}{\mathbf{4}} = \dfrac{\mathbf{4}}{\mathbf{20}}$$

$$\dfrac{3}{4} \times \dfrac{\mathbf{5}}{\mathbf{5}} = \dfrac{\mathbf{15}}{\mathbf{20}}$$

A common denominator can be determined by multiplying the original denominators together. As in the case above, multiply the denominators $2 \times 5 \times 4 = 40$. Note that this process does not always give the lowest common denominator, but it will give one that is common to all denominators.

Exercises

In each of the following problems, write the given fractions as equivalent fractions with denominators that are equal, preferably the lowest common denominator.

1. $\dfrac{1}{2}, \dfrac{3}{4}, \dfrac{5}{16} = \dfrac{\mathbf{8}}{\mathbf{16}}, \dfrac{\mathbf{12}}{\mathbf{16}}, \dfrac{\mathbf{5}}{\mathbf{16}}$ 　　2. $\dfrac{1}{4}, \dfrac{1}{3}, \dfrac{5}{12} =$

3. $\dfrac{2}{3}, \dfrac{3}{4}, \dfrac{2}{6} =$ 　　4. $\dfrac{5}{8}, \dfrac{2}{3}, \dfrac{1}{2} =$

5. $\dfrac{1}{4}, \dfrac{2}{3}, \dfrac{4}{9} =$ 　　6. $\dfrac{4}{8}, \dfrac{3}{8}, \dfrac{7}{12} =$

7. $\dfrac{7}{8}, \dfrac{3}{4}, \dfrac{3}{16} =$ 　　8. $\dfrac{5}{8}, \dfrac{7}{32}, \dfrac{3}{16} =$

9. $\dfrac{11}{16}, \dfrac{3}{4}, \dfrac{9}{64} =$ 　　10. $\dfrac{1}{4}, \dfrac{3}{4}, \dfrac{7}{20} =$

1-3
Determining the Missing Numerator or Denominator

In small fractions this can usually be done by inspection:

Example

$$\dfrac{3}{4} = \dfrac{?}{20}$$

$\dfrac{5}{5}$ would be the multiplier

$$\dfrac{\mathbf{3}}{\mathbf{4}} \times \dfrac{\mathbf{5}}{\mathbf{5}} = \dfrac{\mathbf{15}}{\mathbf{20}}$$

If this multiplier were not obvious, the denominator of 20 could be divided by 4 ($20 \div 4 = 5$) and then the numerator could be multiplied by 5.

Example

$$\dfrac{3}{4} = \dfrac{?}{\boxed{20}}$$

$$\mathbf{20 \div 4 = 5}$$

$$\dfrac{\mathbf{3}}{\mathbf{4}} \times \dfrac{\mathbf{5}}{\mathbf{5}} = \dfrac{\mathbf{15}}{\mathbf{20}}$$

Example

$$\dfrac{2}{3} = \dfrac{?}{\boxed{66}}$$

$$\mathbf{66 \div 3 = 22}$$

$$\dfrac{\mathbf{2}}{\mathbf{3}} \times \dfrac{\mathbf{22}}{\mathbf{22}} = \dfrac{\mathbf{44}}{\mathbf{66}}$$

Exercises Insert the missing numerator or denominator so that the fraction is equivalent to the given fraction:

1. $\dfrac{1}{2} = \dfrac{\mathbf{4}}{8}$ 　　2. $\dfrac{3}{5} = \dfrac{}{20}$ 　　3. $\dfrac{5}{6} = \dfrac{}{48}$

4. $\dfrac{7}{8} = \dfrac{}{56}$ 　　5. $\dfrac{2}{7} = \dfrac{}{42}$ 　　6. $\dfrac{2}{3} = \dfrac{18}{}$

7. $\dfrac{3}{4} = \dfrac{24}{}$ 　　8. $\dfrac{9}{16} = \dfrac{63}{}$ 　　9. $\dfrac{3}{10} = \dfrac{27}{}$

10. $\dfrac{2}{11} = \dfrac{16}{}$ 　　11. $\dfrac{2}{5} = \dfrac{}{70}$ 　　12. $\dfrac{3}{10} = \dfrac{21}{}$

13. $\dfrac{5}{24} = \dfrac{}{72}$

14. $\dfrac{3}{32} = \dfrac{24}{}$

15. $\dfrac{7}{36} = \dfrac{}{216}$

16. $\dfrac{3}{25} = \dfrac{18}{}$

Write each of the following fractions as an equivalent fraction with a denominator of 36:

17. $\dfrac{3}{18} = \dfrac{\mathbf{6}}{\mathbf{36}}$

18. $\dfrac{1}{2} =$

19. $\dfrac{5}{6} =$

20. $\dfrac{3}{4} =$

21. $\dfrac{7}{12} =$

22. $\dfrac{7}{9} =$

23. $\dfrac{13}{18} =$

24. $\dfrac{2}{3} =$

25. $\dfrac{11}{12} =$

26. $\dfrac{17}{18} =$

27. $\dfrac{6}{6} =$

28. $\dfrac{1}{3} =$

1-4 Changing Improper Fractions

An improper fraction is one whose numerator is larger than its denominator, such as $\frac{12}{5}$. It can be changed to a mixed number by dividing the numerator by the denominator ($12 \div 5 = 2$ with a remainder of 2). Place the remainder over the divisor.

Example

$$\dfrac{12}{5} = \mathbf{2\dfrac{2}{5}} \qquad \text{or} \qquad 5\overline{)12} = \mathbf{2\dfrac{2}{5}}$$
$$\underline{10}$$
$$2 \text{ remainder}$$

Exercises Express each of the following fractions as a mixed number:

1. $\dfrac{8}{3} = \mathbf{2\dfrac{2}{3}}$

2. $\dfrac{29}{4} =$

3. $\dfrac{40}{3} =$

4. $\dfrac{26}{7} =$

5. $\dfrac{131}{5} =$

6. $\dfrac{45}{42} =$

7. $\dfrac{35}{4} =$

8. $\dfrac{27}{6} =$

9. $\dfrac{53}{8} =$

1-5 Changing Mixed Numbers to Improper Fractions

A mixed number like $4\frac{2}{3}$ can be changed to an improper fraction by multiplying the denominator of the fraction times the whole number and then adding the numerator. The result is placed over the original denominator of the fraction.

Example $4\overset{\curvearrowright}{}\dfrac{2}{3}$ $\mathbf{3 \times 4 + 2 = 14}$ **or** $\dfrac{\mathbf{14}}{\mathbf{3}}$

Exercises Change the following mixed numbers to improper fractions:

1. $6\dfrac{1}{4} = \dfrac{\mathbf{25}}{\mathbf{4}}$

2. $8\dfrac{1}{3} =$

3. $7\dfrac{2}{5} =$

4. $18\dfrac{2}{3} =$

5. $22\dfrac{1}{2} =$

6. $64\dfrac{2}{3} =$

7. $10\dfrac{1}{4} =$

8. $125\dfrac{3}{5} =$

9. $500\dfrac{1}{2} =$

EVALUATION PROBLEMS

What denominator is common to each of the following?

1. $\dfrac{1}{8}, \dfrac{5}{12}, \dfrac{7}{6} =$

2. $\dfrac{1}{9}, \dfrac{7}{12}, \dfrac{3}{4} =$

3. $\dfrac{5}{16}, \dfrac{3}{8}, \dfrac{1}{32} =$

4. $\dfrac{9}{64}, \dfrac{13}{32}, \dfrac{5}{8} =$

5. $\dfrac{15}{96}, \dfrac{7}{8}, \dfrac{11}{12} =$

6. $\dfrac{4}{5}, \dfrac{3}{4}, \dfrac{7}{10} =$

Express each fraction as a mixed number:

7. $\dfrac{9}{4} =$

8. $\dfrac{18}{5} =$

9. $\dfrac{49}{8} =$

10. $\dfrac{13}{3} =$

11. $\dfrac{425}{16} =$

12. $\dfrac{33}{7} =$

13. $\dfrac{25}{4} =$ 　　　14. $\dfrac{327}{5} =$ 　　　15. $\dfrac{19}{7} =$

Express each of the following as an improper fraction:

16. $7\dfrac{1}{8} =$ 　　　17. $15\dfrac{2}{3} =$ 　　　18. $42\dfrac{1}{2} =$

19. $13\dfrac{1}{3} =$ 　　　20. $120\dfrac{2}{3} =$ 　　　21. $19\dfrac{7}{8} =$

22. $32\dfrac{3}{5} =$ 　　　23. $400\dfrac{3}{4} =$ 　　　24. $26\dfrac{3}{7} =$

1-6
Adding Fractions

Fractions may be added together if we keep in mind the first rule of addition: only like things can be added. Feet and inches cannot be added together, only feet to feet and inches to inches. Fractions are *like things* when the denominators are equal.

To add $\frac{1}{4}$ and $\frac{1}{3}$, a common denominator is needed. The lowest common denominator is more desirable, but any common denominator will work. When a common denominator is not apparent, then multiply the denominators together. In this case the denominator of 12 (4 × 3) is also the lowest common denominator.

Example

$$\frac{1}{4} = \frac{3}{12}$$
$$+\frac{1}{3} = \frac{4}{12}$$
$$\overline{\qquad \frac{7}{12}}$$

Like things

When the answer is an improper fraction, change it to a mixed number and reduce to lowest terms.

Example

$$\frac{7}{8} = \frac{14}{16}$$
$$+\frac{3}{4} = \frac{12}{16}$$
$$\overline{\frac{26}{16}} = 1\frac{10}{16} = 1\frac{5}{8}$$

When both whole units and fractions are added, handle the whole units separately from the fractions.

Example

$$3\frac{3}{4} + 6\frac{2}{3} = \qquad 3\ \Big|\ \frac{3}{4} = \frac{9}{12}$$
$$+6\ \Big|\ \frac{2}{3} = \frac{8}{12}$$
$$\overline{9 \qquad \frac{17}{12} = 1\frac{5}{12} = 10\frac{5}{12}}$$

Add whole units

Exercises Perform the indicated addition and reduce answers to lowest terms:

1. $9\frac{7}{8} + 3\frac{1}{4} = 9\frac{7}{8} + 3\frac{2}{8} = 12\frac{9}{8} = 13\frac{1}{8}$

2. $6\frac{1}{3} + 5\frac{5}{6} =$

3. $2\frac{1}{2} + 4\frac{5}{6} + 3\frac{1}{3} =$

4. $6\frac{1}{4} + 9\frac{5}{6} + 4\frac{2}{3} =$

5. $9\dfrac{1}{4} + 4\dfrac{1}{2} =$

6. $7\dfrac{3}{8} + 3\dfrac{1}{4} =$

7. $5\dfrac{3}{4} + 6\dfrac{3}{4} + 2\dfrac{1}{2} =$

8. $10\dfrac{5}{16} + 4\dfrac{3}{8} + 8\dfrac{1}{2} =$

1-7 Subtracting Fractions

When subtracting fractions, rules similar to those for adding fractions are applied. However, when subtracting mixed numbers, the fraction in the *subtrahend* (the number to be subtracted) may be larger than the fraction in the *minuend* (the number to be subtracted from). The operation of borrowing from the units column must then be used.

Example

$$4\dfrac{1}{3} - 2\dfrac{2}{3} = \text{④}\dfrac{1}{3} = 3\dfrac{1}{3} + \dfrac{3}{3} = 3\dfrac{4}{3}$$

$$-2\dfrac{2}{3} \qquad -2\dfrac{2}{3}$$

$$\overline{} \qquad \overline{1\dfrac{2}{3}}$$

$$\text{Borrow } 1 \leftrightarrow 1 = \left(\dfrac{3}{3}\right)$$

Exercises Perform the indicated subtraction and reduce answer to lowest terms.

1. $24\dfrac{1}{8} - 13\dfrac{5}{8} = 23\dfrac{9}{8} - 13\dfrac{5}{8} = 10\dfrac{4}{8} = 10\dfrac{1}{2}$

2. $15\dfrac{3}{8} - 7 =$

3. $21 - 6\dfrac{3}{8} =$

4. $13\dfrac{5}{8} - 4\dfrac{7}{8} =$

5. $10\dfrac{1}{2} - 6\dfrac{3}{8} =$

6. $18\dfrac{3}{4} - 4\dfrac{7}{8} =$

7. $9\dfrac{5}{8} - 6\dfrac{7}{8} =$

8. $16\dfrac{1}{8} - 15\dfrac{1}{2} =$

1-8 Application of Addition and Subtraction

In a machine-parts catalog, a diagram of a bolt is shown as indicated in Fig. 1-1. This diagram is used to cover several lengths of bolts. The unthreaded shaft size may vary for a series of bolts, while the threaded size may remain constant. To determine the total length of a bolt, it would be necessary to add their dimensions.

Example 1

Find the total length of the bolt in Fig. 1-1.

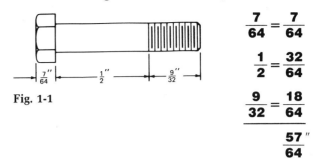

$$\frac{7}{64} = \frac{7}{64}$$

$$\frac{1}{2} = \frac{32}{64}$$

$$\frac{9}{32} = \frac{18}{64}$$

$$\frac{57}{64}''$$

Fig. 1-1

Determining the difference between the diameters in a tapered shaft is an important step when turning such a piece on a lathe. Figure 1-2a illustrates a three-dimensional view of such a taper. Figure 1-2b illustrates a flat view taken from a hardware catalog or one that might be sketched before calculating a taper.

Example 2

Using the dimensions in Fig. 1-2b, calculate the difference between the diameters.

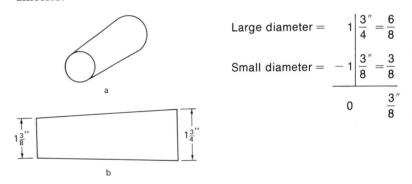

Large diameter $= \quad 1\frac{3}{4}'' = \frac{6}{8}$

Small diameter $= \quad -1\frac{3}{8}'' = \frac{3}{8}$

$$0 \qquad \frac{3}{8}''$$

Fig. 1-2

Round stock can be reduced in diameter on a lathe as illustrated in Fig. 1-3a. As Fig. 1-3b illustrates, the process of measuring this reduction is similar to looking at the end of a piece of pipe and measuring the inside and outside diameter of the pipe.

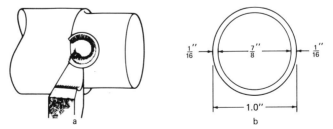

Fig. 1-3

The inside diameter of the pipe represents the finished diameter of the stock, and the outside diameter repesents the original diameter of the stock. The thickness of the pipe represents the depth of cut taken on the lathe.

Example 3

Find the depth of cut required to reduce a 1″-diameter round stock to $\frac{7}{8}$″.

$$1.0'' - \frac{7}{8}^{''} = \frac{1}{8}^{''} \text{ (both thicknesses)}$$

$$\frac{1}{8}^{''} \div 2 = \frac{1}{16}^{''}$$

Note: To divide a fraction by 2, double the denominator.

Exercises
Applications of Fractions

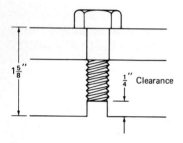

Fig. 1-4

1. What would be the *shank length* (unthreaded portion) of the bolt required to fasten the plate in Fig. 1-4? The threaded portion is $\frac{13}{16}$″ and $\frac{1}{4}$″ clearance is required between the end of the bolt and the bottom of the hole.

_____ Answer

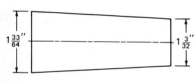

Fig. 1-5

2. Find the difference between the diameters of the tapered shaft shown in Fig. 1-5.

_____ Answer

3. The outside diameter of the plastic pipe in Fig. 1-6 is $3\frac{3}{8}$″. If the pipe is $\frac{7}{32}$″ thick, find the inside diameter.

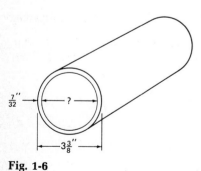

Fig. 1-6

_____ Answer

4. A steel rod $\frac{3}{8}''$ in diameter was cut into five pieces. The lengths of the pieces were as follows: $2\frac{1}{8}''$, $3\frac{3}{8}''$, $7\frac{4}{32}''$, $5\frac{7}{8}''$, and $1\frac{1}{4}''$. What was the original length of the rod? Neglect any waste in cutting the rod.

_____ Answer

5. A piece of round stock with a $1\frac{7}{8}''$ diameter is to be turned down on a lathe. If the cut to be made is $\frac{1}{8}''$, what is the final diameter of the stock?

_____ Answer

6. The rainfall recorded at the San Francisco International Airport for a period of four days was as follows: $\frac{3}{4}''$, $1\frac{1}{2}''$, $\frac{7}{8}''$, and $\frac{3}{4}''$. What was the total rainfall for that period?

_____ Answer

7. Several different steel castings are to be poured. The castings weigh $10\frac{1}{4}$ lb, $40\frac{1}{2}$ lb, and $16\frac{3}{4}$ lb. What will the total weight of the steel used in these castings be?

_____ Answer

8. A plumber cut a 21' length of galvanized pipe into several lengths. If the lengths of the pipe cut were $5\frac{3}{4}'$, $2\frac{1}{3}'$, $1\frac{1}{2}'$, $6\frac{5}{8}'$, how many feet of pipe were cut? How many feet of pipe remained?

_____ Answer

9. The wall thickness of a round piece of tubing is $\frac{5}{16}''$ and the outside diameter of the tubing is $2\frac{5}{8}''$. What is the inside diameter of the tubing?

_____ Answer

10. Find the missing dimension in Fig. 1-7 if the total length is $3\frac{1}{4}''$.

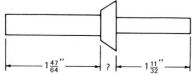

Fig. 1-7

_____ Answer

1-9
Multiplication of
Fractions

This operation is the easiest to perform if the multiplication tables have been mastered. First, multiply the numerators together. Then, multiply the denominators together and reduce the results to lowest terms.

Example
$$\frac{3}{4} \times \frac{5}{8} \qquad \frac{3 \times 5 = 15}{4 \times 8 = 32} = \frac{15}{32}$$

If fractions can be canceled, the operation of multiplication can be simplified.

Example
$$\frac{4}{15} \times \frac{5}{12} \qquad \frac{\overset{1}{\cancel{4}}}{\underset{3}{\cancel{15}}} \times \frac{\overset{1}{\cancel{5}}}{\underset{3}{\cancel{12}}} = \frac{1}{9}$$

Exercises
Perform the indicated functions and reduce all answers to lowest terms.

1. $\dfrac{2}{3} \times \dfrac{4}{7} = \dfrac{\mathbf{8}}{\mathbf{21}}$

2. $\dfrac{7}{9} \times \dfrac{2}{5} =$

3. $\dfrac{\overset{1}{\cancel{4}}}{9} \times \dfrac{5}{\cancel{8}} = \dfrac{\mathbf{5}}{\mathbf{18}}$ 2

4. $\dfrac{7}{27} \times \dfrac{3}{10} =$ 5. $\dfrac{2}{3} \times \dfrac{3}{4} =$ 6. $\dfrac{3}{5} \times \dfrac{10}{27} =$

7. $\dfrac{4}{5} \times \dfrac{35}{24} =$ 8. $\dfrac{28}{10} \times \dfrac{20}{21} =$ 9. $4 \times \dfrac{2}{3} =$

10. $9 \times \dfrac{3}{4} =$ 11. $15 \times \dfrac{3}{20} =$ 12. $\dfrac{16}{3} \times \dfrac{3}{16} =$

1-10
Division of Fractions

To divide fractions, the *divisor* (the fraction to be divided into the other fraction) is inverted, and the operation of multiplication is performed.

Example

$$\dfrac{1}{4} \div \dfrac{2}{3} \quad \text{Invert } \dfrac{2}{3}$$

$$\dfrac{1}{4} \times \dfrac{3}{2} = \dfrac{3}{8}$$

Note: Always invert before cancellation.

Exercises   Divide the following, and reduce all answers to lowest terms.

1. $\dfrac{1}{5} \div \dfrac{1}{2} = \dfrac{1}{5} \times \dfrac{2}{1} = \dfrac{2}{5}$ 2. $\dfrac{1}{4} \div \dfrac{5}{16} =$

3. $\dfrac{2}{3} \div \dfrac{1}{9} =$ 4. $\dfrac{4}{20} \div \dfrac{3}{5} =$

5. $4 \div \dfrac{2}{3} =$ 6. $\dfrac{2}{3} \div 6 =$

7. $\dfrac{9}{35} \div \dfrac{27}{28} =$ 8. $\dfrac{3}{4} \div 6 =$

9. $\dfrac{5}{8} \div \dfrac{9}{13} =$ 10. $6 \div \dfrac{3}{4} =$

11. $\dfrac{26}{45} \div \dfrac{39}{36} =$ 12. $\dfrac{45}{49} \div \dfrac{20}{63} =$

1-11
Multiplication and Division of Mixed Numbers

Change to improper fraction. Cancel when possible.

$$2\dfrac{1}{2} \times 3\dfrac{1}{3}$$

Example

$$\dfrac{5}{2} \times \dfrac{\overset{5}{\cancel{10}}}{3} = \dfrac{25}{3}$$
$$\underset{1}{}$$

Simplify by changing to a mixed number.

$$\frac{25}{3} = 8\frac{1}{3}$$

Example

$$5\frac{1}{2} \div 2\frac{1}{4}$$

Change to improper fraction.

$$\frac{11}{2} \div \frac{9}{4}$$

Invert, cancel, and multiply.

$$\frac{11}{\cancel{2}_{1}} \times \frac{\cancel{4}^{2}}{9} = \frac{22}{9}$$

Simplify.

$$\frac{22}{9} = 2\frac{4}{9}$$

Exercises Perform the indicated operations:

1. $9\frac{1}{7} \times 6\frac{1}{8} = \frac{\cancel{64}^{8}}{\cancel{7}_{1}} \times \frac{\cancel{49}^{7}}{\cancel{8}_{1}} = 56$ 2. $4\frac{2}{5} \times 7\frac{3}{6} =$

3. $3\frac{3}{4} \times 3\frac{1}{5} =$ 4. $9\frac{7}{9} \times 3\frac{3}{11} =$

5. $5\frac{5}{8} \times \frac{1}{9} =$ 6. $3\frac{8}{9} \times \frac{3}{7} =$

7. $5\frac{1}{3} \times 3\frac{3}{4} =$ 8. $11\frac{1}{9} \times 2\frac{4}{25} =$

9. $5\frac{5}{8} \times 6\frac{2}{5} =$ 10. $7\frac{1}{2} \div \frac{5}{6} = \frac{15}{2} \div \frac{5}{6}$

$$= \frac{\cancel{15}^{3}}{\cancel{2}_{1}} \times \frac{\cancel{6}^{3}}{\cancel{5}_{1}} = 9$$

11. $8\frac{2}{6} \div 3\frac{1}{3} =$ 12. $5\frac{2}{8} \div 1\frac{3}{4} =$

13. $7\frac{6}{7} \div 1\frac{4}{7} =$ 14. $5\frac{5}{8} \div \frac{9}{16} =$

15. $3\frac{8}{9} \div \frac{7}{18} =$ 16. $5\frac{4}{9} \div 2\frac{1}{3} =$

EVALUATION PROBLEMS

Collect the fractions and reduce to lowest terms:

1. $\dfrac{13}{16} + \dfrac{5}{24} - \dfrac{5}{48} =$

2. $\dfrac{19}{20} - \dfrac{2}{5} - \dfrac{3}{8} =$

3. $\dfrac{15}{16} + \dfrac{5}{8} - \dfrac{3}{4} =$

4. $\dfrac{23}{24} - \dfrac{17}{36} + \dfrac{5}{24} =$

5. $\dfrac{3}{5} - \dfrac{1}{9} + \dfrac{8}{45} =$

6. $\dfrac{2}{2} - \dfrac{5}{18} + \dfrac{1}{2} =$

7. $\dfrac{17}{28} - \dfrac{3}{14} + \dfrac{5}{7} =$

8. $\dfrac{15}{16} + \dfrac{7}{8} - \dfrac{1}{4} =$

9. $\dfrac{9}{10} + \dfrac{4}{5} - \dfrac{1}{2} =$

10. $\dfrac{7}{36} - \dfrac{5}{18} + \dfrac{5}{6} =$

Multiply each of the following:

11. $12 \times \dfrac{5}{8} =$

12. $\dfrac{3}{4} \times 6 =$

13. $\dfrac{45}{28} \times \dfrac{14}{63} =$

14. $\dfrac{2}{3} \times \dfrac{5}{8} \times \dfrac{2}{5} =$

15. $\dfrac{4}{9} \times \dfrac{15}{22} \times \dfrac{6}{40} =$

16. $\dfrac{16}{63} \times \dfrac{35}{6} \times \dfrac{3}{2} =$

17. $\dfrac{15}{22} \times \dfrac{33}{35} \times \dfrac{14}{39} =$

18. $6 \times \dfrac{21}{52} \times \dfrac{39}{49} =$

19. $\dfrac{40}{63} \times \dfrac{21}{72} \times 15 =$

20. $\dfrac{50}{15} \times 18 \times \dfrac{6}{63} =$

Divide as indicated:

21. $2\dfrac{1}{5} \div 1\dfrac{1}{7} =$

22. $2\dfrac{1}{5} \div 4\dfrac{7}{8} =$

23. $3\dfrac{3}{4} \div 5 =$

24. $15 \div 6\dfrac{1}{4} =$

25. $4\dfrac{11}{16} \div 1\dfrac{21}{24} =$

26. $\dfrac{7}{8} \div 5\dfrac{1}{4} =$

27. $1\dfrac{31}{32} \div 3\dfrac{17}{20} =$

28. $11\dfrac{2}{3} \div 2\dfrac{2}{9} =$

29. $4\dfrac{4}{5} \div \dfrac{4}{15} =$

30. $12\dfrac{3}{5} \div 2\dfrac{2}{10} =$

1-12
Multiple-Hole Layout

Rather than have a drafter make a full layout as shown in Fig. 1-8b, the notation can be done as shown in Fig. 1-8a. Where the distance between the centers of the holes is the same, this notation saves work and does not clutter up the drawing.

Example

Find the distance between the center of the first hole and the center of the last hole in Fig. 1-8.

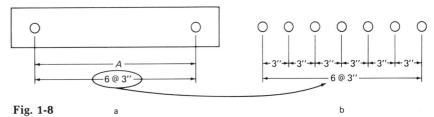

Fig. 1-8   a   b

6 @ 3″ indicates 6 spaces of 3″ each.

6 × 3″ = 18″ Answer

Exercises   Solve each of the following:

1. Sixteen rivets will be placed in the distance B in Fig. 1-9 (16 rivets require 15 spaces). Find the distance B and the total length l.

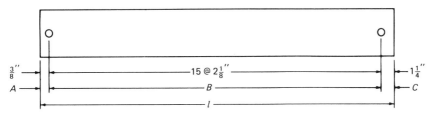

Fig. 1-9

$B =$ _____ Answer

$l =$ _____ Answer

2. Find the total length of the plate in Fig. 1-10.

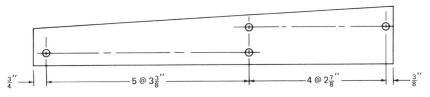

Fig. 1-10

_____ Answer

3. Find distance A and B of the cover plate illustrated in Fig. 1-11.

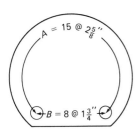

Fig. 1-11

$A =$ _____ Answer

$B =$ _____ Answer

4. Find the dimensions B, C, D, l, in Fig. 1-12.

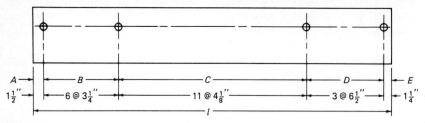

Fig. 1-12

$B =$ _____ Answer

$C =$ _____ Answer

$D =$ _____ Answer

$l =$ _____ Answer

1-13
Adding Feet and Inches

Common ruler measurements are made in feet, inches, and fractions of inches. When adding feet, inches, and fractions of inches, separate units into columns before adding or subtracting.

Example

Add $2'6\frac{1}{2}''$, $3'4\frac{1}{4}''$, and $4'8\frac{1}{2}''$

Add columns separately.

2'	**6**	$\frac{1}{2}'' = \frac{4}{8}$
3'	**4**	$\frac{1}{4}'' = \frac{2}{8}$
4'	**8**	$\frac{1}{2}'' = \frac{4}{8}$
9'	**18**	$\frac{10''}{8}$

Collect full units.

9'	**18**	$1\frac{2}{8}''$
9'	**19**	$\frac{1}{4}''$
10'	**7**	$\frac{1}{4}''$

Exercises Add the feet and inches as indicated:

1. 6' 10"
   8' 3"
   _____

2. $3'\ 4\frac{5}{8}''$
   $2'\ 9\frac{5}{8}''$
   $6'\ 7\frac{3}{4}''$
   _____

3. 2' 2"
   3' 8"
   17' 9"
   11' 10"
   _____

4. $7' \ 2\frac{1}{2}''$

$4' \ 6\frac{1}{2}''$

$10' \ 8\frac{1}{2}''$

$5' \ 4\frac{1}{2}''$

___

5. $12' \ 2''$

$10' \ 11''$

$8' \ 3''$

___

6. $4' \ 9''$

$10' \ 3''$

$18' \ 6''$

$9' \ 5''$

___

7. $6' \ 2\frac{1}{2}''$

$14' \ 10\frac{5}{8}''$

$8' \ 7\frac{7}{8}''$

$9' \ 9\frac{1}{4}''$

___

8. $5' \ 8\frac{1}{4}''$

$4' \ 11\frac{1}{8}''$

$10' \ 7\frac{3}{8}''$

$8' \ 9\frac{3}{4}''$

___

9. $8' \ 6''$

$10' \ 4''$

$5' \ 8''$

$7' \ 6\frac{1}{2}''$

$4' \ 3\frac{1}{2}''$

___

10. $7' \ 10\frac{1}{8}''$

$8' \ 7\frac{3}{8}''$

$2' \ \frac{5}{8}''$

$6' \ 4\frac{1}{2}''$

$5' \ 2\frac{3}{4}''$

___

1-14 Subtracting Feet and Inches

Example

$$6' \ 2\frac{3}{4}''$$

$$- \ 4' \ 3\frac{1}{4}''$$

___

Borrow 1' from the 6', as 1' = 12", and add the 12" to the inch column. Then, subtract as usual.

$$5' \ 14\frac{3}{4}''$$

$$- \ 4' \ \ 3\frac{1}{4}''$$

___

$$1' \ 11\frac{2}{4}'' \qquad \textbf{or} \qquad 1' \ 11\frac{1}{2}''$$

Exercises Subtract the feet and inches as indicated:

1. $\quad 12' \ 6\frac{1}{2}''$

$- \ \ 8' \ 4\frac{1}{4}''$

___

2. $\quad 3' \ 2\frac{1}{4}''$

$- \ 1' \ 1\frac{1}{2}''$

___

3.　32′ 8″
$- \ 4′ \ 9\frac{3}{4}″$
_____

4.　16′ 4″
$- \ 12′ \ 5″$
_____

5.　147′ $6\frac{1}{2}″$
$- \ 38′ \ 4\frac{3}{4}″$
_____

6.　8′ 0″
$- \ 0′ \ 91\frac{1}{2}″$
_____

1-15 Multiplying Feet and Inches

Example

Separate into columns and multiply each column by 3.

4′	8	$\frac{1}{2}″$
×	3	
12′	**24**	$1\frac{1}{2}″$

Collect full units.

12′ 25 $\frac{1}{2}″$

or

14′ 1 $\frac{1}{2}″$

Exercises　Multiply the feet and inches as indicated:

1.　6′ $2\frac{1}{2}″$
$\times \ 2$
_____

2.　3′ $2\frac{1}{4}″$
$\times \ 4$
_____

3.　16′ $6\frac{1}{2}″$
$\times \ 5$
_____

4.　8′ $6\frac{3}{4}″$
$\times \ 10$
_____

5.　10′ $10\frac{1}{2}″$
$\times \ 6$
_____

6.　2′ $\frac{1}{2}″$
$\times \ 8$
_____

1-16 Dividing Feet and Inches

Example

$$6′ \ 2\frac{1}{2}″ \div 4$$

Change all units to inches.

6 × 12 = 72″

$$72'' + 2\frac{1}{2}'' = 74\frac{1}{2}''$$

Divide by conventional method.

$$74\frac{1}{2}'' \div 4$$

$$\frac{149}{2} \times \frac{1}{4} = \frac{149}{8}$$

$$\frac{149}{8} = 18\frac{5}{8}''$$

Exercises   Divide the feet and inches as indicated:

1. $2' \ 5'' \div 2$ 2. $3' \ 6\frac{1}{2}'' \div 4$

3. $12' \ 4'' \div 6$ 4. $1' \ 3\frac{1}{4}'' \div 4$

5. $16' \ 9'' \div 8$ 6. $6' \ 16'' \div 8$

Exercises   Application of fractions.

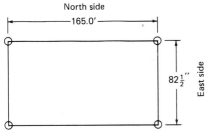

North side

|←———— 165.0' ————→|

$82\frac{1}{2}''$

East side

Fig. 1-13

1. Figure 1-13 illustrates an outline for fencing a rectangular lot. The posts will be set $5\frac{1}{2}'$ between centers. If only the north side of the lot were to be fenced, how many posts would be required?

_____ Answer

2. In Fig. 1-13, if just the east side were to be fenced, how many posts would be required?

_____ Answer

3. How many posts would be required to fence the entire lot in Fig. 1-13.

_____ Answer

4. How many $2\frac{7}{8}''$ plates can be cut from a length of brass stock $52''$ long? Allow $\frac{1}{4}''$ waste for each cut.

_____ Answer

5. How thick is the wall of a pipe whose inside diameter is $16\frac{3}{8}''$ and whose outside diameter is $19\frac{5}{16}''$?

_____ Answer

6. A welder has a pipe $19'8\frac{1}{2}''$ long that will be cut with a pipe cutter. How many $28\frac{1}{2}''$ pieces can be cut from this length? How much pipe will be left over? Allow nothing for waste.

_____ Answer

_____ Answer

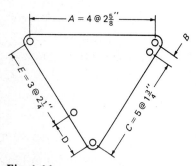

Fig. 1-14

7. The holes in the corners of the triangular plate in Fig. 1-14 are equally spaced. Determine the dimensions A, B, C, D, E.

A = _____ Answer

B = _____ Answer

C = _____ Answer

D = _____ Answer

E = _____ Answer

8. An outline sketch of a bookcase is illustrated in Fig. 1-15. The thickness of wood used in the shelving is $\frac{3}{4}''$. What will be the distance A between the shelves if they are equally spaced? The dimensions given are the outside dimensions of the bookcase.

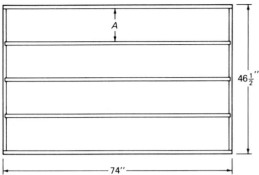

Fig. 1-15

_____ Answer

9. The bookcase in problem 8 is to hold back issues of _National Geographic_. The average magazine is approximately $\frac{5}{16}''$ thick. How many copies will it hold per shelf?

_____ Answer

10. A finished piece of steel casting weighs $82\frac{2}{3}$ lb. Before finishing it weighed $97\frac{1}{4}$ lb. If 800 castings are made, what will be the total loss of steel in the job?

_____ Answer

11. The copper wire used in the electrical service entrance of a home is purchased by the foot. Three pieces of wire will be required, and the wire will run through $14\frac{3}{4}'$ of conduit. If 18″ of excess wire will be needed at each end of the conduit to make the electrical connections, how many feet of wire must be purchased?

_____ Answer

12. A house plan calls for a scale of $\frac{1}{8}'' = 1'$. The distance around an irregular shaped room was measured from the plans and found to be $6\frac{5}{8}''$, $17\frac{5}{8}''$, $9\frac{3}{8}''$, $2\frac{5}{8}''$, $9\frac{1}{4}''$ and $8\frac{1}{4}''$. What is the distance around the room in feet?

_____ Answer

13. A production foreman estimates that he can save $\frac{3}{5}¢$ in production of a garden-hose fitting. If the annual production is $13\frac{1}{4}$ million fittings, how much will the foreman save the company each year?

_____ Answer

REVIEW QUESTIONS

Common Fractions

1. Find the wall thickness of a pipe whose outside diameter is $12\frac{7}{8}''$ and whose inside diameter is $11\frac{9}{16}''$?

_____ Answer

2. Figure 1-16 shows a cut plate. Find dimension A.

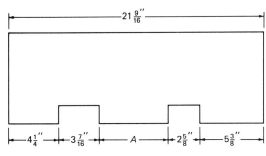

Fig. 1-16

_____ Answer

3. An aluminum pipe 13′4″ long was cut into pieces, each $16\frac{1}{4}''$ long. How many pieces of pipe were cut, and how many inches of pipe were left over?

_____ Answer

_____ Answer

4. How many spacers, each $\frac{7}{16}''$ thick, can be cut from a $31\frac{3}{8}''$ length of brass? Allow $\frac{1}{16}''$ waste for each cut.

_____ Answer

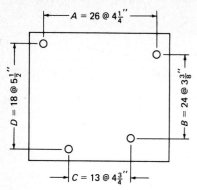

Fig. 1-17

5. Find the dimensions of *A*, *B*, *C* and *D* in Fig. 1-17.

$A = $ _____ Answer

$B = $ _____ Answer

$C = $ _____ Answer

$D = $ _____ Answer

6. A plumber measuring pipe for a job finds the following lengths of pipe are needed: 12′8″, 14′7″, 10′8½″, 15′9¾″, and 13′½″. What total length of pipe is required?

_____ Answer

7. The cost of steel was lowered by ⅔¢ per pound when shipped. If 225,000,000 lb were shipped, how many dollars were saved?

_____ Answer

8. The illustration in Fig. 1-18 is a sketch of a foundation for a child's playhouse. What is the total distance around the outside of the foundation?

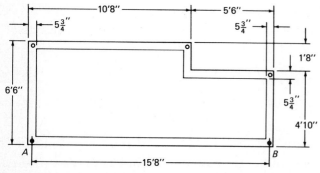

Fig. 1-18

_____ Answer

9. In Fig. 1-18, points *A* and *B* are foundation bolts. If six more foundation bolts are to be equally spaced between points *A* and *B*, how far apart will the centers of the bolts be?

_____ Answer

Fig. 1-19

10. Fourteen additional equally spaced holes will be drilled between points *A* and *B* in Fig. 1-19. Find the distance between the centers of the holes.

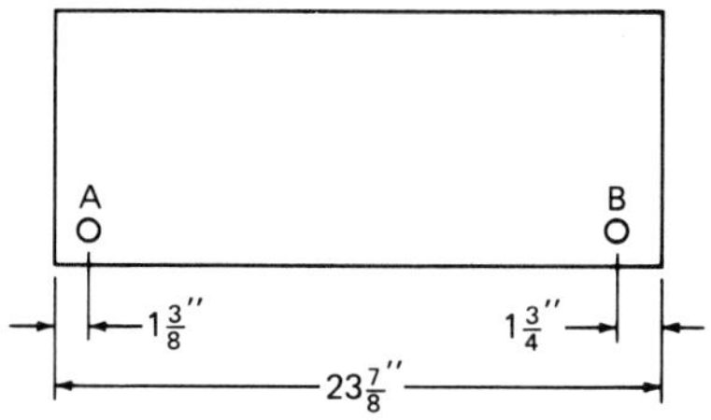

_____ Answer

11. A carpenter determines that the following lengths of 2 × 4's are needed in a construction job: $6'4\frac{1}{2}''$, $4'3\frac{3}{4}''$, $2'11\frac{3}{8}''$, $6'7\frac{3}{4}''$, and $1'\frac{3}{4}''$. If only standard 92″-long studs are available, how many will be needed and what is the total lineal length of 2 × 4's required?

_____ Answer

_____ Answer

12. A round brass shaft is reduced in diameter by $\frac{3}{8}''$. What total depth of cut is required on a lathe to reduce the diameter in one cut?

_____ Answer

CHAPTER TWO
DECIMAL FRACTIONS

Decimal numbers, like common fractions, are fractional parts of whole numbers. They are preferred to common fractions because they are easier to work with and can be more precise.

2-1
Fractional Notation

A fraction indicates the mathematical operation of division. The fraction $\frac{3}{4}$ means 3 divided by 4. When 3 is divided by 4, the result is 0.75 or a decimal fraction.

In a decimal notation, the decimal point separates the whole units from the fractional part of the units, as indicated in Fig. 2-1.

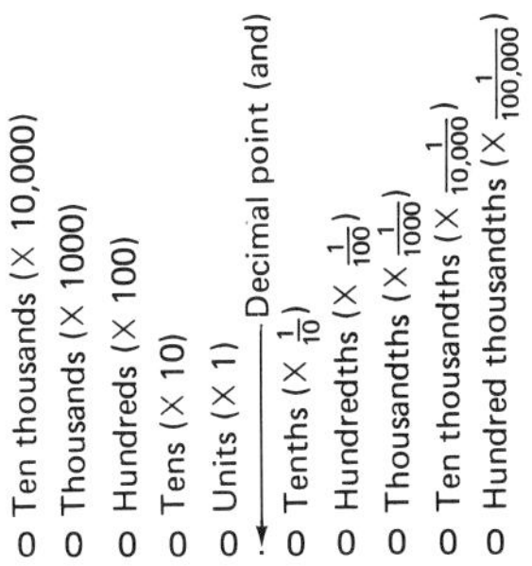

0 Ten thousands ($\times$ 10,000)
0 Thousands ($\times$ 1000)
0 Hundreds ($\times$ 100)
0 Tens ($\times$ 10)
0 Units ($\times$ 1)
. Decimal point (and)
0 Tenths ($\times \frac{1}{10}$)
0 Hundredths ($\times \frac{1}{100}$)
0 Thousandths ($\times \frac{1}{1000}$)
0 Ten thousandths ($\times \frac{1}{10,000}$)
0 Hundred thousandths ($\times \frac{1}{100,000}$)

Fig. 2-1

When reading a decimal number, the decimal point is replaced by the word "and."

Example

Read 46.8

Forty-six and eight tenths.

Read 468.08

Four hundred sixty-eight and eight hundredths.

Exercises

Verbally read the following decimals:

1. 0.8   2. 0.88   3. 0.888
4. 8.888   5. 0.07   6. 0.0068

7. 4.02	8. 183.562	9. 5.100
10. 0.400	11. 68.10	12. 1942.560
13. 400.400	14. 699.99	15. 0.00103

Write the value of each quantity as a decimal:

1. Three hundredths **0.03**
2. Four hundred eighty-two thousand _____
3. Four hundred and eighty-two thousandths _____
4. Nine ten-thousandths _____
5. Six hundred sixty-six and six hundred sixty-six ten-thousandths

    _____

6. Fifty-seven thousandths _____
7. Five hundred fifty-seven thousandths _____
8. Thirty-two and forty-five hundred-thousandths _____
9. Four ten-thousandths _____
10. Seventy-six and four tenths _____

2-2
Addition and Subtraction of Decimals

The essential rule in adding or subtracting decimals is to line up the decimal points, and then perform addition or subtraction.

Example

$$\text{Add} \quad \begin{array}{r} 62 \,.\, 84 \\ 7 \,.\, 93 \\ \hline \mathbf{70}\,.\,\mathbf{77} \end{array} \qquad \text{Subtract} \quad \begin{array}{r} 142 \,.\, 65 \\ 18 \,.\, 72 \\ \hline \mathbf{123}\,.\,\mathbf{93} \end{array}$$

Exercises Perform the indicated function:

1. $0.028 + 1.8 + 3 =$ **4.828**
2. $11.64 + 0.009 + 2.15 =$ _____
3. $849 + 0.875 + 2.15 =$ _____
4. $0.004 + 0.0215 + 10.002 =$ _____
5. $8 + 0.8 + 0.0088 =$ _____
6. $7.46 - 3.32 =$ _____
7. $0.5326 - 0.4215 =$ _____
8. $100.628 - 6.994 =$ _____
9. $3.475 - 1.785 =$ _____
10. $0.111 - 0.0003 =$ _____

2-3
Rounding Off Numbers

First determine the decimal place to which the number is to be rounded off. If the number to the right of that place is 4 or less, drop that number and all others to the right of that point. If the number to the right is greater than 5, increase the preceding digit by one and eliminate all numbers to its right.

Example

Round to three decimal places (thousandths):

$$76.473\textcircled{46} = \mathbf{76.473}$$
Drop

$$76.473\textcircled{58} = \mathbf{76.474}$$
Increase by one.

In a case where the determining number is exactly 5, there is a choice to either round up or drop. In practical terms, each case would be determined by its application. For the purposes of this text, if the number to be rounded is an even number, drop the 5. If the number to be rounded is an odd number, round up, changing it to an even number

Example

Round to two decimal places (hundredths):

$$36.46\textcircled{5} = \mathbf{36.46}$$
Drop

$$36.4\textcircled{7}5 = \mathbf{36.4\textcircled{8}}$$
Round up, making an even number.

Exercises

Round off the following numbers to the nearest thousandth:

1. 0.0146 _____   2. 0.000652 _____

3. 12.90000 _____   4. 276.04215 _____

5. 99.9999 _____   6. 16.49952 _____

7. 38.37305 _____   8. 39.2896 _____

9. 11.11111 _____   10. 32.04088 _____

2-4
Significant Figures

The numbers used in a measurement are referred to as *significant figures*. For example, a measurement made by a micrometer can be read 23 thousandths or written 0.023. The only number read on the micrometer is 23. The operator reading the micrometer adds the other zeros (0.023). Although this number is important as a place holder when writing the number, it is not significant in the measurement.

Remember the following rules for significant figures:

1. All nonzero numbers are significant

2. All zeros between nonzero numbers are significant

3. Zeros to the right of other numerals are significant

4. Zeros used to place the decimal point are not significant

Example

Number	Significant figures	Rule used
675	3	1
675.68	5	1
600.608	6	2
1001	4	2
74.750	5	3
77.00	4	3
0.⟨00⟩274	3	4

Important, but not significant

Numbers may be rounded by referring to the number of significant figures.

Example

Round to three significant figures:

$$0.001486 = 0.00149$$

$$3.646 = 3.65$$

$$457.8 = 458$$

Exercises   Determine the number of significant figures in each number:

1. 72.4 **3**_____   2. 475.06 _____   3. 808 _____

4. 0.01478 _____   5. 7000.42 _____   6. 114,600 _____

7. 88.940 _____   8. 0.000156 _____   9. 0.01970 _____

10. 62,547 _____   11. 10.08 _____   12. 1100.50 _____

Round the following to three significant figures:

13. 0.04215 **0.0422**_____   14. 3.1415 _____

15. 0.6827 _____   16. 0.001054 _____

17. 18.5694 _____   18. 7.892 _____

19. 0.3485 _____   20. 0.1555 _____

2-5
Multiplication of
Decimals

Multiplying decimals is just like multiplying whole numbers, except for placing the decimal point. To determine the placement of the decimal point in the answer:

1. Count the number of digits to the right of the decimal point in each multiplier.

2. Add the number of digits together.

3. Starting at the right of the answer, count to the left the number of digits determined by step 2 and place the decimal point there.

Example:

8.22	Number of digits to right of decimal = 2
1.2	Number of digits to right of decimal = 1
1644	Total = 3 digits
822	
9.864	The answer contains 3 digits to the right of the decimal.

Exercises   Multiply the following and round to three significant figures:

1.   1.972
          6

   11.832
   11.8 (rounded)

2.   0.035
        0.06

3.   30.15
          3.2

4.   3.14
        0.07

5.   0.000146
            2.4

6.   66.6
      0.06

7.   0.0082
        5000

8.   0.0826
           40

9.   9.08
      9.08

2-6
Division of Decimals

The process for division of decimals is the same as the normal process for long division, except for placement of the decimal point in the final answer. Set up the division problem in the following manner:

Number divided by (*divisor*) $\overline{)\text{ number to be divided } (\textit{dividend})}$

Example

Divide 16.42 by 3.32

$$3.32\overline{)16.42}\text{ (Set up)}$$

1.   Count the number of digits to the right of the decimal in the divisor. In this case, the divisor has two (3.32).
2.   Now move the decimal point in the divisor and the dividend two places to the right (3.32 $\overline{)16.42}$).
3.   The decimal point is placed directly above this point in the answer.

Example

```
        4.94
3.32) 16.42.00        Zeros are added to complete the division.
      1328
       3140
       2988
       1520
       1328
        192
```

Divide the following (round off to nearest $\frac{1}{1000}$):

1.
$$\begin{array}{r} 4120.000 \\ 0.02\overline{)82.40.000} \\ 8 \\ \hline 2 \\ 2 \\ \hline 4 \\ 4 \\ \hline 00 \end{array}$$

2. $3\overline{)13.78}$

3. $0.16\overline{)18.3}$

4. $1.5\overline{)33.33}$

5. $0.5\overline{)198}$

6. $9.8\overline{)1.46}$

7. $13\overline{)62.4}$

8. $12.0\overline{)6.0}$

9. $11.1\overline{)88.8}$

10. $0.4215\overline{)6.4215}$

**2-7
Division and
Multiplication by Factors
and Multiples of 10**

This process can be simplified by the following rules:

1. To multiply by 10, 100, 1000, etc., count the number of zeros and move the decimal point in the other multiplier to the right by that amount.

Example

$$6.48 \times 100 = 648$$
Count 2

$$8.97 \times 1000 = 8970$$
Count 3

2. To divide by tens, follow the same process and move the decimal point to the left.

Example

$$8.12 \div 1\underset{\smile\smile}{00} = 0.0812$$
count 2

$$6784 \div 1\underset{\smile\smile\smile}{000} = 6.784$$
count 3

3. To multiply by $\frac{1}{100}$, or 0.01, count the number of zeros in the common fraction or the number of digits to the right of the decimal and move the decimal point that number of digits to the left.

Example

$$46.28 \times 0\underset{\smile\smile}{.01} = 0.4628$$
count 2

$$5.42 \times \frac{1}{100} = \frac{5.42}{100} = 0.0542$$

4. To divide by $\frac{1}{100}$, $\frac{1}{1000}$, etc., count the number of zeros and move the decimal in the answer to the right by that amount.

Example

$$16.423 \div \tfrac{1}{100} = \mathbf{16.423} \times \ \ \mathbf{100} = 16.\underset{\smile\smile}{42}3$$

$$8.267 \div \tfrac{1}{1000} = \ \mathbf{8.267} \times \mathbf{1000} = 8.\underset{\smile\smile\smile}{267}0$$

Exercises   Perform the indicated function by mentally moving the decimal points:

1. $3.1456 \times 100 = \mathbf{314.56}$

2. $32 \times \dfrac{1}{10} =$

3. $26.82 \times 10 =$

4. $7.25 \times 10 =$

5. $66 \times \dfrac{1}{100} =$

6. $29.42 \div 10 = \mathbf{2.942}$

7. $19.402 \div \dfrac{1}{100} =$

8. $16.4 \times 10,000 =$

9. $1.7624 \div \dfrac{1}{1000} =$

10. $8.4 \div 0.00001 =$

11. $0.001 \times \dfrac{1}{100} =$

12. $54.44 \div 1000 =$

13. $1.414 \times 0.1 =$

14. $683 \times \dfrac{1}{10} =$

2-8
Changing Common Fractions to Decimal Fractions

This may be done by dividing the numerator by the denominator and following the rules of division. A table of decimal equivalents (Table 4) for common fractions is helpful and can be found in the Appendix.

Exercises

Without the use of a table, change the following fractions to equivalent decimal fractions (round off to the nearest thousandth)

1. $\dfrac{1}{8} = \underline{\textbf{0.125}}$

$$\begin{array}{r} 0.125 \\ 8\overline{)1.000} \\ \underline{8} \\ 20 \\ \underline{16} \\ 40 \\ \underline{40} \end{array}$$

2. $\dfrac{3}{16} = \underline{\hspace{3cm}}$

3. $\dfrac{6}{7} = \underline{\hspace{3cm}}$

4. $\dfrac{1}{4} = \underline{\hspace{3cm}}$

5. $\dfrac{5}{16} = \underline{\hspace{3cm}}$

6. $\dfrac{9}{32} = \underline{\hspace{3cm}}$

2-9
Changing Decimals to Ruler Fractions

The most convenient way to perform this operation is by using the table of decimal equivalents. When a table is not available, use the following method:

1. Determine the denominator of the desired common fraction.

2. Multiply the decimal to be converted by this denominator and round off the result to the closest whole number.

3. This number becomes the numerator of the fraction.

Example

Change 0.63 to a ruler fraction with a denominator of 16.

$$\textbf{0.63} \times \textbf{16} = \textbf{10.08}$$

Since 10.08 rounded off equals 10, the closest 16th is $\dfrac{10}{16}$.

$$0.63 = \dfrac{10}{16}$$

Exercises   Without the use of a table, change the following decimal fractions to ruler fractions, as indicated:

To 16ths	To 32ds	To 64ths

1. $0.830 = \dfrac{13}{16}$ 5. $0.772 =$ 9. $0.414 =$

  $16 \times 0.83 = 13.28$

2. $0.762 =$ 6. $0.424 =$ 10. $0.825 =$

3. $0.222 =$ 7. $0.126 =$ 11. $0.111 =$

4. $0.158 =$ 8. $0.942 =$ 12. $0.705 =$

2-10
Tolerances   Because measurement is not without error, measurements must have tolerances. They are expressed in plus or minus values:

Example 0.2565 ± 0.0025
Measurement with desired tolerance

The tolerance is then added to or subtracted from the desired measurement:

Example

Added	Subtracted
0.2565	0.2565
+ 0.0025	− 0.0025
0.2590	0.2540

This measure would still be accepted as 0.2565, although it could be anywhere between 0.2540 and 0.2590.

The plus and minus tolerance are not always equal, as in the case of a shaft that must be placed in a bearing. The minus tolerance may be greater than the plus tolerance because the shaft may be allowed to fit loosely. However, if it were too large, the shaft would not fit the bearing.

Example   0.750 $+ 0.025$
$- 0.045$

Plus	Minus
0.750	0.750
+ 0.025	− 0.045
0.775	0.715

It is sometimes necessary to take several measurements and average them to get a more accurate result.

Example

Several micrometer readings were taken on a driving shaft. What is the average reading?

Measurements
0.623
0.620
0.618
0.623
2.484

Divide the sum by the number of readings.

$$4)\overline{\begin{array}{r} \mathbf{0.621} \text{ Average} \\ 2.484 \\ \underline{2\ 4} \\ 8 \\ \underline{8} \\ 4 \\ \underline{4} \\ 0 \end{array}}$$

Exercises   Determine the size of the following within the given tolerance:

1. 0.8816 ± 0.0010″   Smallest value **0.8806**″ ____ Answer

   0.8816   **0.8816**   Largest value **0.8826**″ ____ Answer
− 0.0010 **+ 0.0010**
   0.8806   **0.8826**

2. 0.5000 + 0.0025″   _____ Answer

           − 0.0040″   _____ Answer

3. 0.875 + 0.025″   _____ Answer

           − 0.015″   _____ Answer

4. 2.375 ± 0.012″   _____ Answer

                                   _____ Answer

5. 1.625 ± 0.010″   _____ Answer

                                   _____ Answer

Find the average quantity:

6.   8.627″ $3)\overline{\begin{array}{r} \mathbf{8.6273} \\ \mathbf{25.882} \end{array}}$
       8.620″
       8.635″
      25.882″   **8.627″** ____ Answer

7. 2.370″
    2.355″
    2.365″   _____ Answer

8. 0.888″
    0.875″
    0.882″
    0.880″   _____ Answer

9. 87.6″
    62.5″
    95.8″
    85.0″
    76.5″   _____ Answer

10. 0.0125″
    0.0122″
    0.0125″
    0.0120″
    0.0127″   _____ Answer

EVALUATION PROBLEMS

Multiply each of the following. Round each answer to three significant figures:

1. 0.086
    <u>0.11</u>

2. 6.14
    <u>0.28</u>

3. 0.0078
    <u>0.0032</u>

4. 748
    <u>0.16</u>

5. 0.0046
    <u>40</u>

6. 3.14
    <u>12</u>

Divide each of the following. Round off to the hundredths place:

1. $0.5\overline{)648}$

2. $5\overline{)17.25}$

3. $0.15\overline{)15.46}$

4. $7\overline{)22}$

5. $4.5\overline{)900}$

6. $0.02\overline{).7854}$

Multiply or divide as indicated:

1. $6.48 \times 1000 =$

2. $6.48 \div 1000 =$

3. $0.0068 \times 100 =$

4. $3.14 \div \dfrac{1}{1000} =$

5. $77.7 \div 0.01 =$

6. $4286 \times 0.0001 =$

7. $57.3 \times .01 =$ 8. $0.125 \div 0.10 =$

9. $0.001 \times 1000 =$ 10. $0.01 \div \dfrac{1}{100} =$

Change the common fractions to decimal equivalents:

1. $\dfrac{3}{8} = $ _____   2. $\dfrac{5}{16} = $ _____   3. $\dfrac{9}{16} = $ _____

4. $\dfrac{7}{8} = $ _____   5. $\dfrac{1}{3}$ _____   6. $\dfrac{111}{444}$ _____

7. $\dfrac{24}{64}$ _____   8. $\dfrac{9}{10} = $ _____   9. $\dfrac{20}{100}$ _____

Convert the decimals to the nearest ruler fraction (Use Table 4):

1. $0.865 =$ 2. $0.0158 =$ 3. $0.963 =$

4. $0.756 =$ 5. $0.135 =$ 6. $0.555 =$

2-11
Applying Fractions and
Decimal Fractions

Many measurements are given or measured in both fractional values and decimal values. For example, motor-shaft sizes are specified as $\frac{1}{2}$ in, $\frac{5}{8}$ in, $\frac{3}{4}$ in, etc. However, when machining such a shaft, the machines are calibrated in decimal values. When doing layout work, some instruments, such as rulers, are calibrated in fractional sizes, while vernier calipers are calibrated in decimal values. Therefore, it is often necessary to convert between fractional decimal values.

Example

A $\frac{1}{2}''$ drill bit (Fig. 2-2) is to be reduced in diameter to fit in a $\frac{3}{8}''$ drill chuck. What total depth of cut will be required to reduce the diameter? Since this will be reduced by grinding on a lathe, the depth of the cut will be measured in decimal values.

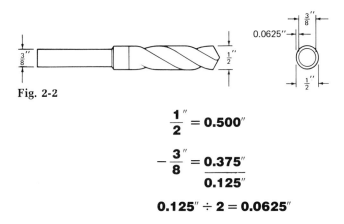

Fig. 2-2

$$\frac{1}{2}'' = 0.500''$$

$$-\frac{3}{8}'' = 0.375''$$
$$\overline{\phantom{-\frac{3}{8}'' = } 0.125''}$$

$$0.125'' \div 2 = 0.0625''$$

A drafter doing a machine-layout drawing may be given the measurement both in fractional and decimal values. Measurements made with rulers are usually fractional, while those made with vernier calipers are usually decimal. Standard specifications may be given in either decimal or fractional notation.

Example

A drafter is given the sketch in Fig. 2-3 and is required to make a scale drawing supplying the missing dimensions. Find the dimensions A and B to the nearest $\frac{1}{1000}''$.

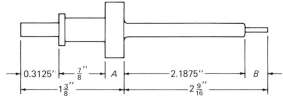

Fig. 2-3

Distance A

$$\frac{7}{8}'' = 0.875''$$

$$0.875'' + 0.3125'' = 1.1875''$$

$$1\frac{3}{8}'' = 1.375''$$

$$1.375'' - 1.1875'' = 0.1875''$$

$$= 0.188'' \text{ Ans.}$$

Distance B

$$2\frac{9}{16}'' = 2.5625''$$

$$2.5625'' - 2.1875'' = 0.375'' \text{ Ans.}$$

Exercises
Application of Decimal Fractions

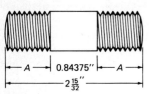

Fig. 2-4

1. Figure 2-4 illustrates a $\frac{5}{16}$″ threaded-stud bolt. The bolt is available in several lengths, and it varies by the length of the unthreaded portion. What is the length of the threaded portion *A*?

_______________ Answer

2. Find the center-to-center distance between 18 equally spaced holes if the distance between the centers of the first and last holes is 47″. (Round to nearest hundredth.)

_______________ Answer

3. A piece of round stock is $3\frac{5}{8}$″ in diameter. How deep a cut on a lathe will be required to turn the finished diameter to 3.487″?

_______________ Answer

4. A precision shaft was measured with a micrometer in five places, and the following readings were recorded: 1.6287″, 1.6284″, 1.6283″, 1.6284″, and 1.6285″. Using the given readings, what is the average diameter of the shaft?

_______________ Answer

5. An automobile engine with a standard *bore* (diameter) of $3\frac{5}{16}''$ was rebored to $\frac{40}{1000}''$ oversize. What did the new bore measure?

_____ Answer

6. Lockwashers in large quantities are generally sold by the pound. How many $\frac{1}{4}''$ lockwashers are in 9 lb if each one weighs 0.48 oz (1 lb = 16 oz)?

_____ Answer

7. An aluminum pipe is cast with an outside diameter of 6.255". The inside diameter of the pipe is 4.625". Find the wall thickness of the casting.

_____ Answer

8. The skin of an airplane wing is fastened to the crossmember with rivets. In one crossmember, the distance between the centers of the rivets is 1.15". If 47 rivets are used in a certain crossmember, what is the distance between the centers of the first and last rivets?

_____ Answer

9. A rough brass casting weighed 12.75 lb before finishing. After finishing the casting weighed 11.65 lb. If 1000 of these castings are made, what is the total amount of waste in this job?

_____ Answer

10. A certain electrical wire was found to weigh 0.0054 lb/ft. After using some of the wire from the roll, the roll was weighed and found to weigh 47.5 lb. If the spool on which the wire was wound weighs 4.5 lb, how many feet of wire are left on the roll?

_____ Answer

11. A motor-shaft bearing has a diameter of $0.7256'' \pm 0.0025''$. What are the largest and smallest acceptable dimensions of the bearing diameter?

_____ Answer

_____ Answer

12. A machinist found the dimension C missing from Fig. 2-5. Find C to the nearest $\frac{1}{100}''$ and the closest ruler fraction.

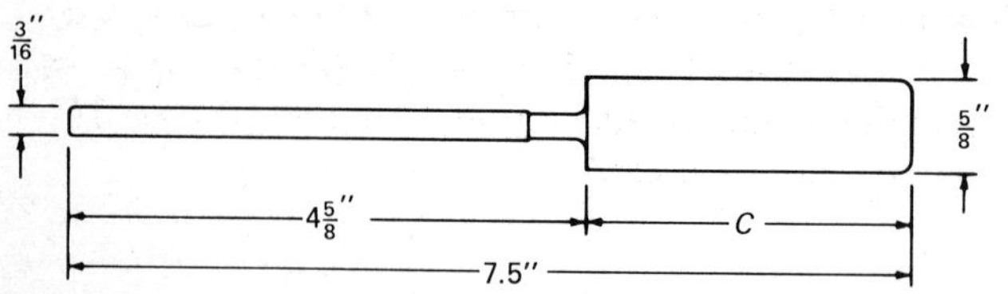

Fig. 2-5

_____ Answer

_____ Answer

13. A steel tape expanded 0.000158″ for each inch in length when it was heated by the sun. How many inches would a 150′ tape expand when heated in this manner?

_____ Answer

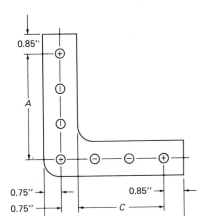

Fig. 2-6

14. In completing the drawing for Fig. 2-6, the drafter was required to determine the distances A, B and C. If the distance between the centers of the holes is 1.65″ each, find A, B, and C.

A = _____ Answer

B = _____ Answer

C = _____ Answer

15. Brass shimstock 3″ wide and 18.75″ long is to be used for 0.62″ spacers. How many may be cut from this piece?

_____ Answer

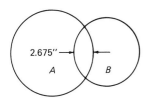

Fig. 2-7

16. Figure 2-7 illustrates the outline of two overlapping pulleys on different shafts. Pulley A is $11\frac{3}{8}″$ in diameter and pulley B is $8\frac{5}{8}″$ in diameter. What is the distance between their centers? (Note: The radius of a circle is $\frac{1}{2}$ the diameter.)

_____ Answer

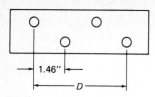

Fig. 2-8

17. The plate in Fig. 2-8 is to be expanded and 15 equally spaced holes will be drilled in the distance D. If the distance between the centers of the holes is 1.46″, what is the distance D?

$D =$ _____ Answer

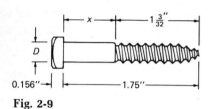

Fig. 2-9

18. If the lag bolt in Fig. 2-9 has the dimensions shown, find the dimension x to the nearest $\frac{1}{1000}''$.

$x =$ _____ Answer

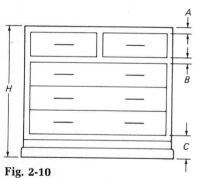

Fig. 2-10

19. Figure 2-10 is a manufacturer's drawing of a cabinet with the following dimensions: $H = 29\frac{3}{4}''$, $C = 2.125''$, $A = B = 0.75''$. If all drawer heights are of equal dimensions, find the height of each drawer.

_____ Answer

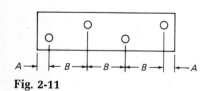

Fig. 2-11

20. In Fig. 2-11, the distance B between the hole centers in the mending plate is 2.3875″ and the distance $A = 0.350''$. How long would a mending plate be if it contained 18 holes?

_____ Answer

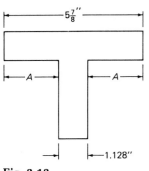

Fig. 2-12

21. Dimension A was missing on the drawing in Fig. 2-12. What is the dimension A to the nearest $\frac{1}{1000}$"?

$A =$ _____ Answer

22. Determine the spacing between 17 equally spaced holes if the distance between the centers of the first and last holes is $27\frac{7}{8}$". Round to the nearest $\frac{1}{100}$" and also to the nearest $\frac{1}{32}$".

_____ Answer

_____ Answer

23. The diameter of a bearing shaft for a 20-hp (horsepower) irrigation-pump motor is 1.4270". It has a plus tolerance of 0.0020" and a minus tolerance of 0.0035". What are the smallest and largest acceptable diameters for the shaft?

_____ Answer

_____ Answer

24. A piece of round stock 1.7820″ in diameter has a ±0.0043″ tolerance. What are the smallest and largest acceptable diameters of the finished piece?

_____ Answer
_____ Answer

REVIEW QUESTIONS

Decimals

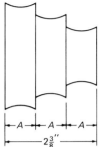

Fig. 2-13

1. An outline of a pulley arrangement is illustrated in Fig. 2-13. Find the distance A, the width of each pulley, to the nearest $\frac{1}{1000}''$.

_____ Answer

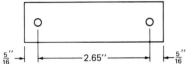

Fig. 2-14

2. The splice plate in Fig. 2-14 will be expanded to include 27 equally spaced holes. The drawing illustrates a typical layout for two holes. What will be the total length of the expanded plate to the nearest $\frac{1}{16}''$?

_____ Answer

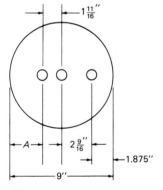

Fig. 2-15

3. In Fig. 2-15, find the distance A to the nearest $\frac{1}{100}''$. Then find A to the nearest $\frac{1}{16}''$.

_____ Answer

_____ Answer

4. A round bar is $1\frac{11}{16}''$ in diameter. How deep a cut is required to bring the diameter down to 1.621"? (Round off to nearest $\frac{1}{1000}''$).

_____ Answer

5. How many 0.723″ pieces of insulating tubing can be cut from a 21″ length of tubing, allowing $\frac{1}{32}$″ for each cut? How much tubing is left? (Round off to nearest $\frac{1}{100}$″.)

_____ Answer

_____ Answer

6. A cylinder bore (diameter) was measured in several places and the following readings were obtained: 2.1268″, 2.1265″, 2.1270″, and 2.1265″. What is the average diameter of the bore?

_____ Answer

7. The diameter of the large circle in Fig. 2-16, is 13.25″, and the diameter of the small circle is 5.21″. Find the missing dimension to the nearest $\frac{1}{100}$″.

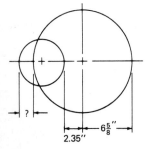

2.35″
$6\frac{5}{8}$″

Fig. 2-16

_____ Answer

8. An alternator armature shaft has an allowable diameter of $0.8355^{+0.0025″}_{-0.0035″}$. The true diameter was measured and found to be 0.8338″. Is it still within tolerance? Justify the answer.

_____ Answer

9. A steel cable used to support a television antenna is $\frac{3}{16}''$ in diameter and is sold in 500' rolls without a spool. A new roll weighs 16.875 lb. If a partially used roll of cable weighs 9.65 lb, how many feet of cable are left?

_____ Answer

Fig. 2-17

10. A sketch of a bracket is illustrated in Fig. 2-17. Find dimension *A*.

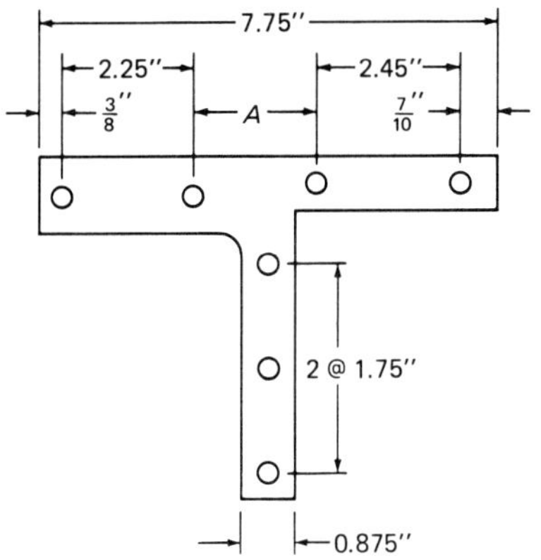

_____ Answer

11. A piece of round stock had an original diameter of 0.875". The diameter was reduced on a cutting lathe to 0.5565". How deep a cut was required to reduce the diameter? (Answer to the nearest ruler fraction and to the nearest $\frac{1}{1000}''$.)

_____ Answer

_____ Answer

12. In problem 11, the tolerance for the finished diameter was ±0.0035". If a cut of $\frac{11}{64}''$ were made, would the finished piece be within acceptable tolerance? Justify the answer by computation.

_____ Answer

CHAPTER THREE
PERCENTAGES

Percentages are a part of everyday living in the form of sales taxes, income taxes, discounts, comparisons, interest on bank accounts and loans, etc. By definition, a *percentage* is a specified part of every hundred. The number 10 is 10 parts out of 100, or 10 percent. It should be remembered that percent notation is just a convenient way to express a decimal fraction and has no significance to the mathematical operation of a problem. It is more convenient to indicate the interest on a loan as "8 percent" rather than "0.08 of the original loan."

**3-1
Fractions, Decimals, and
Percents**

To change a decimal fraction to percent notation, move the decimal point two places to the right (this is the same as multiplying by 100).

Example

$$0.56 \times 100 = 56\%$$

To change a common fraction to a percent, first convert the fraction to a decimal fraction, then move the decimal point two places to the right.

Example

$$\frac{3}{8} = 0.375 \times 100 = 37.5\%$$

To change a percent to a decimal fraction, divide by 100 or move the decimal point two places to the left.

Example

$$42.5\% \div 100 = 0.425$$

**Exercises
Changing to Percents**

Change the following decimals to equivalent percents:

1. $0.32 = $ **32%**	2. $0.64 =$	3. $0.3 =$
4. $0.005 =$	5. $0.04 =$	6. $1.50 =$
7. $0.033 =$	8. $0.0025 =$	9. $3 =$
10. $0.006 =$	11. $1.008 =$	12. $0.304 =$
13. $0.109 =$	14. $0.002 =$	15. $1.59 =$

Express the following fractions as equivalent percents:

16. $\frac{1}{4} =$ **25%** 17. $\frac{1}{2} =$ 18. $\frac{3}{4} =$

19. $\frac{3}{8} =$ 20. $\frac{3}{6} =$ 21. $\frac{3}{40} =$

22. $\frac{11}{20} =$ 23. $\frac{4}{3} =$ 24. $\frac{1}{175} =$

Express the following percents as equivalent decimal fractions:

25. 25% = **0.25** 26. 40% = 27. 7% =

28. 0.6% = 29. 62% = 30. 125% =

31. 15% = 32. 34.5% = 33. 3% =

34. 65% = 35. 83.5% = 36. 17% =

3-2
Determining a Percentage of a Number

This concept is extremely important in solving a wide range of problems, such as determining the amount of discount allowed on automobile parts, the amount of social security deducted from a salary, or the amount of tin in a solder alloy.

Example

The discount on a rebuilt automobile starter is 20%. If the starter cost $65, what would be the amount of the discount?

20% of $65

Change 20% to its decimal equivalent and multiply.

0.20 × $65 = $13 (discount)

Percentages may be expressed in quantities greater than 100%. The amount of water in undried wood is often greater than 100%.

Example

If the water content is 130%, how many pounds of water are there in a pine board that weighs 30 lb dry?

130% of 30 lb

1.3 × 30 = 39 lb of water

An important concept to see at this point is that multiplying by a percent less than 100% will result in an answer less than the original quantity. Multiplying by a percent greater than 100% will result in an answer greater than the original quantity. A percent must always be changed to its decimal equivalent before multiplying.

Exercises Find the values of the following:

1. 30% of 60 =
    0.30 × 60 = 18

2. 6% of 75 =

3. 12.5% of 35.8 =

4. 2% of 0.09 =

5. 0.3% of 39 =

6. 130% of 87 =

7. 55% of 42.8 =   8. 0.09% of 360 =

9. 3.2% of 0.43 =   10. 210% of 16.25 =

3-3 Determining Percentages

Example

Scoring a test by a percentage is a good example of determining a percent of a number. A student answered 40 out of 50 questions correctly. What is the percentage score?

Make a fraction out of the question.

40 questions right
50 total questions

Change to decimal equivalent by dividing 40 by 50.

$$\frac{40}{50} = 0.8$$

Change 0.8 to a percent.
0.8 × 100 = 80%

Example

What percent of 8 is 12?

$$\frac{12}{8} = 1.5 \times 100 = 150\%$$

Express the following as a percent:

1. What percent is 16 of 32? $\frac{16}{32} = 0.5 = 50\%$ _____

2. What percent is 44 of 65? _____

3. What percent is 150 of 1275? _____

4. What percent is 32 of 12? _____

5. What percent is 18 of 740? _____

6. What percent of 480 is 2.8? _____

7. What percent of 124 is 3.2? _____

8. What percent of 0.3 is 0.36? _____

9. What percent of 4 is 1.5? _____

10. What percent of 30 is 13.5? _____

When the percent of discount and the amount of discount is known, the original cost of the item can be computed.

Example

A discount of $14 was given on a new tire. This discount represents 25%. What was the original selling price of the tire?

$14 is 25% of what number?

Change 25% to a decimal.

$$25\% = \frac{25}{100} = 0.25$$

Divide $14 by 0.25.

$$\frac{14.00}{0.25} = \$56 \text{ (original selling price)}$$

The concept to remember is that dividing by a percent less than 100% results in an answer greater than the fractional part. Dividing by a percent greater than 100% results in an answer smaller than the fractional part.

Exercises Find the original number from the given percent and fractional part.

1. 30% of what number is 6? _____ **6 ÷ 0.3 = 18** _____

2. 40% of what number is 16.5? _____

3. 6% of what number is 18.6? _____

4. 120% of what number is 45.9? _____

5. 17% of what number is 6.1? _____

6. 15% of what number is 1.075? _____

7. 37.5% of what number is 1.3150? _____

8. 25% of what number is 0.043? _____

9. 118% of what number is 26.68? _____

10. 9% of what number is 1.5557? _____

EVALUATION SHEET

Percentages

Perform as indicated:

1. What percent of 24 is 98? _____

2. 3% of what number is 12.6? _____

3. What percent of 4.3 is 1.4? _____

4. Find 5.5% of 23.6. _____

5. 100% of what number is 65.5? _____

6. Find 175% of 0.36. _____

7. What percent of 16.5 is 0.324? _____

8. Find 0.01% of 18.25. _____

9. 0.02% of what number is 3.2? _____

10. 12.2% of what number is 12.015? _____

11. Find 66.6% of 6.9. _____

12. What percent of 4800 is 17? _____

13. 33% of what number is 3? _____

14. Find 15% of 86. _____

15. Find 250% of 50. _____

16. What percent of 16 is 32? _____

17. Find 0.05% of 80. _____

18. 16% of what number is 120? _____

19. What percent is 225 of 1200? _____

20. What percent of 100 is 18.5? _____

3-5
Application of Percentages

Example

A customer bought a battery guaranteed for 24 months. After 18 months, the battery failed. What percent of the guarantee was used?

18 months out of 24 were used.

$$\frac{18}{24} = 0.75 \times 100 = 75\% \text{ used}$$

If the new battery cost $36, how much would it cost to replace the battery?

75% of the guarantee was used and 25% remained

$$100\% - 75\% = 25\%$$
$$25\% \text{ of } \$36$$
$$0.25 \times \$36 = \$9 \text{ credit}$$
$$\$36 - \$9 = \$25 \text{ (Cost of replacement battery)}$$
or

$$75\% \text{ of } \$36 = \$25$$

Example

A service station attendant worked 55 (hours) during one week and received time and a half for all hours over 40 and double time for all hours over 50. If the basic rate of pay is $3.80/h, what is the salary before deductions?

Hours		Rate factor		Total
40	×	1 (Regular time)	=	40
10	×	1.5 (time and a half) to 50 h.	=	15
5	×	2 (double time for all hours over 50	=	10 h
				65 h

The attendant has only worked 55 h but will be paid for 65 h at regular pay.

$$65 \times \$3.80 = \$247$$

This method is usually easier than computing a time and a half wage and double-time wage. What will the attendant's take-home pay be if 22% is withheld for taxes?

$$22\% \text{ of } \$247 = \$54.34 \text{ (taxes)}$$

$$\$247 - \$54.34 = \$192.66 \text{ (take-home pay)}$$

Exercises
Problems Involving Percentages

1. Solder is an alloy made up of tin and lead. If there is $7\frac{1}{2}$ lb of tin in each 16 lb of solder, what percent would be tin and what percent would be lead?

Tin _____ Answer

Lead _____ Answer

2. A newly developed tire on the market obtained an average of 43,780 mi (miles). The older tire averaged only 39,580 mi. What percent of increase does this represent over the mileage of the older tire?

_____ Answer

3. An automobile classic was purchased for $450 when new and was recently sold for $4,850. What percent of increase does this represent?

_____ Answer

4. Power line 1 transmits 420 kW (kilowatts) to a pumping station with an 18-kW loss in transmission. As power needs increased for the pumping station, power line 2 was installed. It delivers 850 kW and has a line loss of 30 kW. Which line is the most efficient? Justify the answer with a percentage comparison.

_____ Answer

12. A mechanic made 18% commission on her base salary for a month pay period. If the commission amounted to $138, what was her base salary for that month?

_____ Answer

13. A brass casting weighed 56.8 lb before finishing and cost $14.56 after finishing. After finishing, it was determined that $12\frac{1}{2}$% of the brass was waste and could be sold at 15¢/lb. What would be the actual cost of making similar castings if the scrap were reclaimed and this amount were deducted from the cost.

_____ Answer

14. A truckload of redwood 2 × 6's weighs 15,860 lb, and the wood contains 45% moisture content. What will be the weight of the redwood after it is dried?

_____ Answer

15. The hourly rate of a welder is $8.40 for the first 36 h, time and a half for each additional hour up to 45 h, and double time for each hour over 45. What is his salary before deductions for that pay period if he worked five days at 9 h each, one day at 11 h, and one day at $6\frac{1}{2}$ h?

_____ Answer

16. If the deductions for the welder's pay in problem 15 were 22% for federal tax, 12% for state tax, 5.8% for social security, and 4.2% for retirement, how much was taken out for:

Federal tax _____ Answer

State tax _____ Answer

Social security _____ Answer

Retirement _____ Answer

17. In a series of exams, all questions were of equal weight in determining a percentage grade. A student earned 8 out of 10 on the first test, 9 out of 15 on the second, 12 out of 16 on the third, 15 out of 15 on the fourth, and 6 out of 9 on the fifth. What is the student's average percentage score?

_____ Answer

REVIEW QUESTIONS

Percentages

1. a. What percent of 42.5 is 16.37?

_____ Answer

   b. Find 32.8% of 0.0184

_____ Answer

   c. 15.6% of what number is 63.47?

_____ Answer

   d. Find 256% of 87.5

_____ Answer

   e. 125% of what number is 8.87?

_____ Answer

2. A new welding machine allows its operator to increase his output from 85 jobs to 108 jobs per week. What is the percent increase in the output?

_____ Answer

3. A welder is earning $6.87/h and time and a half for all hours over 36. She worked 57½ h and has the following deductions: federal tax, 17.5%; state tax, 7.7%; and social security, 6.05%. Find

Base pay _____ Answer

Federal tax _____ Answer

State tax _____ Answer

Social security _____ Answer

Take-home pay _____ Answer

4. A wooden pattern for an iron casting weighs 91 lb. This is 16½% of the weight of the casting. What does the casting weigh?

_____ Answer

5. A contractor estimates that a job will cost $4560 for material and labor. The contract price is $6850. What is the percent profit based on contractor cost?

_____ Answer

6. A machinist earns $3.25/h, with time and a half for overtime. If he works 40 h straight time and 14 h overtime, what percent of his regular pay is his overtime pay?

_____ Answer

7. A mixture of mortar contains 900 lb of sand, lime, and cement. If 23.5% of the weight is cement and 12.75% is lime, how many pounds of sand does the mixture contain?

_____ Answer

8. An auto parts supplier marked up the cost of a wheel bearing 42%. If the bearing cost $14.33, what is the selling price?

_____ Answer

9. The bearing in problem 8 was later discounted to the customer by $16\frac{2}{3}$%. What would the customer now pay for the bearing?

_____ Answer

10. Gasoline was selling for 70.9¢/gal, and the dealer made a profit of 6.2% based on the selling price of gasoline. What did the gasoline cost the dealer?

_____ Answer

11. In problem 10, the dealer's cost was increased by 8.5%. What is the percent of profit of the gas sold for 79.9¢/gal?

_____ Answer

12. Cast iron weighs 449 lb/ft³ (pounds per cubic foot) and wrought iron weighs 490 lb/ft³. In terms of percent, how much more does wrought iron weigh than cast iron?

_____ Answer

13. An automobile tire is guaranteed for 36,000 mi, and it costs $46.85. The tire failed at 25,850 mi. If the guarantee is applied toward the new tire, what percent of the guarantee is left and how much should the new tire cost?

_____ Answer

14. The directions on a can of lacquer paint read "thin to 150% for normal use." How much thinner should be added to a quart of lacquer paint for normal use?

_____ Answer

CHAPTER FOUR
METRIC SYSTEM

The United States has long been using the English system of measure with awkward standards like 12 in = 1 ft, 32 oz = 1 qt, 5280 ft = 1 mi, etc. Although the metric system has been a legal system of measure in the United States since 1866, it has not been given much attention until recent years. Through world agreement, the SI (Système International) metric system has been established. The SI metric system establishes the *meter* as a unit of length, the *kilogram* as a unit of mass (weight), and the *liter* as a unit of volume.

4-1
Prefixes

There are many prefixes used in the metric system. Figure 4-1 illustrates prefixes. Only three of these (milli, centi, and kilo) are commonly used in everyday measurements.

```
                            ┌──────────┐
                            │ meter (m)│
                            │ liter (L)│
                            │ gram (g) │
                            └──────────┘
 kilo (k)   hecto (h)  deka (dk)              deci (d)   centi (c)   milli (m)
  unit        unit       unit                   unit       unit        unit
   3           2          1          0            1          2           3
◄──────────────────────────────────────────────────────────────────────────►
Left                                                                    Right
```

Fig. 4-1
Basic measurements

The prefixes "milli", "centi", and "kilo" can be added to the basic unit of measure as follows:

1. When the prefix "milli" is added to meter, the result is millimeter (mm) or $\frac{1}{1000}$ m (meter).

2. When the prefix "centi" is added to meter, the result is centimeter (cm) or $\frac{1}{100}$ m.

3. When the prefix "kilo" is added to meter, the result is kilometer (km) or 1000 m.

4. The prefixes can also be used with the liter and gram, resulting in:

$$\text{One milliliter (ml)} = \frac{1}{1000}\text{ L (liter)}$$

$$\text{One centiliter (cl)} = \frac{1}{100}\text{ L}$$

One kiloliter (kL) = 1000 L

One milligram (mg) = $\dfrac{1}{1000}$ g (gram)

One centigram (cg) = $\dfrac{1}{100}$ g

One kilogram (kg) = 1000 g

4-2
Conversion by Moving Decimal Points

An easy way to change the prefix of the unit of measurement is to move the decimal point.

Example

Change 8.56 m to cm.

As there are 100 cm to 1 m, multiply the meter measurement (8.56) by 100, and then change the prefix to centimeters. Multiplying by 100 means shifting the decimal point two places to the right.

8.56. m = 856 cm

Note: A centimeter is smaller than a meter. Therefore, converting a number from meters to centimeters will mean that the resulting number will have to be larger.

Changing prefixes can also be accomplished by using the chart in Fig. 4-1 and moving the decimal point.

Example

Convert 250 mL to L

1. Locate the given prefix ("milli" units) on the chart.

2. Count the number of places required to adjust the decimal point to accommodate the new classification (liter). In this case, it would be three places to the left.

250. mL = 0.25 L

Example

Convert 15 m to cm.

To change from meters to centi units would require a two-decimal-place move to the right.

15.00. m = 1500 cm

Example

Convert 3,500,000 mm to km.

To change from "milli" units to "kilo" units requires a six-decimal-place move to the left.

3.500000. = 3.5 km

Example

Convert 180 mm to cm.

To change from "milli" units to "centi" units requires a one-decimal-place move to the left

18.0. mm = 18 cm

Exercises Convert the following to accommodate the new units.

1. 2200 g to _____ kg
2. 4285 L to _____ kL
3. 1280 m to _____ km
4. 252 kg to _____ g
5. 1870 mm to _____ cm
6. 0.084 m to _____ cm
7. 0.528 kL to _____ L
8. 427 mm to _____ m
9. 84 g to _____ kg
10. 96 cm to _____ mm
11. 872 m to _____ cm
12. 8.4 kg to _____ g
13. 6784 mm to _____ m
14. 0.044 cm to _____ mm

4-3
English to Metric Conversion

When either the metric or English system is continually used, the ability to estimate measurements or sizes is developed. Selecting a $\frac{1}{2}$-in socket or open-end wrench from a group becomes routine to a mechanic, but can the same mechanic associate a 13-mm wrench with the correct size bolt? What is 13 mm? A conversion of some common English measurements to metric will be helpful in understanding this concept.

Example

Change $\frac{1}{2}''$ to _____ cm; to _____ mm
   $1'' = 2.54$ cm

$$\frac{1}{2} \times 2.54 \text{ cm} = 1.27 \text{ cm}$$

1.27 cm $\times$ 10 = 12.7 mm   or   **(rounded off) 13 mm**

Converting fractions from English to metric-system units by multiplying with a common factor could result in tedious work which is not really important to the understanding of the relationship of the two systems. Table 4 has been provided in the Appendix to simplify this work and should be used when available. For other conversions, use the multiplier provided in conversion tables.

Exercises A common nine-piece socket set contains the following sizes. What is the closest metric size to each of these?
Note: This does not mean these sockets are interchangeable.

1. $\frac{3}{8}''$ to _____ cm; to _____ mm
2. $\frac{7}{16}''$ to _____ cm; to _____ mm
3. $\frac{1}{2}''$ to _____ cm; to _____ mm
4. $\frac{9}{16}''$ to _____ cm; to _____ mm
5. $\frac{5}{8}''$ to _____ cm; to _____ mm
6. $\frac{11}{16}''$ to _____ cm; to _____ mm
7. $\frac{3}{4}''$ to _____ cm; to _____ mm
8. $\frac{13}{16}''$ to _____ cm; to _____ mm
9. $\frac{7}{8}''$ to _____ cm; to _____ mm

EVALUATION PROBLEMS

Convert as indicated:

1. 4600 g to _____ kg; to _____ dg

2. 4000 mL to _____ L; to _____ kL

3. 0.6 m to _____ cm; to _____ in

4. 31″ to _____ cm; to _____ mm

5. 800 km to _____ m; to _____ dkm

6. $\frac{7}{64}$″ to _____ mm; to _____ cm

7. 8 mm to _____ cm; to _____ in

8. $\frac{9}{32}$″ to _____ cm; to _____ mm

9. 84 cm to _____ m; to _____ in

10. 680 kL to _____ L; to _____ mL

11. 2″ to _____ cm; to _____ mm

12. 86 km to _____ m; to _____ hm

13. 12″ to _____ cm; to _____ mm

14. 6 mi to _____ km; to _____ m

15. 4 gal to _____ L; to _____ qt

16. 100 km to _____ mi; to _____ m

17. 8′ to _____ m; to _____ mm

18. 0.001″ to _____ mm; to _____ cm

19. 25 L to _____ qt; to _____ gal

20. 800 mL to _____ L; to _____ qt

21. 0.64 cm to _____ mm; to _____ m

22. 3000 mi to _____ km; to _____ m

4-4
Application of Metric Concepts

Measurement tools, like micrometers, precision gauges, etc. are expensive, and it may not be practical for small shops and businesses to have both metric- and English-calibrated equipment for all jobs. It will be necessary to make measurements in one system and convert to the other.

Example

The valve clearance on an automobile engine is 0.4 mm. A mechanic has only English-calibrated gauges to use. What gauge should be used?

0.4 mm × 0.03937 = 0.0157″   or   0.016

(0.0393 taken from Appendix)

Example

A parts cleaner holds 3.5 gal. How many liters should be used in the cleaner?

3.5 gal × 3.785 = 13.24 L   or   13 L

(3.785, taken from Appendix)

Exercises
Application of Metric Concepts

1. A spark plug gap is 0.025″. What would this be in millimeters?

_____ Answer

2. What would be the metric equivalent of ignition-point settings of 0.016″?

_____ Answer

3. Convert each of the feeler-gauge sizes listed below to their closest metric equivalent:

$0.002″ =$ _____

$0.004″ =$ _____

$0.006″ =$ _____

$0.010″ =$ _____

$0.022″ =$ _____

4. If a $\frac{1}{8}''$ welding rod were ordered using the metric system, what size rod would be ordered?

_____ Answer

5. A metal splicing plate has been used to hold two beams together. The original plate used $\frac{5}{8}''$ by 10″ bolts to secure it. If the bolts are replaced with metric sizes, what will be the closest metric size?

_____ Answer

6. How much would it cost to fill a 20-gal gas tank if gas sells for 20¢/L?

_____ Answer

7. Some typical legal speed limits are listed below. How many km/h would they be?

15 mi/h = _____

25 mi/h = _____

40 mi/h = _____

50 mi/h = _____

55 mi/h = _____

8. Convert the distances between the following cities from miles to kilometers:

New York to Chicago–840 mi _____ km

Miami to Atlanta–667 mi _____ km

Phoenix to Dallas–1029 mi _____ km

Seattle to Portland–175 mi _____ km

9. The distance between San Francisco and Los Angeles is 405 road miles. At an average speed of 80 km/h, how long would it take to travel between the cities?

_____ Answer

10. An average cruising speed for a jet airliner is 600 mi/h. How many km/h is its cruising speed?

_____ Answer

11. A typical cruising altitude for a jet airliner is 27,000'. Approximately how many kilometers is this altitude?

_____ Answer

12. How many bushings 30 mm thick can be cut from a piece of round brass stock 1.52 m in length? Allow 0.75 mm for waste. How much stock is left?

_____ Answer

_____ Answer

13. In problem 12, what would the thickness of the bushings be and the length of the stock in English measurement?

_____ Answer

_____ Answer

14. For fractional values below 1", the approximation that $\frac{1}{8}$" = 3 mm (3.175 actual) can be used to convert metric equivalents. Approximate the following metric equivalents?

$\frac{3}{8}$" = _____

$\frac{1}{2}$" = _____

$\frac{5}{8}$" = _____

$\frac{3}{4}$" = _____

15. What would be the depth of a cut in millimeters to reduce the diameter of a piece of round stock from 32 mm to 27 mm?

_____ Answer

16. What would be the approximate English measurement of the original size, finished size, and depth of cut in problem 15?

_____ Answer

_____ Answer

_____ Answer

17. Determine the length of the splice plate illustrated in Fig. 4-2.

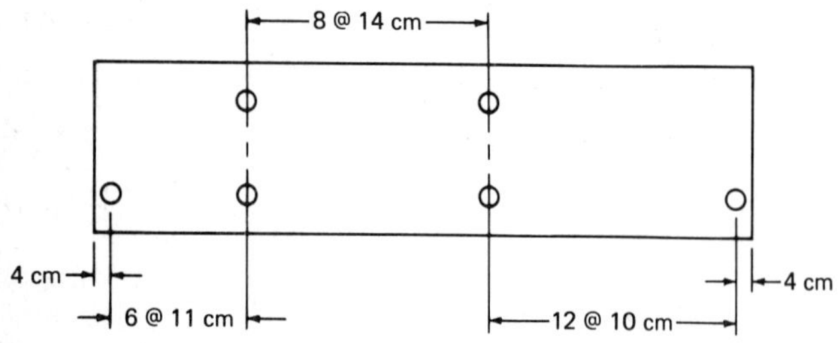

Fig. 4-2

_____ Answer

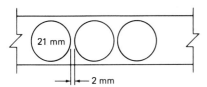

Fig. 4-3

18. Determine the number of blanks that can be cut from a 96-m roll of the aluminum in Fig. 4-3. Each hole is 21 mm in diameter. Neglect the starting waste.

_____ Answer

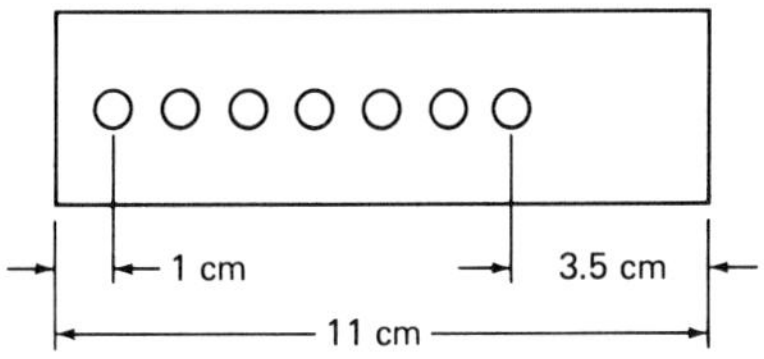

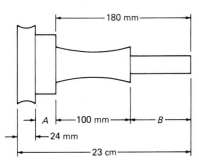

Fig. 4-4

19. Determine the distance between the centers of the holes in Fig. 4-4. Each hole is 5 mm in diameter.

_____ Answer

20. The diameter of a motor-shaft bearing is 0.8 mm larger than the shaft. What is the diameter of the bearing if the motor shaft is 6.0 cm in diameter?

_____ Answer

21. Determine the missing dimensions on the step pulley illustrated in Fig. 4-5.

_____ Answer

_____ Answer

Fig. 4-5

22. Telephone poles are spaced 28 m apart. How many poles will be required in 3500 m?

_____ Answer

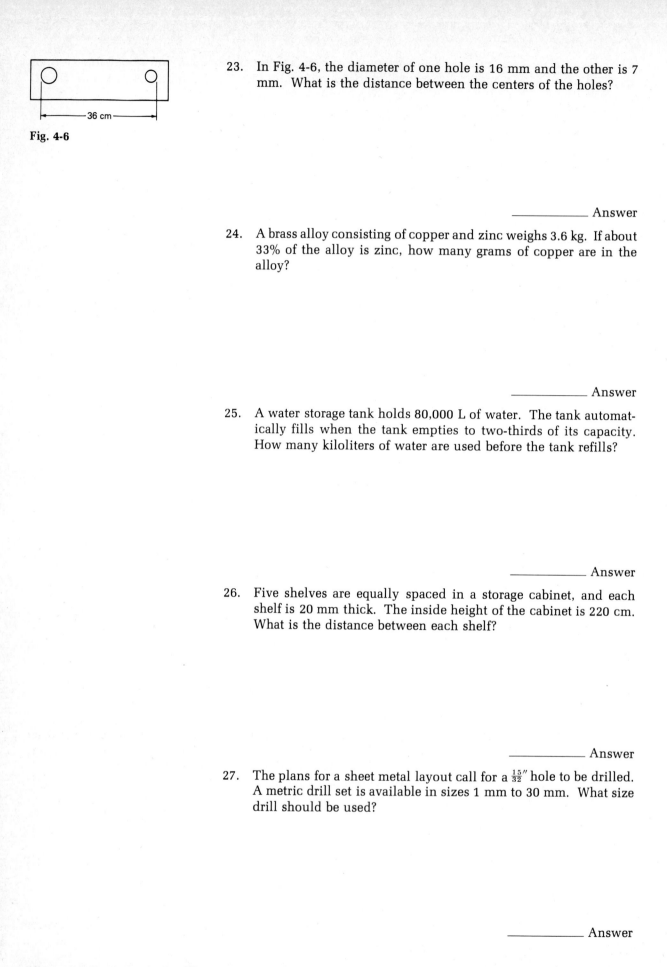

Fig. 4-6

23. In Fig. 4-6, the diameter of one hole is 16 mm and the other is 7 mm. What is the distance between the centers of the holes?

_____ Answer

24. A brass alloy consisting of copper and zinc weighs 3.6 kg. If about 33% of the alloy is zinc, how many grams of copper are in the alloy?

_____ Answer

25. A water storage tank holds 80,000 L of water. The tank automatically fills when the tank empties to two-thirds of its capacity. How many kiloliters of water are used before the tank refills?

_____ Answer

26. Five shelves are equally spaced in a storage cabinet, and each shelf is 20 mm thick. The inside height of the cabinet is 220 cm. What is the distance between each shelf?

_____ Answer

27. The plans for a sheet metal layout call for a $\frac{15}{32}''$ hole to be drilled. A metric drill set is available in sizes 1 mm to 30 mm. What size drill should be used?

_____ Answer

REVIEW QUESTIONS

Metric

1. Make the following conversions:

   18 kg to _____ g

   1485 L to _____ kL

   0.065 cm to _____ mm

   12,560,000 cm to _____ km

   8,766 g to _____ kg

   86 kL to _____ L

   1600 mm to _____ m

   64.8 kg to _____ g

   19.87 cm to _____ m

   6,876,572 mm to _____ km

2. The main bearings of a foreign automobile were measured with an English-calibrated micrometer and found to be 0.00875" undersize. How many millimeters undersize would this be?

_____ Answer

3. An airplane pilot is required to make an emergency landing, and the plane requires a minimum of 1200 yd (yards) to land. If the emergency landing strip is 1500 m, will the plane have enough runway to land? Justify the answer.

_____ Answer

4. An American-made truck is rated at 10,000 lb for the capacity of its load. The truck is being loaded with boxes from Japan which each weigh 575 kg. How many boxes could the truck hold and not exceed the rated capacity? The physical size of the truck or boxes is not a concern.

_____ Answer

5. In Europe, a touring motorist finds that gasoline is in short supply and only 12 L is available. The next gasoline stop is 62 km away. If the tourist's automobile averages 15 mi/gal, can the trip be made and how far should the automobile be able to travel?

_____ Answer

_____ Answer

6. If 4' × 8' plywood sheets were manufactured using metric dimensions, what would be the closest metric size?

_____ Answer

7. A piece of round stock is to be reduced in diameter from $\frac{3}{4}''$ to $\frac{5}{8}''$ on a lathe calibrated in the metric system. What will be the depth of cut required in millimeters?

_____ Answer

8. An automobile averages 16.5 mi/gal, and a full tank of gasoline is 68 L. How many miles will the automobile travel on a full tank of gas if 15% of the fuel is to remain in reserve?

_____ Answer

9. Twenty-eight rivet holes are drilled in a straight line in an aluminum sheet. If the holes are equally spaced with 16 mm between centers, what is the distance from the center of the first hole to the center of the last hole?

_____ Answer

10. A sand and gravel truck is loaded with 10,000 lb of sand, which is $\frac{3}{4}$ of its capacity. How many kilograms will the truck hold at full capacity?

_____ Answer

11. The cost of sending first-class mail overseas from the United States is 31¢/$\frac{1}{2}$oz. How much postage would be required to send a letter that weighs 68 g?

_____ Answer

12. A manufacturer of lawn furniture assembles most of the furniture with $\frac{3}{16}''$ nuts and bolts. It has been decided to replace these nuts and bolts with their metric equivalents. What size should be used?

_____ Answer

13. A bottle of cleaning liquid is priced at 79¢ and contains 13 oz. A second bottle is marked 69¢ and contains 400 mL. Which is the better buy? Justify the answer.

_____ Answer

14. The diameter of electrical wire is measured in terms of the unit called the *mil* ($\frac{1}{1000}''$). Number 8 gauge wire is 128 mils in diameter. What would be the diameter of the approximately similar metric size?

_____ Answer

15. If the wire mentioned in problem 9 had an insulation thickness of 0.05″, what would be the thickness of the wire in millimeter?

_____ Answer

CHAPTER FIVE
SQUARES AND
SQUARE ROOTS

Square units are a part of practical measurement. They describe measurements such as the surface area of a floor or a building lot. Squaring numbers and extracting square roots are operations that are performed in many equations, such as for the area of circles or right-triangle solutions. Because the applications are so varied, a good foundation for squaring and extracting square roots is essential.

5-1
Roots of Numbers

The *square root* of a number is defined as one of its two equal factors. For example, 3×3 are the equal factors of 9 and are its roots. In 16, the two equal factors are 4×4, and 4 is the square root of 16.

A *radical sign* is used to indicate the root of a number:

Example $\sqrt{64} = 8$ $\sqrt{36} = 6$ $\sqrt{100} = 10$

Some numbers are *perfect squares*, like 1, 4, 9, 16, 25, 36, 49, 64, and 81. The roots of these numbers should be obvious. All the roots are exactly even. Numbers like 5, 7, 10, 13, 15, etc. have roots that include fractions. Larger numbers, like 4789, may or may not be perfect squares, and the roots are not obvious.

There are three ways of finding a square root of a number. The easiest way, naturally, is to use a calculator with a square-root key. This will give the root of a number, limited only by the number of digits in the calculator's display. The second way of determining the square root of a number is by using tables, such as Table 5 in the Appendix. The third method demands a good deal of work with a paper and pencil. However, because calculators and tables are so convenient, this book will not cover the third method.

Table 5 gives square roots of numbers 1 through 999. There are many methods for expanding this table to find the square root of any number. If extremely accurate answers are needed, other methods than the ones discussed in the text should be used. For fractional numbers between 1 and 10, use the following procedure:

Example $\sqrt{3.46} = \sqrt{3.46 \times \dfrac{100}{100}} = \sqrt{\dfrac{346}{100}}$

As $\sqrt{346} = 18.60$ (from table) and $\sqrt{100} = 10$

$\sqrt{\dfrac{346}{100}} = \dfrac{18.60}{10} = 1.86$ answer

For numbers less than 1:

$$\sqrt{0.0068} = \sqrt{0.0068 \times \frac{10,000}{10,000}} = \sqrt{\frac{68}{10,000}}$$

as $\quad \sqrt{68} = 8.246 \quad$ and $\quad \sqrt{10,000} = 100 \quad$ from Table 5

$$\sqrt{\frac{68}{10,000}} = \frac{8,246}{100} = 0.08246 \cong 0.08$$

(This will result in only an approximate square root.)

$$\sqrt{0.788} = \sqrt{0.788 \times \frac{100}{100}} = \sqrt{\frac{78.8}{100}}$$

$$= \sqrt{\frac{79}{100}} = \frac{8.8882}{10} = 0.88882 \cong 0.889$$

For numbers greater than in Table 5:

$$\sqrt{54,658} = \sqrt{54,658 \times \frac{100}{100}} = \sqrt{546.58 \times 100}$$

By rounding off 546.58 to 547,

$$\sqrt{547} = 23.38 \quad \text{and} \quad \sqrt{100} = 10 \quad \text{from Table 5}$$

$$23.38 \times 10 = 233.8$$

$$\sqrt{54,658} \cong 233.8 \cong 234$$

Example

$$\sqrt{12,500} = \sqrt{125,00 \times \frac{100}{100}} = \sqrt{125 \times 100}$$

$$\sqrt{125} = 11.1803 \quad \text{and} \quad \sqrt{100} = 10 \quad \text{From Table 5}$$

$$11.1803 \times 10 = 111.803$$

$$\sqrt{12,500} = 111.803 \cong 112$$

Exercises   Determine the approximate square root of the following using Table 5:

1. 8.6	2. 38.78
3. 1.62	4. 0.462
5. 0.0084	6. 5672
7. 8888	8. 14,728
9. 42.7	10. 52,876
11. 1.47	12. 3.14

13. 22.8   14. 0.072

15. 0.625   16. 126

5-2
Squaring Numbers Using
Table 5

To square a number means to multiply it by itself, as $6 \times 6 = 36$, $5 \times 5 = 25$, $15 \times 15 = 225$, etc. These operations may be indicated by the use of exponents.

Example

$$6^2 \; 5^2 \; 15^2$$
Exponents

where 2 written to the upper right of the number to be squared is called an *exponent*. This would mean to multiply the number by itself. If the exponent were 3, as in 2^3, this would mean *cube* 2 or multiply 2 three times.

Example

$$2^3 = \mathbf{2 \times 2 \times 2 = 8}$$

Again, the easiest way to perform this operation is with an electronic calculator. Table 5 in the Appendix can be used, but only to an accuracy of three significant figures, which will suffice for this text. For numbers between 1 and 10:

Example 8.25^2

Choose a multiplier that will make the number fit the table.

$$\left(\frac{8.25 \times 100}{100} \right)^2$$

$$\left(\frac{825}{100} \right)^2$$

$$825^2 = 680{,}625 \qquad 100^2 = 10{,}000$$

(From Table 5)

$$\frac{680{,}625}{10{,}000} = 68.0625$$

$$8.25^2 = 68.0625 \cong 68.1$$

For numbers less than 1:

$$0.68^2$$

Choose a multiplier that will make the number fit the table.

$$\left(\frac{0.68 \times 100}{100} \right)^2$$

$$\left(\frac{68}{100} \right)^2$$

$$68^2 = 4624 \qquad 100^2 = 10{,}000$$

$$\frac{4624}{10{,}000} = 0.4624$$

$$0.68^2 = 0.4624 \cong 0.462$$

For numbers greater than the table:

$$1486^2$$

Divide by 10 first.

$$\left(\frac{1486 \times 10}{10}\right)^2 = (148.6 \times 10)^2$$

$$148.6 \cong 149$$

$$149^2 = 22{,}201 \qquad 10^2 = 100$$

$$22{,}201 \times 100 = 2{,}220{,}100$$

$$1486^2 = 2{,}220{,}100 \cong 2{,}220{,}000$$

Actual value is 2,208,196

Exercises Square the following numbers using Table 5:

1. 425

2. 0.036

3. 1642

4. 0.75

5. 0.0089

6. 2485

7. 32.4

8. 8.62

EVALUATION PROBLEMS

Perform the operations as indicated:

1. 86^2

2. 8.6^2

3. 0.86^2

4. 866^2

5. $\sqrt{75}$

6. $\sqrt{7.5}$

7. $\sqrt{750}$

8. 3.14^2

9. 9874^2

10. 55.05^2

11. $\sqrt{95.95}$

12. 9.3^2

13. 8.2^2

14. 1.25^2

15. $\sqrt{2.5}$

16. 25^2

17. $\sqrt{256}$

18. 0.0046^2

19. 0.042^2

20. $\sqrt{.0077}$

21. $\sqrt{0.00025}$

22. $416{,}000^2$

23. $\sqrt{5280}$

24. $\sqrt{3.35}$

5-3
Right-Triangle Solutions

A common application of squaring numbers and determining square roots can be applied to right triangles. Several thousand years ago, a Greek named Pythagoras determined that the sum of the squares of the two short sides (the *legs*) of a right triangle equal the square of the longest side (*hypotenuse*). This is graphically illustrated by Fig. 5-1.

Example

Altitude squared plus the base squared equals the hypotenuse squared.

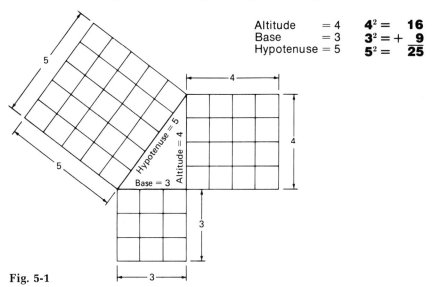

Altitude   = 4 $4^2 =$ **16**
Base   = 3 $3^2 = +$ **9**
Hypotenuse = 5 $5^2 =$ **25**

Fig. 5-1

In standard right-triangle notations shown in Fig. 5-2, the base is given the letter b, altitude the letter a, and hypotenuse the letter c. This relationship is described in the Pythagorean formula $c^2 = a^2 + b^2$.

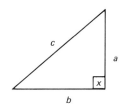

Fig. 5-2

1. To find c: $c = \sqrt{a^2 + b^2}$

2. To find a: $a = \sqrt{c^2 - b^2}$

3. To find b: $b = \sqrt{c^2 - a^2}$

Example

Find the altitude of a right triangle whose base is 15 and whose hypotenuse is 23.

Select the correct form of the Pythagorean formula.

$$a = \sqrt{c^2 - b^2} \qquad c = 23, \, b = 15$$
$$= \sqrt{(23)^2 - (15)^2}$$

Square 23 and 15.

$$= \sqrt{529 - 225}$$

Subtract.

$$= \sqrt{304}$$

Extract square root.

$$= 17.4 \text{ Answer}$$

Exercises Solve the following problems by selecting the correct form of the Pythagorean formula:

1. If $a = 7$ and $b = 6$ find c.

$c =$ _____ Answer

2. If the given hypotenuse equals 680 and the altitude equals 80, find the base.

$b =$ _____ Answer

3. Find a, if $c = 486$ and $b = 127$.

$a =$ _____ Answer

4. Find b, if $c = 8.46$ and $a = 2.26$.

$b =$ _____ Answer

5. Given the base of 0.68 and the altitude of 0.425, find the hypotenuse.

$c =$ _____ Answer

5-4
Applications of the Pythagorean Formula

The Pythagorean formula can be applied any time measurements are applicable to the right triangle.

Example

The length of the rafter illustrated in Fig. 5-3 can be calculated if the rise and run are known.

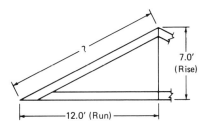

7.0′ (Rise)

12.0′ (Run)

Fig. 5-3

Select the correct form of the Pythagorean formula where rise equals the altitude a and run equals the base b.

$$c = \sqrt{a^2 + b^2} \qquad a = 7, b = 12$$
$$= \sqrt{7^2 + 12^2}$$
$$= \sqrt{49 + 144}$$
$$= \sqrt{193} = 13.89$$
$$\cong 14'$$

Example

A distance across a body of water can be measured as indicated in Fig. 5-4.

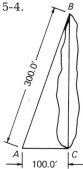

B

300.0′

A   C
100.0′

Fig. 5-4

The distances AB and AC can be measured since they are on land. BC can be calculated by the Pythagorean formula,

where AB = hypotenuse

AC = the base

BC = the length of the body of water

$$a = \sqrt{c^2 - b^2} \qquad c = 300, b = 100$$
$$= \sqrt{300^2 - 100^2}$$
$$= \sqrt{90{,}000 - 10{,}000}$$
$$= \sqrt{80{,}000}$$
$$= 282.8' \cong 283'$$

Solve the following:

1. A 33' television antenna is to be erected on a flat roof and held with guy wires. The guy wires will be anchored 37' from the base of the antenna. How long will the guy wires be?

_____ Answer

2. A 35' ladder is available to attempt to reach a window 28' above the ground. Because of construction, the foot of ladder must be placed 15' from the bottom of the building. Will the ladder reach the window? How far up the building will the ladder reach?

_____ Answer

3. A drafter has determined that a dimension missing on a drawing is part of a right triangle. The base dimension is 17 cm and the hypotenuse is 38 cm. What is the length of the missing dimension?

_____ Answer

4. A maintenance engineer needs to know the length of the diagonal distance of a room. However, a work station in the center of the room makes this measurement difficult to obtain with a ruler. If the room is 28' by 45', what is this distance.

_____ Answer

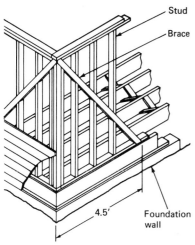

Stud

Brace

4.5′

Foundation wall

Fig. 5-5

5. A diagonal brace is to be placed in the corner of a building. The height of the wall is 8′ and the brace is to be 4.5′ from the corner. What is the length of the brace in Fig. 5-5?

_____ Answer

6. In the sketch of the roof truss (Fig. 5-6), the distance from *A* to *B* (called the *run*) is 18′, and the distance from *A* to *C* (the *roof rafter*) is 19′. What is the approximate distance of the vertical rise from *B* to *C*?

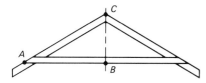

Fig. 5-6

_____ Answer

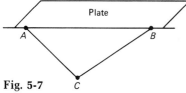

Plate

Fig. 5-7

7. The steel brace illustrated in Fig. 5-7 is used to help support a steel plate. It will be welded to the plate at points *A* and *B*, a distance of 82 cm. If the distance from *B* to *C* is 68 cm, what is the length from *A* to *C*? Angle *C* is a right angle.

_____ Answer

8. How many meters of fence will be needed to fence the lot illustrated in Fig. 5-8. (Determine the missing dimension.)

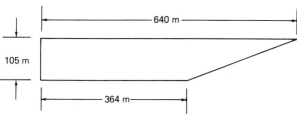

640 m

105 m

364 m

Fig. 5-8

_____ Answer

CHAPTER SIX
PERIMETERS, AREAS, AND VOLUMES

Certain basic geometric figures are common to all technical areas. Most of the figures used in technical computations are based on the rectangle, triangle, and circle. For example, the calculation of piston displacement in an automobile engine uses a circle. An understanding of Figs. 6-1 to 6-10 and associated terminology is essential in any technical field.

6-1
Basic Geometric Figures

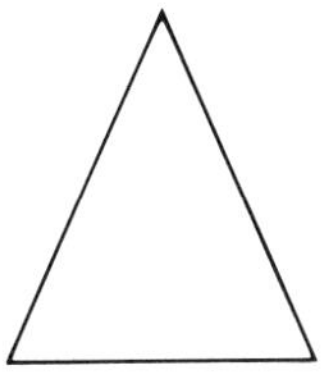

Fig. 6-1
Isosceles triangle: Two sides are equal.

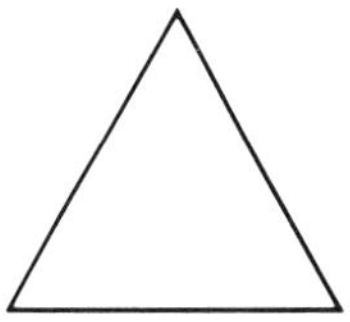

Fig. 6-2
Equilateral triangle: Three sides are equal.

Fig. 6-3
Scalene triangle: No sides are equal.

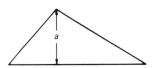

Fig. 6-4
Height, or altitude, of a triangle.

Fig. 6-5
Rectangle: Opposite sides are equal.

Fig. 6-6
Square: A rectangle with all sides equal.

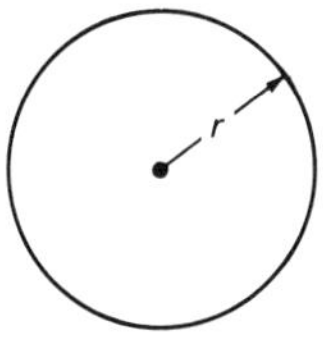

Fig. 6-7
Radius of a circle.

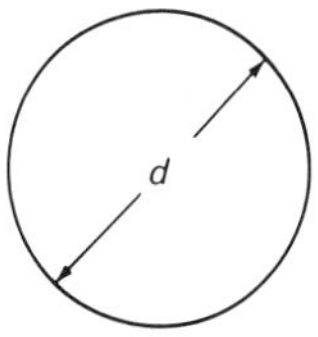

Fig. 6-8
Diameter of a circle.

Fig. 6-9
Parallelogram.

Fig. 6-10
Trapezoid.

6-2
Perimeter
The *perimeter* of any figure is the distance around its edge. For straight-sided figures, like the square, triangle, parallelogram, or rectangle, the perimeter is the sum of the sides (see Fig. 6-11).

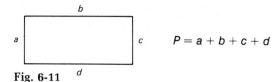

$$P = a + b + c + d$$

Fig. 6-11

In a rectangle, since the opposite sides are equal, several equations apply, as illustrated in Fig. 6-12.

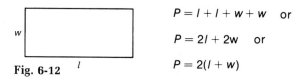

$$P = l + l + w + w \quad \text{or}$$

$$P = 2l + 2w \quad \text{or}$$

$$P = 2(l + w)$$

Fig. 6-12

Likewise, a triangle's perimeter is the distance around its edge, as shown in Fig. 6-13.

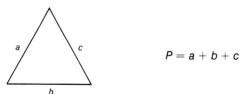

$$P = a + b + c$$

Fig. 6-13

The equation of some triangles can be simplified as shown by Fig. 6-14*a*. For an isosceles triangle,

Isoceles

$$P = a + a + b \quad \text{or} \quad P = 2a + b$$

For an equilateral triangle,

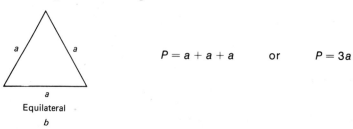

Equilateral

$$P = a + a + a \quad \text{or} \quad P = 3a$$

Fig. 6-14

Determine the perimeter of the rectangles with the dimensions given:

	Length	Width	Perimeter
1.	4.5"	2.5"	_____
2.	6.5'	6"	_____
3.	0.75'	0.04'	_____
4.	0.11"	1.5"	_____
5.	452 yd	640 yd	_____
6.	1050'	1000'	_____

Determine the perimeter of triangles with the dimensions given:

	Base	Side 1	Side 2	Perimeter
7.	3.5"	6.4"	4.8"	_____
8.	32 cm	160 mm	160 mm	_____
9.	4' 8"	56"	56"	_____
10.	800 mm	120 cm	1200 mm	_____
11.	6000'	4000'	2300'	_____
12.	0.075"	0.05"	0.0287"	_____

6-3
Circumference of a Circle

The perimeter of a circle is referred to as its *circumference*. The relationship that exists between the circumference and diameter is illustrated in Fig. 6-15. If the radius of a circle is curved to fit the contour of the circumference, it will fit approximately 6.28 times on the circumference. Likewise, the diameter will fit approximately 3.14 times. The relationship of the diameter to the circumference (3.14) is given by the Greek symbol π (pronounced "pie").

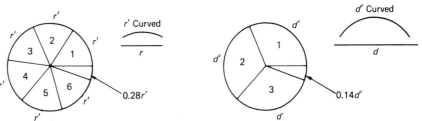

Fig. 6.15
Circumference = 6.28 × radius. Circumference = 3.14 × diameter.

Determine the circumference of the following circles with the given dimensions.

	Radius	**Circumference**
1.	1'	_____
2.	30 m	_____
3.	2.5"	_____

	Diameter	
4.	$\frac{1}{2}''$	_____
5.	5.5 cm	_____
6.	850'	_____

EVALUATION PROBLEMS

1. A rectangular lot is to be fenced with field fence. Each roll of fence contains 330' and sells for $45 per roll. What will it cost to fence a lot 680' by 275'? Fence must be purchased in full rolls.

_____ Answer

2. Weatherstripping around a rectangular automobile window is to be replaced. How many inches of weatherstripping will be needed if the window is $19\frac{1}{2}''$ by $23\frac{5}{8}''$?

_____ Answer

3. How many bricks $5\frac{1}{2}''$ long would be required to build a circular brick planter 12.5' in diameter? The planter will be three bricks high. Neglect the width of the mortar.

_____ Answer

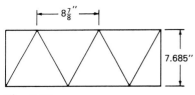

Fig. 6-16

4. Figure 6-16 illustrates a bracket that is to be welded together from $\frac{1}{2}''$ angle iron. The triangles are all equilateral and are $8\frac{7}{8}''$ on each side. What is the total length of angle iron required?

_____ Answer

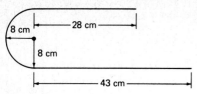

Fig. 6-17

5. Figure 6-17 illustrates the bending outline for a piece of 10 mm copper tubing. What is the total length of tubing needed to make the layout?

_____ Answer

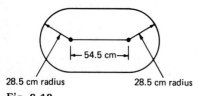

Fig. 6-18

6. A tubular rubber seal will be placed under the coverplate illustrated in Fig. 6-18. What is the total length of seal which will be required?

_____ Answer

6-4
Area of Rectangles,
Triangles,
and Circles

The *area* of a figure is defined as the amount of surface enclosed within its perimeter. This is referred to as the *square measurement* of the surface. An example of this is illustrated in Fig. 6-19 using a rectangle 3in by 4in.

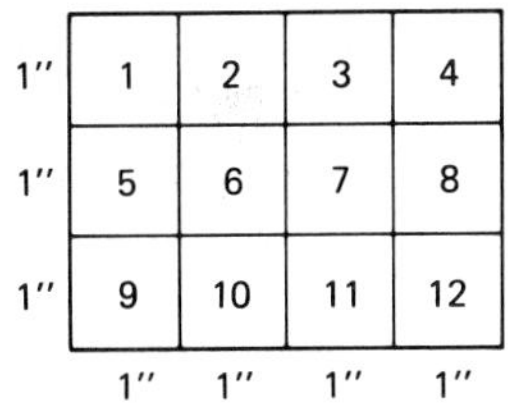

Fig. 6-19
This figure can be divided into 12 squares, each 1 in. × 1 in.—that is, 12 square inches.

Since this figure has 12 squares, 1 in on each side, it has an area of 12 in² (square inches). The area can be determined by multiplying the length times the width ($A = lw$), as shown in Fig. 6-20.

$A = lw$

Fig. 6-20

A triangle is one-half of a square, rectangle, or parallelogram, as illustrated in Fig. 6-21.

  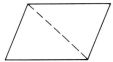

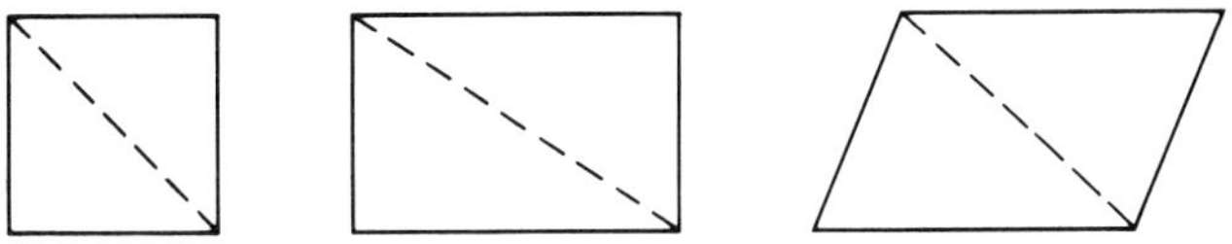

Fig. 6-21

The area of a triangle, therefore, is one-half that of a rectangle, and the equation for area of a triangle is

$$A = \frac{1}{2} ba.$$

The base and altitude are defined as illustrated in Fig. 6-22.

 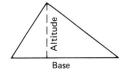

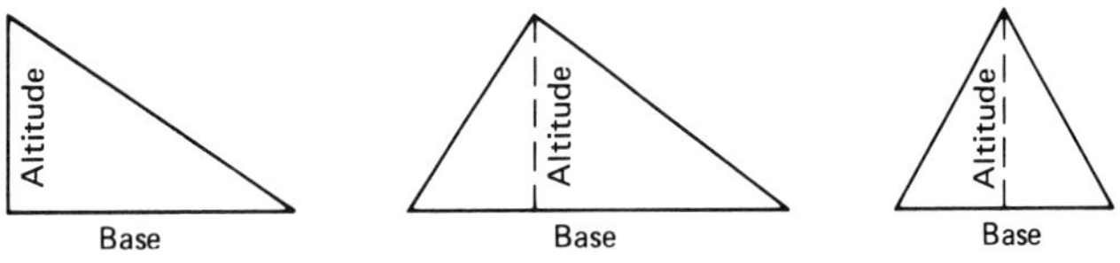

Fig. 6-22

$$A = \frac{1}{2} ba \qquad \text{or} \qquad A = \frac{ba}{2}$$

The area of a circle in terms of the radius can be determined by

$$A = \pi r^2 \qquad \text{or} \qquad A = 3.14r^2$$

where r = the radius of a given circle and π (pi) = 3.14

Since the diameter of a circle is usually what is measured in a practical application, an equation using the diameter may be more useful.

$$A = 0.785d^2$$

where d = the diameter of a circle

Exercises
Area Problems

Determine the area of the following figures:

Rectangles $\quad A = lw$

	Length	Width	Area
1.	16″	2.5″	_____
2.	35 cm	16 mm	_____
3.	3′ 4″	22″	_____
4.	180 mm	4.5 cm	_____

Triangles $\quad A = \dfrac{ba}{2}$

	Base	Altitude	Area
5.	16″	8″	_____
6.	1′ 4″	1′ 6″	_____
7.	0.06 m	14 cm	_____
8.	1800 mm	260 cm	_____

Circles $\quad A = 0.785d^2 \quad$ or $\quad A = 3.14r^2$

	Diameter	Radius	Area
9.	36 cm	_____	_____
10.	1′	_____	_____
11.	_____	50 cm	_____
12.	_____	3′ 8″	_____

6-5
Composite Areas
In technical applications, the area of most geometric figures can be found by finding the areas of all component parts. For instance, a parallelogram is a four-sided figure with opposite sides parallel. The angles, however, are not right angles, as Fig. 6-23 illustrates.

Fig. 6-23

To determine the area of a parallelogram, divide the parallelogram into three parts: two triangles and a rectangle, as shown in Fig. 6-24.

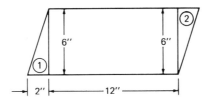

Fig. 6-24

Area of triangle 1

$$A_1 = \frac{ba}{2} = \frac{6 \times 2}{2} = 6 \text{ in}^2$$

Area of triangle 2

$$A_2 = \frac{ba}{2} = \frac{6 \times 2}{2} = 6 \text{ in}^2$$

Area of rectangle R

$$A_R = lw = 6 \times 12 = 72 \text{ in}^2$$

Area of parallelogram

$$A_1 + A_2 + A_R$$
$$6 \text{ in}^2 + 6 \text{ in}^2 + 72 \text{ in}^2 = 84 \text{ in}^2$$

This can be simplified to give the equation for the area of a parallelogram

$$A = ab$$

where a = altitude and b = base (see Fig. 6-23).

EVALUATION PROBLEMS

Determine the area of each of the Figs. 6-25 through 6-30.

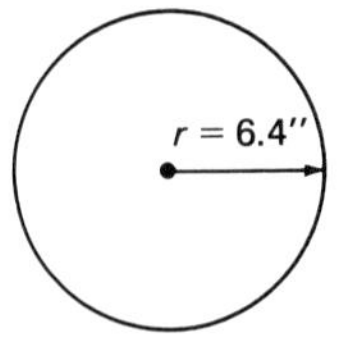

Fig. 6-25

_____ Answer

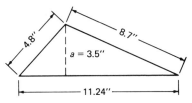

Fig. 6-26

_____ Answer

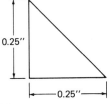

Fig. 6-27

_____ Answer

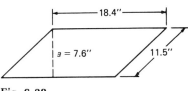

Fig. 6-28

_____ Answer

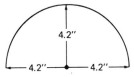

Fig. 6-29

_____ Answer

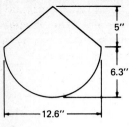

Fig. 6-30

_____ Answer

6-6
Area of Geometric Shapes

Figures 6-31a, b, and c represent the cross-sectional area of common structural material, such as angle iron, U-channel, etc. The shaded area in Fig. 6-31a is the cross-sectional area of a piece of angle iron with a uniform thickness of 0.25 in.

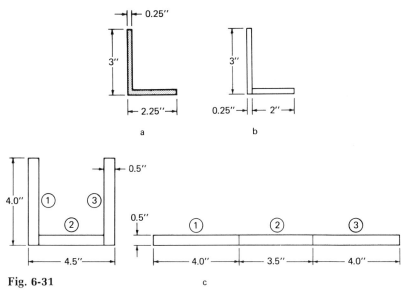

Fig. 6-31

If the cross section is divided into two basic rectangles as in Fig. 6-31b, the area of each rectangle can be found and the sum of the two areas will equal the cross-sectional area.

Example

Area of the larger rectangle:

$$A = lw$$
$$= 3'' \times 0.25''$$
$$= 0.75 \text{ in}^2$$

Area of smaller rectangle:

$$A = lw$$
$$= 2'' \times 0.25''$$
$$= 0.50 \text{ in}^2$$

Cross-sectional area $= 0.75 \text{ in}^2 + 0.50 \text{ in}^2 = 1.25 \text{ in}^2$

Example

Determine the cross-sectional area of Fig. 6-31c. The figure has a uniform thickness of 0.5".

Since the figure is uniform, the area can be considered for one long rectangle rather than three small rectangles. The length is equal to the sum of the sides

$$l = 4'' + 3.5'' + 4'' = 11.5''$$

The area is then

$$A = lw$$

$$= 11.5'' \, (0.5'')$$

$$= 5.75 \text{ in}^2$$

Another geometric shape whose area should be considered is a cylinder. A closed cylinder is composed of two circles which form the ends of the cylinder and the curved surface area of the cylinder which forms a rectangle when unfolded as indicated in Fig. 6-32. A cylinder used as a storage tank may be mounted with one end on the ground, and this end would not be included in the surface area. A large smokestack would only have a curved surface area and no ends.

Example

Find the area of a closed cylinder if it is 8″ in diameter and 10″ long.

Area of the ends

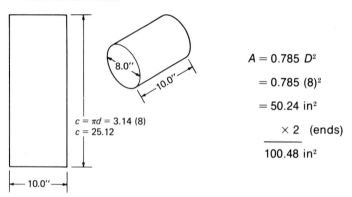

$$A = 0.785 \, D^2$$

$$= 0.785 \, (8)^2$$

$$= 50.24 \text{ in}^2$$

$$\underline{\times 2 \quad (\text{ends})}$$

$$100.48 \text{ in}^2$$

c = πd = 3.14 (8)
c = 25.12

Fig. 6-32
Length will equal the circumference.

Area of the curved surface

$$A = lw$$

$$= 25.12 \, (10)$$

$$= 251.2 \text{ in}^2$$

Total surface area

$$100.48 + 251.2 = 351.68 \text{ in}^2 \cong 352 \text{ in}^2$$

Exercises Find the area of the following figures:
Geometric Shapes

1. In Fig. 6-33, A = 3.25″, B = 3.25″, and C is a uniform thickness of 0.65″.

Fig. 6-33

_____ Answer

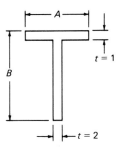

Fig. 6-34

2. In Fig. 6-34, $A = 3''$, $B = 4\frac{1}{2}''$, $t - 1 = 0.5''$, and $t - 2 = 0.6''$

_____ Answer

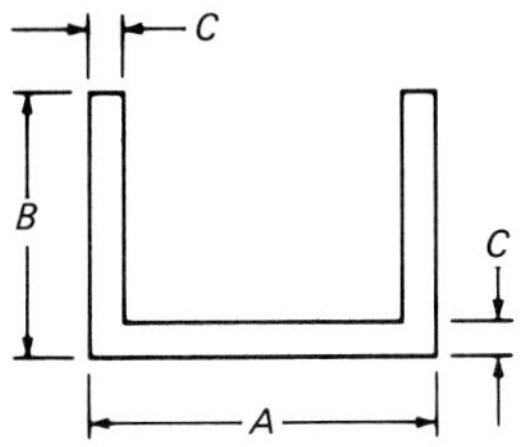

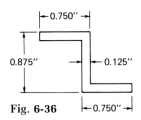

Fig. 6-35

3. In Fig. 6-35, $A = 4.375''$, $B = 3.25''$, and C is a uniform thickness of $0.400''$.

_____ Answer

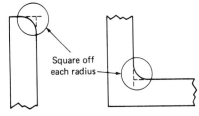

Fig. 6-36

4. In Fig. 6-36, 0.125 is a uniform thickness, and all other dimensions are as indicated.

_____ Answer

6-7
Area of Nonuniform
Geometric Figures

The following figures do not contain strictly uniform dimensions because they have inside and outside radii. The areas can be approximated using the same techniques used in Exercise 6-5. Neglect the radii and consider the figure to have square corners. In most cases, the area lost on an outside curve will be gained on a similar inside curve as shown in Fig. 6-37. (This method will be satisfactory for the purposes of this text.)

Square off
each radius

Fig. 6-37

Exercise 6-7   Find the areas of the following figures, using the dimensions illustrated:

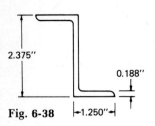

Fig. 6-38 |←1.250"→|

1.   In Fig. 6-38, 0.188" is a "uniform" thickness.

_____ Answer

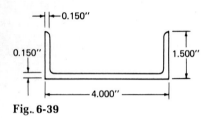

Fig.. 6-39

2.   In Fig. 6-39, 0.150" is a uniform thickness.

_____ Answer

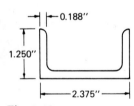

Fig. 6-40

3.   In Fig. 6-40, 0.188" is a uniform thickness.

_____ Answer

EVALUATION PROBLEMS

Determine the area of the following figures:

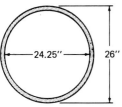

Fig. 6-41

1. Find the area of the shaded portion in Fig. 6-41.

_____ Answer

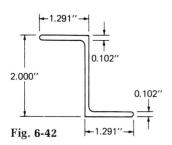

Fig. 6-42

2. In Fig. 6-42, 0.102 is a "uniform" thickness.

_____ Answer

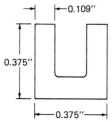

Fig. 6-43

3. In Fig. 6-43, 0.109 is a "uniform" thickness.

_____ Answer

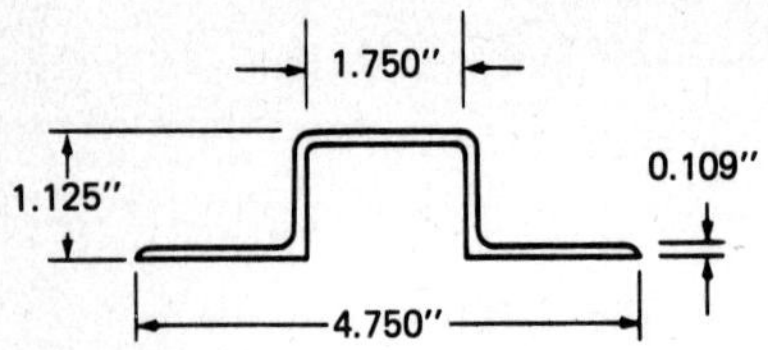

Fig. 6-44

4. In Fig. 6-44, 0.109 is a "uniform" thickness.

_____ Answer

The *volume* of an object can be defined as the amount of space it oc-
cupies. The volume of a rectangular solid 2″ × 3″ × 4″ (Fig. 6-45)
would occupy a space of 24 in³ (cubic inches).

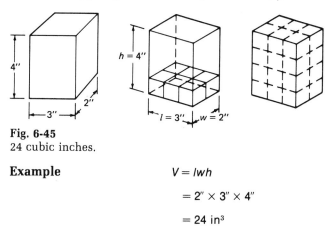

Fig. 6-45
24 cubic inches.

Example

$$V = lwh$$

$$= 2'' \times 3'' \times 4''$$

$$= 24 \text{ in}^3$$

The formula $V = lwh$ is convenient to use when working with rectangular figures. However, volumes of triangular solids, prisms, cylinders,
or structural materials like I-beams can be determined using the cross-
sectional area and the length or height of the figure. Illustrated in Fig.
6-46 is a triangular solid. To determine the volume, first determine the
area of the triangle (shaded area), and then multiply the area by the
length of the solid. Observe caution when computing volume to make
sure all dimensions are in the same units.

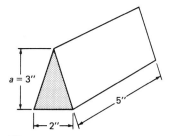

Fig. 6-46

The volume of any figure with a uniform length can be determined by
this method. For instance, the volume of the I-beam in Fig. 6-47 could
be determined by computing the cross-sectional area of the end of the
beam and multiplying by the length. Similarly, the volumes of the cylinder and elliptical tank in Fig. 6-47 can be found by the same basic
procedure.

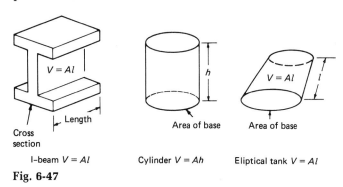

Fig. 6-47

$$\text{Area of triangle} = \frac{1}{2}ba$$

$$A = \frac{1}{2}(3)(2)$$

$$= 3 \text{ in}^2$$

$$\text{Volume} = A \times (\text{length of the object})$$

$$V = 3 \text{ in}^2 \times 5''$$

$$= 15 \text{ in}^3$$

Exercises Determine the volume of the following figures:

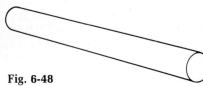

Fig. 6-48

1. The diameter of the cylinder in Fig. 6-48 is 2.6″ and the length is 11″.

_____ Answer

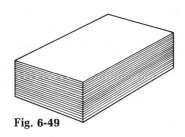

Fig. 6-49

2. The rectangular solid in Fig. 6-49 has a length of 4.5″, a width of 3.75″, and a height of 1.5″.

_____ Answer

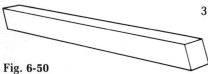

Fig. 6-50

3. The solid in Fig. 6-50 is 1.5″ square and 2.5′ long.

_____ Answer

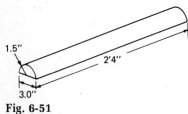

1.5″

2′4″

3.0″

Fig. 6-51

4. Find the volume of the solid shown in Fig. 6-51.

_____ Answer

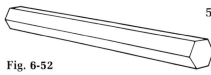

Fig. 6-52

5. The hexagonal solid in Fig. 6-52 is $4\frac{1}{2}'$ long, and the side of the hexagon is 1.6".

_____ Answer

6-9
Determining Weight
through Use of Volume

The weight of objects can be determined if two things are known: the volume, and the weight of material per unit volume. Table 3, a table of weight per unit volume of common materials, is provided in the Appendix.

Once the required information is known, determine the volume of the object, and then multiply by the weight per unit volume.

Example

If the triangular solid used in Fig. 6-46 were made of steel, its weight would be 4.25 lb.

$$\text{Weight} = \text{Volume (in}^3) \times 0.2833 \text{ 1b/in}^3 \text{ (from Table 3)}$$

$$= 15.0 \text{ in}^3 \times 0.2833$$

$$= 4.25 \text{ 1b}$$

Exercises
Weight and Volume

Determine the weight of the objects by using volume and the conversions in Table 3.

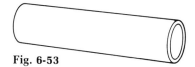

Fig. 6-53

1. The outside diameter of the steel boiler pipe is 1.25", and the inside diameter is 0.75". If the pipe is 21' long, how many cubic inches of steel does it contain? What is the weight of the pipe?

$V = $ _____

$W = $ _____

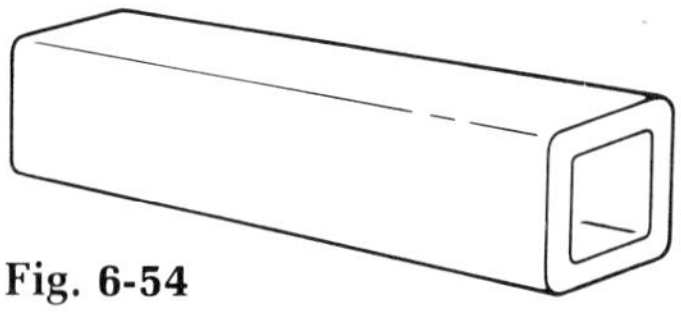

2. The outside square of the aluminum square channel in Fig. 6-54 is 2.25" on a side, and the inside square is 1.75" on a side. If the length is 12', what is the volume of the channel? What is the weight of the channel?

Fig. 6-54

$V = $ _____

$W = $ _____

EVALUATION PROBLEMS

1. How many yards of dirt must be removed when digging for a foundation of a rectangular building if the excavation is 94′ long, 36′ wide, and 25′ deep? (In trade terminology, a yard of concrete, gravel, dirt, etc. is assumed to be a cubic yard.)

_____ Answer

2. How many cartons can be stored to a height of 9′ in a space 10′ by 12′, if each carton is 2′ by 1′ 6″ by 1′? (Calculate by volume.)

_____ Answer

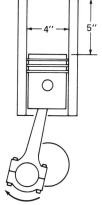

Fig. 6-55

3. Find the *displacement* of a piston (volume of the engine cylinder illustrated in Fig. 6-55 whose *bore* (diameter) is 4″ and whose *stroke* (height the piston moves) is 5″.

_____ Answer

4. How many gallons of oil does a railroad tank car hold if it is 8′ in diameter and 42′ long (1 ft^3 = 7$\frac{1}{2}$ gal)?

_____ Answer

5. A cylinder is to be chrome plated. The cost is determined by the surface area. What is the square-inch outside surface area of a closed cylinder 2.5″ in diameter and 14″ long.

_____ Answer

6. The inside of a measuring cylinder is to be chrome plated. The cylinder has no top, and the inside diameter is 4.25″. If the depth of the cylinder is 6.5″, what is the square-inch surface area to be plated.

_____ Answer

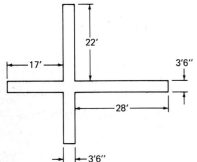
Fig. 6-56

7. Figure 6-56 is a drawing of a sidewalk of a uniform thickness of 4″. How many cubic yards of concrete would be required to pour the sidewalk?

_____ Answer

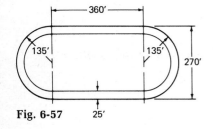
Fig. 6-57

8. Figure 6-57 is the sketch of an oval race track. Find the area of the track.

_____ Answer

9. The dirt has been removed from the track in Fig. 6-57 and filled with an all-weather track material to a depth of 3". How many yards of the material will be required to fill the track?

_____ Answer

10. Figure 6-58 is a field sketch of a go-cart track built by a neighborhood organization. The track will require a surface of compact clay to a depth of 5". If the cost is $8.80/yd, what will be the approximate cost for the clay surface?

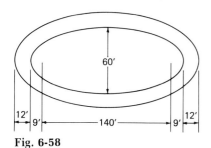

Fig. 6-58

_____ Answer

11. Several structural shapes are illustrated in Figs. 6-59 to 6-63. The cross-sectional area of the end of each shape is given. Determine the volume and weight of each piece (refer to Table 3).
   a. Cross-sectional area is 1.65 in²; material, aluminum; length is 12".

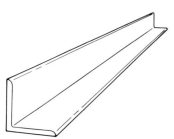

Fig. 6-59
Equal angle.

$V = $ _____

$W = $ _____

   b. Cross-sectional area is 4.75 in²; material, steel; length is 15'.

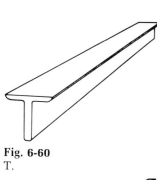

Fig. 6-60
T.

$V = $ _____

$W = $ _____

   c. Cross-sectional area 2.65 in²; material, brass; length is 25'.

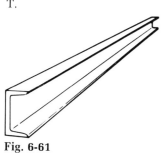

Fig. 6-61
Channel.

$V = $ _____

$W = $ _____

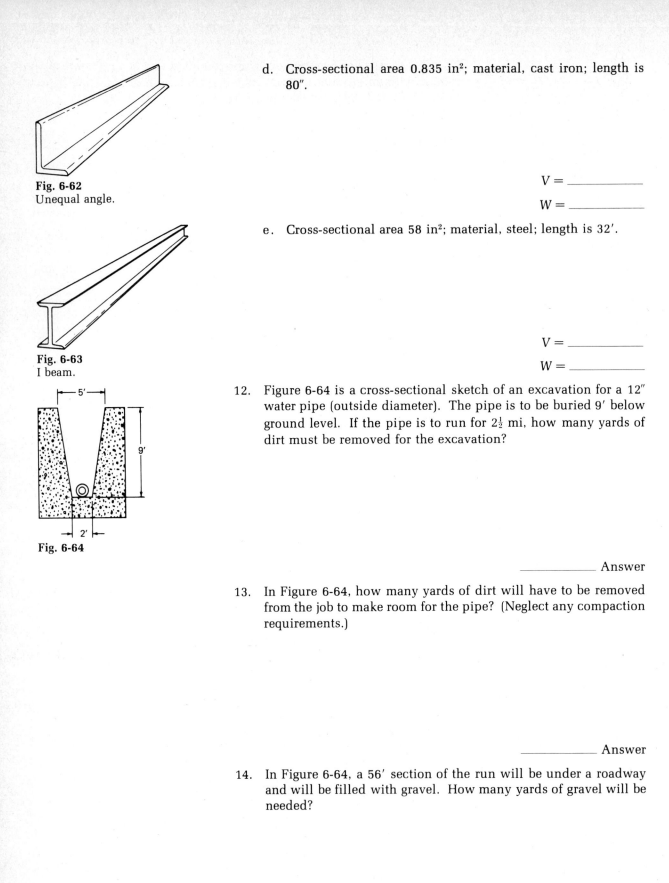

Fig. 6-62
Unequal angle.

Fig. 6-63
I beam.

Fig. 6-64

d. Cross-sectional area 0.835 in²; material, cast iron; length is 80″.

V = _____

W = _____

e. Cross-sectional area 58 in²; material, steel; length is 32′.

V = _____

W = _____

12. Figure 6-64 is a cross-sectional sketch of an excavation for a 12″ water pipe (outside diameter). The pipe is to be buried 9′ below ground level. If the pipe is to run for $2\frac{1}{2}$ mi, how many yards of dirt must be removed for the excavation?

_____ Answer

13. In Figure 6-64, how many yards of dirt will have to be removed from the job to make room for the pipe? (Neglect any compaction requirements.)

_____ Answer

14. In Figure 6-64, a 56′ section of the run will be under a roadway and will be filled with gravel. How many yards of gravel will be needed?

_____ Answer

6-10
Concrete Foundations

A slab foundation for a rectangular building will be made of footings in the shape of rectangles and a floor which will also be a rectangular solid. If the foundation were removed from the ground, it would appear to be a four-sided box without a top.

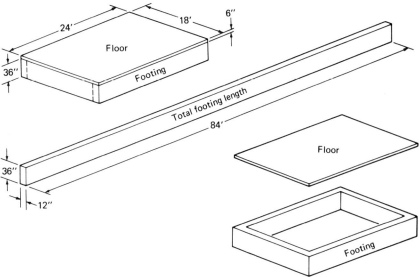

Fig. 6-65
Note that the actual length of the footing may be reduced by 4 ft because of the corners, but in a practical application this would not be necessary.

In Fig. 6-65, the footing is 12″ wide at the bottom, 84′ long, and 36″ from the ground to the bottom of the floor. The floor is 6″ thick and 24′ by 18′. The total amount of concrete in cubic yards needed to pour the foundation can be calculated by finding the volume of both the footing and the floor and then adding them. This will give the answer in cubic feet; the answer in cubic yards can be found by dividing this volume by 27, the number of cubic feet in a cubic yard. (The actual length of the footing can be reduced by 4 ft. because of the corners, but in practical application this would not be necessary.)

Volume of footing:

$$V = lwh$$
$$= 1' \times 3' \times 84'$$
$$= 252 \text{ ft}^3$$

Volume of floor:

$$V = lwh$$
$$= 24' \times 18' \times 0.5'$$
$$= 216 \text{ ft}^3$$

Total volume:

$$252 \text{ ft}^3 + 216 \text{ ft}^3 = 468 \text{ ft}^3$$

$$468 \text{ ft}^3 \div 27 \text{ ft}^3/\text{yd} = 17.33 \text{ yd}^3 \text{ of concrete}$$

Exercises   1.   a.   Figure 6-66 shows a sketch of the top view and side view of a
Volumes and Concrete   slab foundation. It will be poured in a frost-free climate with
                                    the footings only 12″ deep. How many cubic yards of concrete
                                    will be needed to pour the footings?

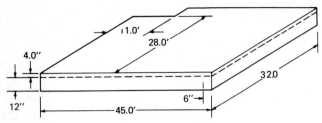

Fig. 6-66

_____ Answer

b.   How many cubic yards needed for the slab floor poured in Fig.
6-66? The floor is 4.0″ thick.

_____ Answer

c.   If concrete sells for $32.50/yd, how much will the concrete cost
for the footing and floor in Fig. 6-66?

_____ Answer

d.   A bag of cement weighs 94 lb and its volume is equal to 1 ft³. If
a five-bag mixture (five bags of cement for each cubic yard) is
used for the job in Fig. 6-66, how many bags of cement will be
required (calculated to the closest whole yard)?

_____ Answer

e. What will be the approximate weight of the concrete used in the job in Fig. 6-66?

_____ Answer

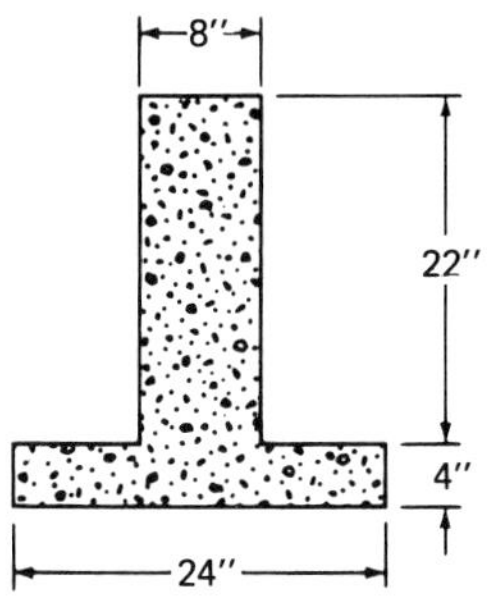

2. If the footing in Fig. 6-66 were modified to that illustrated in Fig. 6-67, how many yards of concrete would be required for the footing? The floor is poured separately with this type of footing.

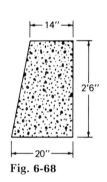
Fig. 6-67

_____ Answer

3. A concrete retaining wall will be poured for length of 36′. The cross section is given in Fig. 6-68. How many yards of concrete will be required?

Fig. 6-68

_____ Answer

4. In Fig. 6-68, a six-bag mixture of concrete (refer to problem 1d) is required for the wall. How many bags of concrete are needed (calculated to the closest whole yard)?

_____ Answer

REVIEW QUESTIONS

1. How many floor tiles 9″ square are required to cover a floor 12′ by 16′?

_____ Answer

2. How many square yards of surface area are on a spherical tank 26′ in diameter? (Refer to Table 2 in the Appendix for the equation.)

_____ Answer

3. How much would the contents of a 12′ spherical tank weigh if it were filled with gasoline?

_____ Answer

4. A circular cement pillar is used to hold a freeway bridge. The pillar is 42″ in diameter and 18′ 6″ in length. If 22% of the pillar volume is comprised of reinforcing steel, find (a) yards of concrete used, (b) weight of concrete, (c) weight of steel, and (d) total weight of pillar?

(a) _____

(b) _____

(c) _____

(d) _____

5. A cylindrical gasoline storage tank is 32′ in diameter and 24′ high. The top and side of the tank are to be painted. If the paint to be used covers 465 ft²/gal, how many gallons of paint will be required to paint the tank?

_____ Answer

6. A cross section of a simplified concrete-slab foundation is illustrated in Fig. 6-69, showing the foundation footing and slab floor. How many yards of concrete would be needed for a foundation 36′ by 28′? Remember that the footing will be under all sides of the slab floor.

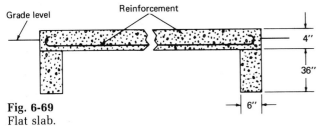

Fig. 6-69
Flat slab.

_____ Answer

7. The footing for a wood-floor house is illustrated in Fig. 6-70. How many yards of concrete will be needed for a footing 262′ in length?

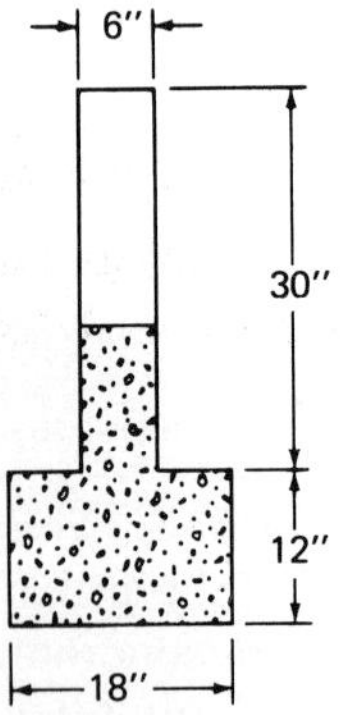

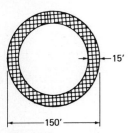

Fig. 6-70

_____ Answer

8. A circular walkway around a planter is to be resurfaced. What is the area of the walkway indicated by the shaded area in Figure 6-71?

Fig. 6-71

_____ Answer

9. Determine the surface area to be painted of a closed cylindrical tank if it is 40′ long and 25′ in diameter and will be painted on all sides.

_____ Answer

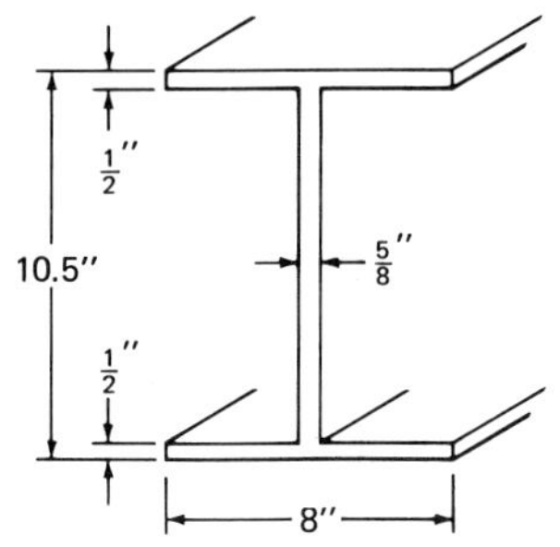

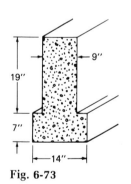

Fig. 6-72

10. If the steel I-beam in Fig. 6-72 has a length of 22′, what is its volume and weight?

Volume _____

Weight _____

11. How much does a concrete floor weigh if it is 4″ thick and 20′ × 18′?

_____ Answer

12. Figure 6-73 is the cross section of a foundation footing. If 160′ of footing is to be poured, how many yards of concrete will be required?

Fig. 6-73

_____ Answer

13. If 15% of the volume of the footing in Fig. 6-73 were steel, how much would the steel weigh?

_____ Answer

14. A piece of aluminum hexagonal stock is 0.265″ on each side. What will be the weight of a 12′ length?

_____ Answer

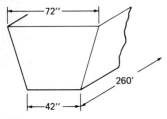

Fig. 6-74

15. How many yards of dirt will be removed from the excavation sketched in figure 6-74 if the depth is 4.5′?

_____ Answer

16. A cylindrical oil tank mounted vertically on a concrete foundation has a diameter of 22′ and a height of 22′. The tank is to be painted, and the manufacturer of the paint states that each gallon will cover 595 ft². How many gallons will be required?

_____ Answer

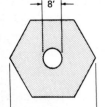

Fig. 6-75

17. The top view of the concrete foundation for the bottom of a reflecting pool is sketched in Fig. 6-75. The shaded portion will be concrete to a depth of 5″. What will the concrete cost if it sells for $38.50/yd³? The 8′ center section will house the filter and control units and will not need a foundation.

_____ Answer

CHAPTER SEVEN
RATIO AND PROPORTION

Ratios are used for the comparison of two or more things. The statement "That man weighs twice as much as that boy" is an example of a ratio used as a comparison. This ratio is expressed as 2 to 1 (for every 2 lb the man weighs, the boy weighs 1). In a technical area, relative speeds of motors, mixture quantities of antifreeze and water, and the scale of a building plan are examples of ratio comparisons.

A *proportion* is a mathmatical expression showing the equality of two ratios. The relative speeds of two belted pulleys, the relationship between meshing gears, and lever action are all applications of proportions.

7-1
Ratio

Ratio is commonly used to compare numbers which are usually written in the same unit values. For example, 5 cm is half of 10 cm and may be expressed as a ratio that can be written

5 to 10   or   5:10   or   5/10

When the fraction $\frac{5}{10}$ is reduced, it could be expressed as

1 to 2

The ratio of 5 to 10 is the same as the ratio 1 to 2. It is sometimes more convenient to express a ratio "to 1." For instance, if the fraction $\frac{5}{10}$ is changed to its decimal equivalent, the ratio can be expressed as 0.5 to 1, which is the same as 5 to 10 or 1 to 2. Having one part of a ratio equal to a whole unit or 1 may make it more understandable and easier to handle.

Remember to use the same unit value when expressing ratio, such as centimeters to centimeters, grams to grams, feet to feet, hours to hours, etc.

Exercises
Expressing Ratio

Express each of the ratios in like units and also "to 1" by dividing the numerator by the denominator.

4 h to 2 h

4 to 2   **is**   **4 ÷ 2**   **or**   **2 to 1**

18″ to 2′

1.5′ to 2′

1. 600 kg to 20 kg **600 to 20** or **30 to 1**

2. 40 km to 400 m _____ or _____

3. $1.80 to $0.30 _____ or _____

4. $\frac{1}{2}$ kL to $\frac{3}{4}$ kL _____ or _____

5. 600 rpm to 400 rpm _____ or _____

6. 6 h to 30 min _____ or _____

7. 60 kL to 100 L _____ or _____

8. 180 cm to 100 mm _____ or _____

9. 8.4 km to 12 m _____ or _____

10. 8 kg to 16 g _____ or _____

7-2 Application of Ratio

In preparing mortar for laying bricks, a mixture of sand, cement, and lime is generally used. The mixture chosen for this mortar is

3 parts sand   1 part cement $\frac{1}{4}$ part lime

The total parts in this mixture would be $4\frac{1}{4}$, and $\frac{3}{4.25}$ of the total would be sand, $\frac{1}{4.25}$ cement and $\frac{0.25}{4.25}$ lime. To apply this ratio, assume a total volume of mortar needed for the job was 3.0 m³. To determine the correct quantity of sand, cement, and lime needed, apply the ratio as follows:

Example

$$\text{Sand} = \frac{3}{4.25} \times 3.0 \text{ m}^3 = 2.12 \text{ m}^3$$

$$\text{Cement} = \frac{1}{4.25} \times 3.0 \text{ m}^3 = 0.706 \text{ m}^3$$

$$\text{Lime} = \frac{0.25}{4.25} \times 3.0 \text{ m}^3 = 0.176 \text{ m}^3$$

Check: 2.12 + 0.706 + 0.176 = 3 m³

Example

Divide $84 into a ration of 5:7.

Total number of parts   5 + 7 = 12

$$\frac{5}{12} \times \$84 = \$35 \qquad \frac{7}{12} \times \$84 = \$49$$

Check: $35 + $49 = $84

Exercises Solve the following problems with applications of ratio.

1. Specific gravity is defined as the ratio of a material to an equal volume of water, usually at 4°C. If a cubic centimeter of water weighs approximately 1 g and a cubic centimeter of steel weighs 7.84 g, what is the specific gravity of the steel?

_____ Answer

2. A cubic foot of water weighs 62.4 lb and a cubic foot of lead weighs 705 lb. What is the specific gravity of lead?

_____ Answer

3. A gallon of diesel fuel weighs approximately 5.84 lb. What is its specific gravity? A gallon of water weighs 8.33 lb.

_____ Answer

4. The ratio of gasoline to oil used in a two-cycle engine is 18 to 1. If 16 L of mixture are required, how much gas and oil will be needed?

Gas _____ Answer

Oil _____ Answer

5. Eight property owners are sharing expenses on a road assessment. Each parcel of land is assessed by the amount of land fronting the road. Three property owners have 65′ fronts, four have 82′ fronts, and one has 150′ fronting the road. If the total assessment is $30,000, what will each one pay?

4 property owners each _____ Answer

3 property owners each _____ Answer

1 property owner _____ Answer

575 cm³

67 cm³

Fig. 7-1

6. The compression ratio of a gasoline engine is defined as the ratio of cylinder volume at the bottom of the stroke to the volume at the top of the stroke. A cylinder of an engine has a full volume of 575 cm³ at the bottom of the stroke and 67 cm³ at the top. What is the compression ratio? (See Fig. 7-1.)

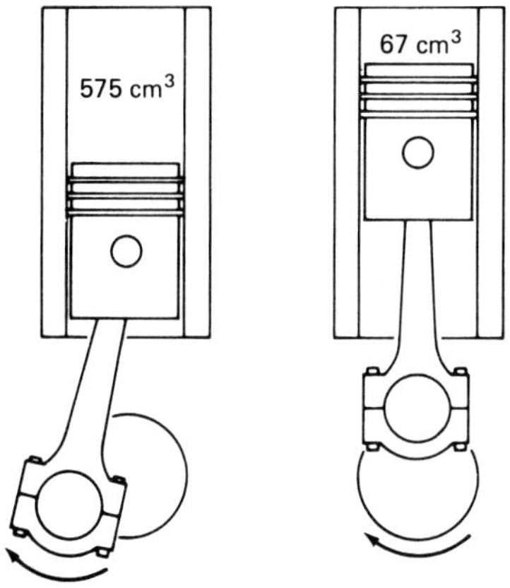

_____ Answer

7. A mixture of antifreeze for several automobile radiators is mixed at a ratio of 3.5 parts antifreeze to 5.5 parts water. How many quarts of each will be needed to mix 80 qt?

Antifreeze _____ Answer

Water _____ Answer

8. Three partners shared in a land investment. The first invested $8000 the second invested $12,500 and the third invested $16,500. The land sold for a profit of $45,000.00. What will each partner receive based on the original investment?

First investor _____ Answer

Second investor _____ Answer

Third investor _____ Answer

9. The effeciency of a machine is expressed as a ratio of the output to the input. For convenience, this is usually expressed as a percent. What is the percent efficiency of an electric motor that delivers 1.5 hp and requires 1375 W (watts) to operate (1 hp = 746 W)?

_____ Answer ·

10. A building plan is drawn to the scale 10 mm = 1 m (a ratio of 1 to 100). What will be the size of a rectangular building if the plan is 132 mm by 260 mm?

_____ Answer

EVALUATION PROBLEMS

Express the following as a ratio "to one":

1. 85 km to 15 m _____

2. 40 L to 8 kL _____

3. 36 h to 30 min _____

4. $0.37 to $3.70 _____

5. 465 ft to 15 mi _____

6. 25,000 L to 250 kL _____

Solve the following:

7. A sewage assessment is to be paid by property owners according to the number of feet that front the main highway. An assessment of $38,500 is to be paid by 15 property owners. Ten lots have 75′ fronting the road, three have 150′, and two have 200′. How much will each lot be assessed?

75′ front _____ Answer

150′ front _____ Answer

200′ front _____ Answer

8. A cleaning solvent used to clean grease from automotive parts is cut with kerosene at a ratio of 5 parts solvent to 2 parts kerosene. How many quarts of each are required to produce 12 gal of solution?

Solvent _____ Answer

Kerosene _____ Answer

9. An airplane is hired to seed rice fields, and the cost is to be shared by three parties. Each party will pay according to the amount of land seeded. The amount seeded was 20 acres, 15 acres, and 12 acres. If the total seeding cost is $880, what will each share cost?

20 acres ＿＿＿＿＿＿ Answer

15 acres ＿＿＿＿＿＿ Answer

12 acres ＿＿＿＿＿＿ Answer

10. What is the percent efficiency of an electric motor if it requires 1100 W input to produce a 1.25-hp output?

＿＿＿＿＿＿ Answer

When one ratio is equal to another, they are of *equal proportions*.

Example

$$\frac{1}{2} = \frac{4}{8} \qquad \frac{4}{3} = \frac{12}{9} \qquad \frac{2}{8} = \frac{1}{4} \qquad \text{etc.}$$

In the above examples, as in all equal proportions, the cross products are equal.

Example

$$\frac{1}{2} \times \frac{4}{8}$$

$$8 \times 1 = 2 \times 4$$

$$8 = 8$$

$$\frac{4}{3} \times \frac{12}{9}$$

$$4 \times 9 = 3 \times 12$$

$$36 = 36$$

$$\frac{2}{8} \times \frac{1}{4}$$

$$2 \times 4 = 8 \times 1$$

$$8 = 8$$

If any three parts of the proportion are known, the fourth part can be determined.

Example

$$\frac{1}{2} \times \frac{x}{4}$$

2x = 4

Divide 4 by 2.

x = 2

$$\frac{4}{y} \times \frac{12}{9}$$

12y = 36

Divide 36 by 12.

y = 3

$$\frac{2}{8} \times \frac{1}{z}$$

2z = 8

Divide 8 by 2.

z = 4

In each of the problems, determine the unknown by cross multiplication.

1. $\dfrac{4}{x}$ $\dfrac{10}{3}$ ___ **x = 1.2** ___

   10x = 12

   Divide by 10.

2. $\dfrac{x}{16} = \dfrac{5}{3}$ _____

3. $\dfrac{a}{12} = \dfrac{3}{8}$ _____

4. $\dfrac{1}{3} = \dfrac{400}{y}$ _____

5. $\dfrac{860}{320} = \dfrac{z}{10}$ _____

6. $\dfrac{1400}{x} = \dfrac{2000}{4500}$ _____

7. $\dfrac{3.5}{0.7} = \dfrac{R}{0.80}$ _____

8. $\dfrac{8.4}{1.2} = \dfrac{1200}{x}$ _____

9. $\dfrac{a}{0.5} = \dfrac{1500}{3}$ _____

10. $\dfrac{10.6}{y} = \dfrac{800}{40}$ _____

7-4 Direct Proportions

Direct proportion means that one ratio varies in the same manner as the other. For instance, the amount of gas consumed by a car varies directly with the distance traveled; i.e., the longer the trip, the more gas will be used.

Example

> A steel bar 40 cm long weighs 800 g.
> How much would a similar shaped steel bar weigh
> if it were 100 cm long?

This is a direct relationship since the longer bar will weigh more than the shorter bar. To solve for the weight of the longer bar, express the given terms as ratios. It is important to keep ratios expressed in the same units.

$$\dfrac{40 \text{ cm}}{100 \text{ cm}} \quad \text{and} \quad \dfrac{800 \text{ g}}{x} \text{ (weight of new bar)}$$

The ratios are equal to each other.

$$\dfrac{40 \text{ cm}}{100 \text{ cm}} = \dfrac{800 \text{ g}}{x}$$

The weight of the 40-cm bar is placed directly opposite 40 cm because it is a direct proportion. The unknown value of the 100-cm bar goes directly opposite 100 cm.

$$\dfrac{40 \text{ cm}}{100 \text{ cm}} \xrightarrow[\text{directly opposite}]{\text{directly opposite}} \dfrac{800 \text{ g}}{x}$$

Solve for the unknown by cross-multiplication.

$$\frac{40 \text{ cm}}{100 \text{ cm}} \diagdown\diagup \frac{800 \text{ g}}{x}$$

$$40x = 100 \times 800$$

$$x = \frac{80,000}{40}$$

$$= 2000 \text{ g (weight of the new bar)}$$

Exercises

Applications of Direct Proportion

1. An automobile can travel 60 km on 12 L of gas. How far can it travel on 42 L?

_____ Answer

2. There are two gears in a transmission that mesh, and one has a diameter of 7 cm and has 28 teeth. If the other gear has a diameter of 350 mm, how many teeth does it have? (Note that there is a direct relationship between the diameter and the number of teeth on gears in a system.)

_____ Answer

3. A steel I-beam 4 m long weighs 220 kg. How much will a similar I-beam weigh if it is 14 m long?

_____ Answer

4. An automobile service center charges $57 for a job it took two men 3 h to perform. If three men performed a job in 3 h 40 min, how much should the job cost? (Work ratio in man-hours.)

_____ Answer

5. A roll of single-strand electrical wire weighs 15 lb and contains 450′ of wire. If a roll of the same wire weighs 6.5 lb, how many feet of wire remain on the roll? (The wire is not on a spool.)

_____ Answer

6. Concrete pillars 14.5′ long are used to support a second floor in a parking lot. Each pillar weighs 1375 lb, and similar pillars 12′ long will be used to support the third floor. How much will each pillar weigh?

_____ Answer

7. Under certain wind conditions, a sailboat travels 8 km in 1.3 h. With the same wind conditions, could the boat travel 14 km in 2.3 h? Justify the answer.

_____ Answer

8. The ratio of the diameters of two gears on a lathe is 3.2 to 2. If the larger gear has 32 teeth, how many teeth will the smaller gear have?

_____ Answer

9. A truck hauling concrete has a ratio of 5 parts dry mix to $\frac{1}{2}$ part water. The contents of the truck weigh 5050 kg. How much will the same load weigh if the water content is increased to $\frac{3}{4}$ part?

_____ Answer

10. A contractor purchased a new truck to haul diesel fuel and desires to use the old truck to haul water for road work. The truck has a rated capacity of 8500 lb, but when filled with diesel fuel, it only weighs 7700 lb. The weight ratio of diesel fuel to water is 0.7 to 1 (specific gravity). Will the truck exceed the 8500 lb when filled with water? How much will it weigh?

_____ Answer

_____ Answer

7-5
Indirect Proportion

Indirect or *inverse proportions* work in reverse to direct proportions. In the indirect proportion, as one quantity increases the other quantity decreases. The example of a pulley arrangement in Fig. 7-2 will help explain this relationship.

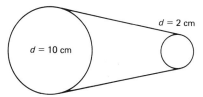

d = 2 cm

d = 10 cm

Fig. 7-2

The smaller pulley will move faster than the larger pulley. Since the diameter of the larger pulley is 5 times larger than that of the smaller pulley, the smaller pulley will move 5 times faster.

Example

The speed of the larger pulley is 8 rpm. How fast will the smaller pulley travel?

$$\frac{10 \text{ cm}}{2 \text{ cm}} \xrightarrow{\text{inverse position}} = \frac{x}{8 \text{ rpm}}$$

The diameter of 10 cm is associated inversely with 8 rpm, and 2 cm is associated inversely with x. Notice how this differs from the example of direct proportion.

Solve by cross-multiplication:

$$\frac{10 \text{ cm}}{2 \text{ cm}} \diagdown\!\!\!\!\diagup \frac{x}{8 \text{ rpm}}$$

$$2x = 8 \times 10$$

$$x = \frac{80}{2}$$

$$x = 40 \text{ rpm (or 5 times faster than the larger pulley)}$$

1. The motor of a circular saw drives a saw blade with a $2\frac{1}{4}''$ pulley. If the motor pulley is 4.5" and the motor is driving at 1750 rpm, how fast is the $2\frac{1}{4}''$ pulley traveling?

 Answer

The transfer case in a tractor has a gear of 42 teeth that meshes with a gear of 14 teeth. If the smaller gear travels at 73 rpm, how fast does the larger gear travel?

_____ Answer

3. Five punch-presses produce blanks for a certain job in $12\frac{3}{4}$ h. If two of the presses are shut down, how many hours will it take to complete the same amount of work?

_____ Answer

4. The smaller gear in Fig. 7-3 travels at 750 rpm. How fast is the larger gear traveling?

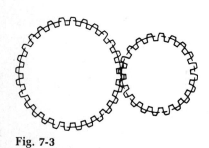

Fig. 7-3

_____ Answer

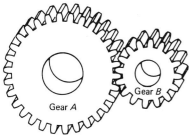

Fig. 7-4

5. In Fig. 7-4, how fast will the faster gear travel if the slower one rotates at 450 rpm?

_____ Answer

6. In Fig. 7-4, if a third gear having 7 teeth is also meshed with gear A and has a speed of 900 rpm, how fast will gear B travel?

_____ Answer

7. If gear B in Fig. 7-4 meshes with a driving gear of 82 teeth traveling at 60 rpm, how fast would gear A travel?

_____ Answer

EVALUATION PROBLEMS

1. An automobile uses 82 L of gas to travel 380 km. How much would it use under the same conditions to travel 260 km?

_____ Answer

2. Four men can produce 320 pieces on a lathe in 65.75 h. How long would it take seven men with the same skill to produce the 320 pieces?

_____ Answer

3. Two gears are in the ratio of 7.8 to 2. If the larger gear has a diameter of 8 cm, what is the diameter of the smaller gear?

_____ Answer

4. A steel crossmember is to be added to the bed of a large truck, but is too akward to weigh. A similar piece of crossmember weighs 8.5 lb and is 18″ long. How much weight would be added if four 5.5′ crossmembers were attached to the truck?

_____ Answer

5. A gear traveling at 2200 rpm is 1.75″ in diameter and is driven by a gear 3.5″ in diameter. What is the speed of the larger gear?

_____ Answer

6. A full roll of steel antenna cable weighs 32 lb and contains 500′ of cable. How many feet of cable remain on the roll when it weighs 25 lb?

_____ Answer

7. A gear traveling at a speed of 120 rpm is driven by a gear traveling at 480 rpm. If the smaller gear has 16 teeth, how many will the larger gear have?

_____ Answer

8. A gear 4 cm in diameter has 24 teeth, and it meshes with a gear having 36 teeth. What is the diameter of the other gear?

_____ Answer

7-6
Levers and Indirect
Proportions

A *lever* is a device used to make mechanical work easier. An example might be moving a large rock with a pipe (Fig. 7-5). One end of the pipe is placed under the rock, and a block of wood is placed under the pipe. A force (the weight of a person) placed at point B will move the rock if the force is great enough.

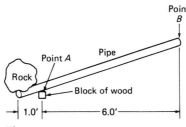

Fig. 7-5

Example

If the rock weighs 500 lb, it would be impossible for a person weighing 180 lb to move it. By using the *lever* or *fulcrum principle*, it can be moved. The pipe is 7' long: 6' from point B to point A (the *fulcrum point*) and 1' from point A to the end of the pipe. Fig. 7-6 shows a schematic drawing of this lever relationship.

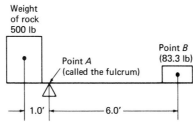

Fig. 7-6
Since the rock is an irregular shape, this is only an approximation.

Since it will require less effort or weight to move the rock, this illustrates an indirect proportion.

$$\frac{1'}{6'} = \frac{x}{500 \text{ lb}}$$

$$6x = 500$$

$$x = 83.3 \text{ lb}$$

A lifting force of 83.3 lb could apply a force of 500 lb at the end of the pipe. If a person put all his weight (180 lb) at the end of the pipe, how much lifting force could he apply?

$$\frac{1'}{6'} = \frac{180 \text{ lb}}{x}$$

$$x = 1080 \text{ lb}$$

Since the force applied to the rock is greater than the weight of the rock, the rock will move.

The principle of levers and fulcrums can be applied to many common tools, like pliers, wrenches, pry bars, etc.

A

32 kg

|← 85 mm →|←——— 282 cm ———→|

Fig. 7-7

1. Figure 7-7 is a schematic of a simple lever. Determine the force applied to point A.

_____ Answer

2. What force is applied to the pipe if an 80-lb force is placed at point A on the pipe wrench? Draw a schematic of the lever action similar to the one in Fig. 7-7.

_____ Answer

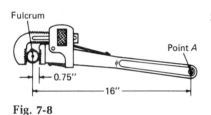

Fulcrum

Point A

0.75″

16″

Fig. 7-8

3. If the handle of the wrench in Fig. 7-8 was extended by 4′, what force would be applied to the pipe using the same 80-lb force at the end of the extended wrench.

_____ Answer

12 mm

35 cm

Fulcrum

Fig. 7-9

4. The principle of the fulcrum point used in problem 2 can also be applied to the socket wrench in Fig. 7-9. If a 75-lb force is applied to the handle of the wrench, what force would be applied to the bolt head? Draw a schematic of the lever action.

_____ Answer

5. Using Fig. 7-9, replace 12 mm with $\frac{3}{8}$″ and repeat problem 4.

_____ Answer

7-7
Similar Figures

Similar figures can be described as figures with the same shape but with different sizes. A baseball is similar in shape to a basketball but is different in size. Squares, rectangles, circles, etc. may be similar in shape but different in area.

Triangles are good examples of similar figures. If the corresponding interior angles of a triangle are equal, the triangles are similar (Fig. 7-10).

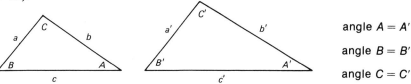

angle $A = A'$

angle $B = B'$

angle $C = C'$

Fig. 7-10
Corresponding interior angles are equal.

If the figures are similar, their sides are in direct proportion.

$$\frac{a}{a'} = \frac{b}{b'} = \frac{c}{c'}$$

Example

If the side $a = 3$, $b = 4$, $c = 5$, and $a' = 6$, then b' and c' can be determined by a direct proportion as follows. Find side b'.

$$\frac{a}{a'} = \frac{b}{b'} \qquad \text{or} \qquad \frac{3}{6} = \frac{4}{b'}$$

Cross-multiply and $b' = 8$

Find side c'.

$$\frac{a}{a'} = \frac{c}{c'} \qquad \text{or} \qquad \frac{3}{6} = \frac{5}{c'}$$

Cross-multiply and $c' = 10$

Areas of similar figures vary with the square of the ratio.

Example

In Fig. 7-11, what is the area of a square with 2 cm sides, if the area of a 4 cm square is 16 cm²?

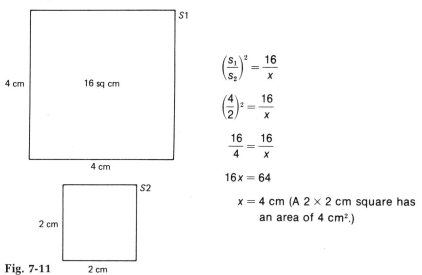

$$\left(\frac{s_1}{s_2}\right)^2 = \frac{16}{x}$$

$$\left(\frac{4}{2}\right)^2 = \frac{16}{x}$$

$$\frac{16}{4} = \frac{16}{x}$$

$16x = 64$

$x = 4$ cm (A 2 × 2 cm square has an area of 4 cm².)

Fig. 7-11

Volumes of similar figures vary with the cube of the ratio.

Example

In Fig. 7-12, what is the volume of a sphere with a diameter of 4 cm if a 12 cm diameter sphere has a volume of 905 cm³?

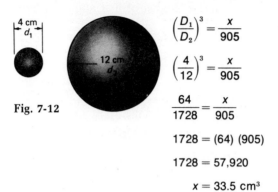

Fig. 7-12

$$\left(\frac{D_1}{D_2}\right)^3 = \frac{x}{905}$$

$$\left(\frac{4}{12}\right)^3 = \frac{x}{905}$$

$$\frac{64}{1728} = \frac{x}{905}$$

$$1728 = (64)\,(905)$$

$$1728 = 57{,}920$$

$$x = 33.5 \text{ cm}^3$$

Exercises
Applications of Similar Figures

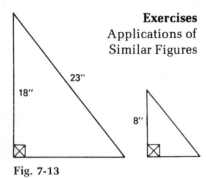

23″

18″

8″

Fig. 7-13

1. If the right triangles in Fig. 7-13 are similar, find the hypotenuse of the smaller triangle.

_____ Answer

2. A square bar of aluminum 3 cm on a side weighs 5 kg. How much will an aluminum bar 6 cm on a side weigh (bars of equal length)?

_____ Answer

3. A 12′ piece of bar stock has an end the shape of an octagon, and it weighs 62 lb. The large diameter of the octagon was measured, and it is 1.5″. A second 12′ octagon bar was too heavy to weigh on the scale. Its large diameter is 2.5″ inches. How much does it weigh?

_____ Answer

4. Spherical tanks are often used to store extremely high-octane fuels. The diameter of a tank is 3 m and it has a capacity of 14 kL. What will be the capacity of a tank 6 m in diameter?

_____ Answer

5. The surface area of the 3-m sphere in problem 4 is 28.3 m². What is the surface area of the 6-m sphere?

_____ Answer

6. A scale model and the actual object upon which it is based are similar figures. The surface area of the scale model of a missile is 500 cm². If the scale is 1 to 40, what is the surface area of the missile?

_____ Answer

7. What is the fuel capacity of the missile in problem 6 if the model holds 7.5 liters?

_____ Answer

8. A 32'-diameter circular swimming pool has a water surface area of 804 ft². What will be the surface area of a swimming pool with a diameter 1.5 times larger?

_____ Answer

9. A tank in the shape of a sphere holds 6785 gal of fuel oil and has a diameter of 12 ft. How much fuel oil will a tank hold if its diameter is 5 ft?

_____ Answer

REVIEW QUESTIONS

1. A drafter is scaling down a building and making a working drawing. The scale to be used on the building plan is 1 to 100 (1 cm = 1 m). What will be the dimensions on the drawing for a rectangular building 32 m by 18 m?

_____ Answer

2. The average height of a Roman soldier was approximately 5′ 2″, and the average height of an American soldier during the 1960s was approximately 179 cm. Determine the ratio of the height of the American soldier to the height of the Roman soldier.

_____ Answer

3. The scale of a workshop floor plan is drawn 1 to 8 ($\frac{1}{8}'' = 1'$). If the area of a room on the plan is 18.75 in², what is the area of the workshop?

_____ Answer

4. A wrench with a handle of 24″ is used to tighten a $1\frac{1}{2}''$ pipe. What is the approximate force applied to the pipe if a 60-lb force is applied to the end of the wrench? (Figure 7-8 illustrates the problem.)

_____ Answer

5. A model of a water storage tank is made to a scale of 1 to 5. If the volume of the model is 6000 cm³, what is the volume of the tank in kiloliters?

_____ Answer

6. Two partners share in a profit of $850. If the money is to be divided in a ratio of 3 to 5, how much will each receive?

_____ Answer

_____ Answer

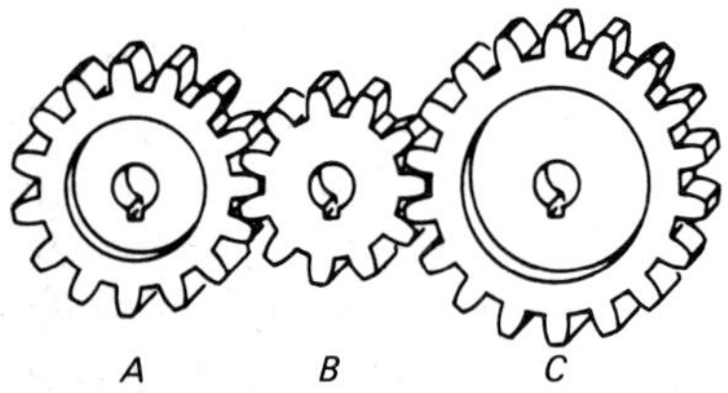

A   B   C

Fig. 7-14

7. In Fig. 7-14, if gear A travels at 250 rpm, how fast is gear C traveling?

_____ Answer

8. Gear B in Fig. 7-14 travels at 675 rpm, how fast will gears A and C travel?

A = _____ Answer

C = _____ Answer

9. In Fig. 7-14, gear B is 2 cm in diameter, what is the diameter of gears A and C?

A = _____ Answer

C = _____ Answer

10. In Fig. 7-14, a fourth gear having 8 teeth and traveling at 1750 rpm meshes with gear B. How fast would gears A and C travel?

A = _____ Answer

C = _____ Answer

Fan

Alternator

Fig. 7-15   Crankshaft

11. A typical pulley arrangement on an automobile might be set up as illustrated in Fig. 7-15. The automobile idles at 600 rpm, and the crankshaft pulley is 11 cm in diameter. What size pulley should be used on the alternator to drive it at a speed of 900 rpm?

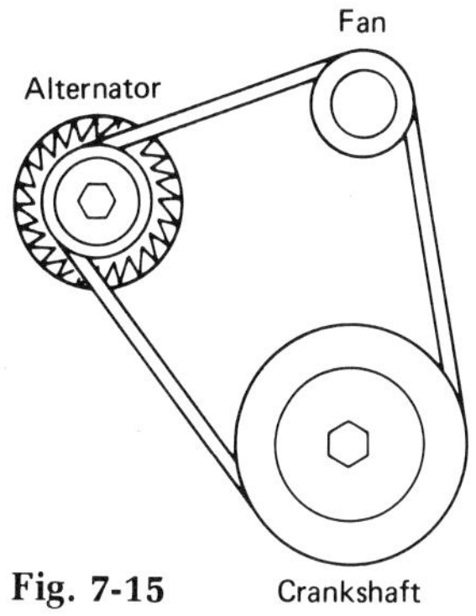

_____ Answer

12. How fast is the fan in Fig. 7-15 traveling if it has a diameter of 6 cm?

_____ Answer

13. A power-steering unit is added to the configuration in Fig. 7-15. The operating power is taken off another 11 cm pulley attached to the crankshaft pulley. What will be the diameter of the power-steering pulley if it is to idle at 850 rpm?

_____ Answer

14. The *slope* of a roof is defined as the ratio of the rise to the run. What is the slope of the roof in Fig. 7-16? (The ratio is usually expressed as 1 to something.)

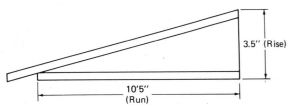

3.5″ (Rise)

10′5″
(Run)

Fig. 7-16

_____ Answer

15. The model of a newly designed automobile provides for a gas tank with a volume of 10 cm³. If the scale is 1 to 20, how many liters of fuel will the new car hold?

_____ Answer

CHAPTER EIGHT
ALGEBRA FUNDAMENTALS

Algebra is a system of math which provides a broader view of the solution of equations and formulas. In Unit 5, a formula such as $A = lw$ was presented and was solved for the value of A. If A and w were known, how would it be solved to find l? Understanding a few basic principles of algebra will help in the solution of many such equations.

8-1
Equations

A *formula* or *equation* like $A = lw$ is a shorthand method of stating that "the area A is equal to the product of length l times the width w." The symbols A, l, and w are used to represent each quantity, and the equation is general for all problems dealing with the area of a rectangle.

Likewise, an equation can represent the theory of the figure or operation. If the equation $A = \frac{1}{2}ba$ is understood, it should be apparent that the figure involved is a triangle. Exercise 8-1 does not represent any particular figure or operation, but provides practice in putting words into an algebraic notation.

Example

"Four times a number z plus the number 4 is equal to x" written as an algebraic notation is

$$4z + 4 = x$$

Exercises

Write an equation for each of the following cases:

1. A number x is equal to 4 times another number a.

    _____**x = 4a**_____ Answer

2. One number b minus 16 is equal to another number c.

    _____ Answer

3. Three times a number z is equal to a number b minus 4.

    _____ Answer

4. Five times a number x divided by a number c is equal to 32.

    _____ Answer

5. A number p divided by 3 is equal to 45.

    _____ Answer

6. A number n divided by a number x is equal to 3 times the number x minus a number c.

_____ Answer

7. Two and one-half times a number p is equal to a number b minus 6.

_____ Answer

8. Eight times a number p minus a number 3 times p is equal to 35.

_____ Answer

9. Six-tenths times a number x plus 3 times the number x plus 2.9 times the number x is equal to the product of the numbers x and y.

_____ Answer

10. Two-thirds of a number t plus three-quarters of a number t minus five-tenths of a number t is equal to 687.

_____ Answer

8-2
Signs of Numbers

Signs of numbers can be explained by use of a *number line* as shown in Fig. 8-1. An arbitrary point, usually the center point, is chosen and considered to be zero. All numbers to the right of that point are considered positive numbers (+), and those to the left are negative (−).

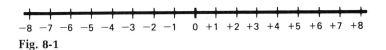

Fig. 8-1

The *sign of a number* does not determine a value, but shows the direction taken from the zero point. The number +5 has the same value as the number −5. Each number has five units between zero and 5, but negative numbers are to the left and positive numbers are to the right. When no sign is affixed to a number, it is considered positive.

A practical example of these numbers is a thermometer for measuring temperature. In reading a thermometer, +10° is 10° above zero, and −10° is 10° below zero. They represent ten degrees difference between zero and ten, but each represent a different point or temperature.

Algebra requires the use of positive and negative numbers. A system of operations or rules has been established, as illustrated by these examples.

Addition:

a. To add two or more numbers of like signs, find their sum and the sign of the answer will be the common sign.

Example

$$
\begin{array}{ccc}
& & +\ 3 \\
+\ 4 & -\ 4 & +\ 2 \\
+\ 2 & -\ 2 & +\ 7 \\
\hline
+\ 6 & -\ 6 & +\ 12
\end{array}
$$

b. To add a positive and negative number, find the difference between the numbers and the sign of the answer will be the sign of the larger number.

Example

$$\begin{array}{r} +8 \\ -2 \\ \hline +6 \end{array} \qquad \begin{array}{r} -12 \\ +7 \\ \hline -5 \end{array} \qquad \begin{array}{r} +3 \\ -2 \\ \hline +1 \end{array} \qquad \begin{array}{r} +4 \\ -7 \\ \hline -3 \end{array}$$

Subtraction:

a. To subtract one number from another, change the sign of the *subtrahend* (bottom number) and algebraically add, following the rules for addition.

Example
Subtract:

+ 8 = + 8 (minuend) ⟶change sign.

+ 3   −3 (subtrahend)
─────
+ 5 (remainder or answer)

Example
Subtract

$$\begin{array}{r} 25 \\ -\ 8 \\ \hline \end{array} = \begin{array}{r} \mathbf{25} \\ \mathbf{+\ 8} \\ \hline \mathbf{+33} \end{array} \qquad \begin{array}{r} -16 \\ +\ 4 \\ \hline \end{array} = \begin{array}{r} \mathbf{-16} \\ \mathbf{-\ 4} \\ \hline \mathbf{-20} \end{array} \qquad \begin{array}{r} -15 \\ -\ 5 \\ \hline \end{array} = \begin{array}{r} \mathbf{-15} \\ \mathbf{+\ 5} \\ \hline \mathbf{-10} \end{array}$$

Exercises Perform the indicated operation of signed numbers.
Add:

1. $\begin{array}{r} 16 \\ -10 \\ \hline \mathbf{-6} \end{array}$ 2. $\begin{array}{r} -45 \\ 18 \\ \hline \end{array}$ 3. $\begin{array}{r} -19 \\ -31 \\ \hline \end{array}$

4. $\begin{array}{r} -340 \\ -692 \\ \hline \end{array}$ 5. $\begin{array}{r} 66.42 \\ -32.21 \\ \hline \end{array}$ 6. $\begin{array}{r} -0.0025 \\ 0.4716 \\ \hline \end{array}$

7. $\begin{array}{r} 92.6 \\ 30.4 \\ -287.0 \\ 13.0 \\ \hline \end{array}$ 8. $\begin{array}{r} -36.4 \\ -14 \\ -86 \\ 200 \\ \hline \end{array}$ 9. $\begin{array}{r} 5\frac{1}{4} \\ -3\frac{1}{2} \\ \hline \end{array}$

10. $\begin{array}{r} \frac{1}{2} \\ -\frac{1}{8} \\ \hline \end{array}$

Subtract:

11. $\begin{array}{r} 25 \\ 85 \\ \hline \end{array}$ $\begin{array}{r} \mathbf{25} \\ \mathbf{-85} \\ \hline \mathbf{-60} \end{array}$ 12. $\begin{array}{r} 14 \\ -6 \\ \hline \end{array}$ 13. $\begin{array}{r} 44 \\ -92 \\ \hline \end{array}$

14. $\begin{array}{r} -285 \\ -650 \\ \hline \end{array}$ 15. $\begin{array}{r} -35 \\ 68 \\ \hline \end{array}$ 16. $\begin{array}{r} -63 \\ -22 \\ \hline \end{array}$

17.   0.025   18.   76.25   19. $6\frac{1}{2}$

      -0.016 32.15

                                                   $-2\frac{1}{5}$

20. -16.45

      $-\ \ 3.25$

21. The following are changes in a temperature recorded on a thermometer. What is the range or temperature change recorded by the thermometer. (The range will always be stated as a positive value.)

    a. $+10°$ to $+54° =$ **54 − (10) = 44°**   _____**44°**_____ Answer

    b. $-10°$ to $+44°$ _____ Answer

    c. $+60°$ to $95°$ _____ Answer

    d. $-15°$ to $-5°$ _____ Answer

    e. $+85°$ to $115°$ _____ Answer

22. The highest and lowest ocean tides for a certain 8-day period in San Francisco were recorded as follows. What is the difference between the low and high tide for each day? (The difference will always be a positive valve.)

Low	High		Difference	
$-0.4'$	$6.1'$	**6.1 =** **6.1** **− 0.4** **+ 0.4** **6.5**	_____**6.5'**_____	Answer
$-0.3'$	$6.4'$		_____	Answer
$-0.8'$	$6.6'$		_____	Answer
$-1.2'$	$6.8'$		_____	Answer
$-1.4'$	$6.8'$		_____	Answer
$-1.3'$	$6.8'$		_____	Answer

$$-1.2' \qquad 6.7'$$

_____ Answer

$$-0.8' \qquad 6.3'$$

_____ Answer

8-3
Multiplication and Division of Signed Numbers

Multiplication rules:

1. The product of two numbers with like signs will result in an answer with a positive sign.

2. The product of two numbers with unlike signs will result in an answer with a negative sign.

Example

Multiply:

$$\begin{array}{r} +4 \\ +2 \\ \hline +8 \end{array} \qquad \begin{array}{r} -4 \\ -2 \\ \hline +8 \end{array} \qquad \begin{array}{r} +4 \\ -2 \\ \hline -8 \end{array} \qquad \begin{array}{r} -4 \\ +2 \\ \hline -8 \end{array}$$

Division rules:

The rules for division of signed numbers are the same as those for multiplication. Like signs will result in a positive answer, and unlike signs will result in a negative answer.

Example

Divide:

$$(+4) \div (+2) = +2$$

$$(-4) \div (-2) = +2$$

$$(+4) \div (-2) = -2$$

$$(-4) \div (+2) = -2$$

Exercises   Perform the indicated multiplication or division

1. $4\,(-36) =$ ___**−144**___

2. $-3\,(6)\,(12) =$ _____

3. $-0.75\,(-16) =$ _____

4. $-156\,(3)\,(-8) =$ _____

5. $(-3)\,(-20)\,(-3) =$ _____

6. $(-6)\,(-4)\,(-2)\,(-7) =$ _____

7. $\dfrac{16}{-4} =$ _____

8. $\dfrac{-340}{20} =$ _____

9. $\dfrac{-150}{-25} =$ _____

10. $\dfrac{-6.4}{1.6} =$ _____

11. $\dfrac{8\ (4)}{-16} =$ _____

12. $\dfrac{(9)\ (-4)}{-18} =$ _____

13. $\dfrac{(-14)\ (9)\ (2)}{(-7)\ (-1)} =$ _____

14. $\dfrac{(18)\ (3)}{(9)\ (-3)} =$ _____

8-4
Evaluating Algebraic Expressions

The algebraic expression can be evaluated by substituting numerical values for unknown or general numbers stated in the expression. A *general number* (sometimes called a *literal number*) is an unknown quantity and can be expressed as a, b, z, x, A, B, W, etc.

For instance, A, l, and w are general numbers in the equation $A = lw$. The expression below is given in general numbers.

Example

$$x + 2y - 3z + 2xy$$

In this example, if $x = 5$, y, $= 3$ and $z = -4$, the result can be obtained by substituting the numerical values for the corresponding unknowns in the expression, such as is done in an equation. Use parentheses where two numbers or double signs are used.

Example

$$x + 2y + 3z + 2xy$$

Substitute.

$$5 + 2\ (3) + 3\ (-4) + 2\ (5)\ (3)$$

Perform multiplication.

$$5 + 6 + (-12) + 30$$

Collect like signed numbers.

$$31 + (-12)$$

Answer: 19

Example

$$x - 2z + 4y + 8z$$

Substitute.

$$5 - 2\ (-4) + 4\ (3) + 8\ (-4)$$

Multiply.

$$5 + 8 + 12 + (-32)$$

Collect like signed numbers.

$$25 + (-32)$$

Answer: -7

If $a = 2$, $b = 3$, $c = 4$, and $d = -2$, evaluate the following algebraic expressions:

1. $a + 2ab + b =$

     2 + 2 (2) (3) + 3 =

     2 + 12 + 3 = 17

2. $a + a - 6 =$

3. $\dfrac{a - b}{a + b} =$

4. $\dfrac{a + b}{3c} =$

5. $\dfrac{a + b + c}{a + b + c} =$

6. $c + 2cd + d =$

7. $2c (2b + 3d) =$

8. $2cd (a + b + c) =$

8-5 Adding Algebraic Expressions

Recall from basic arithmetic that only like things can be added or subtracted. In an algebraic expression, terms are identical only if their general numbers (the letters) are the same.

Example
Add:

     5ab
     3ab
     8ab

$5ab$ can be added to $3ab$ since the ab is identical.

Example
Add:

     5a
   + 3ab
   5a + 3ab

$5a$ and $3ab$ can be added by expressing the result as $5a + 3ab$ since both terms do not contain the same letters.

Perform the indicated addition or subtraction:
Add:

1.   **−10a**
     6a
   − 4a

2. $3a$
   $-6a$

3. $66x$
   $-54x$

4. $12ab$
   $-21ab$

5. $-91xy$
   $\underline{-12xy}$

6. $12x - 3y + 4x - x =$

7. $4a - 3a + 25b + 3a =$

8. $14xy + 3xy - 36xy + 42xy =$

9. $8z + 62z - 42z - 300 =$

10. $72p - 3p + 70p + 2p - 3p =$

Subtract:

11. $12xy - 9xy =$ **3xy**

12. $-6x - (-4x) =$

13. $25y - (-3y) =$

14. $3(a - b) - 6(a - b) =$

15. $1.7cd - 2.9cd =$

16. $1.2x - (-0.7x) =$

17. $16ab - (-25ab) =$

18. $82ax - 14ax =$

19. $139a - 36a =$

20. $0.525ax - (-0.025ax) =$

8-6 Multiplying Monomial Expressions

Unlike quantities may be multiplied, and where the general numbers are alike, square the like literal numbers.

Example

$(3x)(4x) =$ **12x²**

3 (4) = 12   and squaring x **x(x) = x²**

Example

$(8a)(2a) =$ **16a²**

$3(9y) =$ **27y**

$(6xy)(2x) =$ **12x²y**

$(7ab)(3ab) =$ **21a²b²**

Exercises Multiply the following expressions:

1. $(3ab)(2a) =$ **6a² b**

2. $(-5c)(-4d) =$

3. $(-25xy)(5x) =$

4. $(30xy)(3x) =$

5. $(3ab)(-16ab) =$

6. $(17x)(10xy) =$

7. $(ab)(a) =$

8. $(-36x)(0.5x) =$

9. $(8a)(-12) =$

10. $(-90b)(10b) =$

8-7 Division of Simple Expressions

Divide the numerical quantities and cancel the like general numbers:

Example

$$\frac{18a}{-9a} = \textbf{-2} \qquad \textbf{18} \div \textbf{-9 = -2}$$

The a's are cancelled $\left(\dfrac{\cancel{a}}{\cancel{a}}\right)$

Example

$$\frac{36B}{4} = \mathbf{9B} \qquad \frac{-16xy}{4x} = \mathbf{-4y} \qquad \frac{14ab}{-2ab} = \mathbf{-7}$$

Exercises Perform the indicated division.

1. $\dfrac{24a}{6a} = \mathbf{4}$

2. $\dfrac{16xy}{-16xy} =$

3. $\dfrac{25xy}{-5xy} =$

4. $\dfrac{10a - 15a - 60a}{5a} =$

5. $\dfrac{12w - 16w}{4w} =$

6. $\dfrac{37.5x - 62.5x}{12.5x} =$

7. $\dfrac{12x - 8x + 4x}{-2x} =$

8. $\dfrac{36x}{10x} =$

9. $\dfrac{42ab - a}{a} =$

10. $\dfrac{xy}{2xy} =$

8-8
Removing Parentheses

In some equations a quantity is enclosed by parentheses. The parentheses indicate an operation of multiplication. Multiply each term within the parentheses by the term in front of the parentheses.

Example

$$6x\,(2x + y) = \mathbf{12x^2 + 6xy}$$
$$-2a\,(4a + b - 3ab) = \mathbf{-8a^2 - 2ab + 6a^2\,b}$$

When no term precedes the parentheses, multiply each term by 1 using the sign (+ or −) that precedes the parentheses.

Example

$$4x + (6x - 2b) = \mathbf{4x + 6x - 2b = 10x - 2b}$$
$$3a - (6x - a) = \mathbf{3a - 6x + a = 4a - 6x}$$

These examples illustrate that when a term in parentheses is preceded by a plus sign, the parentheses may be removed. If the term in parentheses is preceded by a minus sign, the sign of each term is changed before removing the parentheses.

Exercises Simplify the following by removing the parentheses and collecting like terms.

1. $3x(6y - 4x) = \mathbf{18xy - 12x^2}$

2. $3x(x + y) =$

3. $-6x(x - 4) =$

4. $2x - 6x - (3x - 2) =$

5. $-5(x + y - z) =$

6. $2a(3a - 9 + b) =$

7. $5b - (b - a) =$

8. $6(x - 3y) - 15y + 9x =$

9. $14b + x(x - y + 4) =$

10. $3a + (4x - 3a + 2) =$

8-9 Solving Equations of the Type x + 5 = 8

An *equation* is an equally balanced expression containing a left member and a right member. The important rule to remember is always keep it equally balanced. Whatever is done to one side of an equation must be done to the other. One side of an equation may be added to, subtracted from, multiplied or divided by as long as the same operation is performed on both sides.

Left member	=	**Right member**
+ add		+ add
− subtract		− subtract
× multiply		× multiply
÷ divide		÷ divide

Example

$$\begin{aligned} x + 5 &= 8 \\ -5 &= -5 \\ \hline x &= 3 \end{aligned}$$

To solve for x, add -5 to both sides of the equation.

Exercises Solve the following:

1. $\begin{aligned} x + 7 &= 12 \qquad \underline{\quad \mathbf{x = 5} \quad} \\ -7 \quad &\quad -7 \\ \mathbf{x} = \quad &\quad \mathbf{5} \end{aligned}$

2. $x + 9 = 19$ $x =$ _____

3. $a + 2 = -12$ $a =$ _____

4. $x + 15 = 45$ $x =$ _____

5. $c + 15 = -12$ $c =$ _____

6. $8 + x = -4$ $x =$ _____

7. $x - 4 = 21$ $\qquad$ $x =$ _____

8. $b - 20 = 70$ $\qquad$ $b =$ _____

9. $n - 20 = 7$ $\qquad$ $n =$ _____

10. $a - 6 = -12$ $\qquad$ $a =$ _____

11. $z - 3 = 6$ $\qquad$ $z =$ _____

12. $x + 11 = 22$ $\qquad$ $x =$ _____

13. The equation for determining the *total resistance* (opposition to electron flow) in a series circuit is

$$R_T = R_1 + R_2 + R_3 + \cdots$$

where R_T = total resistance, Ω (ohms)

R_1, R_2, R_3, etc. = resistance of each resistor, Ω

If the total resistance of a circuit is 350 Ω and $R_1 = 125$ Ω and $R_2 = 35$ Ω find R_3.

_____ Answer

14. Referring to the series-circuit equation in problem 13, find R_1, if $R_2 = R_3 = 1150$ Ω, $R_T = 2800$ Ω, and R_4 is added and equals 150 Ω.

_____ Answer

15. The sum of the voltage across each individual component in a series circuit equals the applied voltage, or can be described by the equation

$$E_T = E_1 + E_2 + E_3 + \cdots$$

where E_T = total applied voltage to the circuit, V (volts)

E_1, E_2, E_3 = voltage across each component, V

Find the voltage E_2 if the total applied voltage is 120 V and $E_1 = 36$ V and $E_3 = 45$ V.

_____Answer

16. The temperature range for a given period can be found by taking the highest temperature and subtracting the lowest temperature. This can be described by the equation

$$T_R = T_h - T_l$$

where T_R = temperature range, °F

T_h = highest temperature for the period, °F

T_l = lowest temperature for the period, °F

In a 24-hour period, the highest recorded temperature in Buffalo, New York, was 15° and the range was 32°. What was the lowest temperature for that period?

_____ Answer

17. Referring to problem 16, if the lowest recorded temperature was −6° and the range was 18.5°, what was the highest temperature recorded for that period?

_____ Answer

18. The total cost of an automobile can be determined by

$$C = P + T + S - R$$

where C = total customer cost

P = sticker price

T = sales tax

S = dealer-preparation charge

R = rebate from factory

What would be the dealer-preparation charge if the total cost was $6250, the sticker price was $6155, the sales tax was $369.30, and the rebate offered was $500?

_____ Answer

19. Referring to problem 18, what would the rebate be if the total cost of an automobile was $4635, the sales tax was $279, the dealer-preparation charge was $185, and the sticker price was $4171.

_____ Answer

20. Referring to problem 18, what would the sticker price be if the cost of an automobile was $8535, the sales tax was $435, the rebate was $600, and the dealer-preparation charge was $250?

_____ Answer

Example

$$3x = 12$$

Divide each side of the equation by 3.

Cancel the 3's of left side.

$$\frac{\cancel{3}x}{\cancel{3}} = \frac{12}{3}$$

$$\mathbf{x = 4}$$

Example

$$8y = 3$$

$$\frac{\cancel{8}y}{\cancel{8}} = \frac{3}{8}$$

$$y = \frac{3}{8} \qquad \text{or} \qquad \mathbf{0.375}$$

Exercises Solve the following

1. $\dfrac{\cancel{2}a}{\cancel{2}} = \dfrac{18}{\cancel{2}}$ $a =$ ____**9**____

2. $20x = 4$ $x =$ _____

3. $-6x = 18$ $x =$ _____

4. $-4x = -32$ $x =$ _____

5. $7x = 30$ $x =$ _____

6. $0.5x = 19$ $x =$ _____

7. $250x = -75$ $x =$ _____

8. $-18a = 9$ $a =$ _____

9. $750y = 250$ $y =$ _____

10. $0.33b = -33$ $b =$ _____

11. The circumference of a circle can be determined by $C = \pi D$. What is the diameter of a circle whose circumference is 37 cm?

_____ Answer

12. The area of a rectangle can be computed by $A = lw$. Find the length of one side of a rectangle whose area is 560 in² and whose width is 42".

_____ Answer

13. The voltage in an electrical circuit can be determined by the equation

$$E = IR$$

where E = the voltage, V

I = current, A (amperes)

R = resistance, Ω

What is the resistance of a circuit with a voltage of 9 V and a current of 0.025 A?

_____ Answer

14. In problem 13, what is the current in a small motor if the voltage is 117 V and resistance 560 Ω?

_____ Answer

15. Power is consumed in the form of heat in an electrical circuit and is measured in the unit of a watt W. The power can be calculated by the equation

$$P = I^2 R$$

where P = power dissipated, W

I = current, A

R = resistance, Ω

Find the current in a circuit that dissipates 150 W and has a resistance of 8 Ω.

_____ Answer

16. Referring to problem 15, if the resistance of a circuit is 0.5 Ω, what is the current if the power dissipated is 7.5 W?

_____ Answer

17. The volume of a rectangular solid can be computed by the equation $V = lwd$. Determine the length of a rectangular tank that has a volume of 3.375 ft³ and is limited by a width of 18″ and depth of 9″.

_____ Answer

18. Referring to problem 17, a rectangular gas tank requires a volume of 30,000 cm,³, but is limited by a length of 65 cm and a width of 28 cm. What would be the depth of the tank?

_____ Answer

8-11
Solving Equations of the Type $\frac{x}{2} = 12$.

Example 1

$$\frac{x}{2} = 12$$

Multiply each side of the equation by 2. Cancel 2's on the left side.

$$(2)\,\frac{x}{2} = 12(2)$$

$$x = 24$$

Example 2

$$16 = \frac{x}{4}$$

Multiply each side by 4. Cancel 4s on right side.

$$(4)16 = \frac{x}{\cancel{4}}\,(4)$$

$$x = 64$$

Example 3

$$\frac{6}{x} = 3$$

Multiply each side by x. Cancel x's on left side.

$$(x)\,\frac{6}{x} = 3(x)$$

Divide by 3.

$$\frac{6}{3} = \frac{3x}{3}$$

$$x = 2$$

Exercises   Solve the following:

1. $(\overset{1}{\cancel{6}})\,\dfrac{x}{\underset{1}{\cancel{6}}} = 3(6)$ $x =$ _____18_____   2. $\dfrac{x}{5} = 15$ $x =$ _____

3. $\dfrac{x}{3} = \dfrac{1}{2}$ $x =$ _____   4. $\dfrac{a}{2} = 150$ $a =$ _____

5. $\dfrac{n}{1.5} = 15$ $n =$ _____   6. $\dfrac{a}{6} = 3\dfrac{1}{2}$ $a =$ _____

7. $\dfrac{w}{2.5} = 11$ $w =$ _____   8. $\dfrac{y}{1} = 88$ $y =$ _____

9. $\dfrac{4}{x} = 2$ $x =$ _____   10. $\dfrac{16}{y} = 8$ $y =$ _____

11. $\dfrac{2.5}{a} = 0.5$ $a =$ _____   12. $\dfrac{100}{z} = 10$ $z =$ _____

13. $\dfrac{x}{880} = 22$ $x =$ _____   14. $\dfrac{f}{144} = 1728$ $f =$ _____

15. $\dfrac{12}{c} = 144$ $c =$ _____   16. $\dfrac{c}{27} = 3$ $c =$ _____

17. $12 = \dfrac{96}{p}$ $p =$ _____   18. $6 = \dfrac{8.5}{z}$ $z =$ _____

19. $96 = \dfrac{x}{14}$ $x =$ _____   20. $1072 = \dfrac{a}{10}$ $a =$ _____

21. The area of a triangle can be calculated with the equation $A = ab/2$ (Chap. 6). What is the altitude of a triangle with an area of 16.8 in² and a base of 3.5"?

_____ Answer

22. The specific gravity of a material can be defined by the equation

$$\text{S.G.} = \dfrac{W_1}{W_2}$$

where S.G. = specific gravity

W_1 = weight of a material

W_2 = weight of an equal volume of water

What is the weight of a cubic foot of white pine if it has a specific gravity of 0.5. (Water weighs 62.4 lb/ft³.)

_____ Answer

23. The speed of an automobile can be determined by the equation

$$S = \frac{D}{T}$$

where S = speed, km/h

D = distance, km

T = time, h

How long would it take to travel from Los Angeles to San Francisco at an average speed of 80 km/h if the distance is 650 km?

_____ Answer

24. Referring to problem 24, if an automobile was traveling at a speed of 95 km/h for a time of 90 min, how far could it travel?

_____ Answer

25. The greek symbol π indicates the ratio of the circumference of a circle to its diameter and can be expressed as $\pi = C/D$. What is the diameter of circle whose circumference is 31.5 cm?

_____ Answer

8-12 Solving Equations by Transposing Terms

Example

$$3x + 2 = 8 + 6x$$

Collect like terms by moving them to the same side of the equation. Each time a term is moved from one side to the other, change its sign.

$$3x + 2 = 8 + 6x$$

$$3x - 6x = 8 - 2$$

Collect like terms.

$$-3x = 6$$

The example can then be solved for the unknown by dividing each side by -3.

$$\frac{-3x}{-3} = \frac{6}{-3}$$

$$x = -2$$

Example

$$6a + 4 - 2a + 2 = 3a - 16 - a$$

Collect like terms, transpose, and change signs.

$$4a + 6 = 2a - 16$$

$$4a - 2a = -16 - 6$$

Divide both sides by 2.

$$\frac{2a}{2} = \frac{-22}{2}$$

$$a = -11$$

Example

Clear parentheses by multiplication.

$$2(a + 3) - 4 = 20$$

Collect like terms.

$$2a + 6 - 4 = 20$$

Transpose terms and change sign.

$$2a + 2 = 20$$

Subtract.

$$2a = 20 - 2$$

Divide by 2.

$$2a = 18$$

$$\frac{2a}{2} = \frac{18}{2}$$

$$a = 9$$

Exercises Solve the following:

1. $3r - 7 = 16 - 24r$ $\qquad r = \underline{\quad \textbf{23/27} \quad}$

2. $3x + 10 = 2x - 18$ $\qquad x = \underline{\qquad\qquad}$

3. $3(x - 2) - 4 = 15$ $\qquad x = \underline{\qquad\qquad}$

4. $10x - 10 = 4x + 2$ $\qquad x = \underline{\qquad\qquad}$

5. $7.5c + 25 = 20c$ $\qquad c = \underline{\qquad\qquad}$

6. $5a + 3(8 - a) = 36$ $a = \underline{\hspace{2cm}}$

7. $6(b + 1) - 3 = 12b - 4(2b + 1)$ $b = \underline{\hspace{2cm}}$

8. $6a - 12 = 4a + 2$ $a = \underline{\hspace{2cm}}$

9. The inside diameter of a piece of pipe can be determined by the equation

$$D_i = D_o - 2T$$

where D_i = inside diameter

D_o = outside diameter

T = wall thickness of the pipe

Find the outside diameter of a piece of pipe having an inside diameter of 1.75 cm and a wall thickness of 3 mm.

$\underline{\hspace{3cm}}$ Answer

10. Referring to problem 9, what is the wall thickness of a piece of pipe whose outside diameter is 6 cm and inside diameter is 3.85 cm?

$\underline{\hspace{3cm}}$ Answer

11. The temperature on a Celsius thermometer may be converted to its Fahrenheit equivalent by using the equation $F = 1.8c + 32$. What is the temperature in Celsius if the Fahrenheit reading is 68°?

$\underline{\hspace{3cm}}$ Answer

12. To determine the increase in length of a brass bar caused by a temperature change, the following equation can be used

$$L_i = 0.000125 \; L \; (T_2 - T_1)$$

where L_i = increase in length, in

L = original length, ft

T_2 = new temperature in °F

T_1 = original starting temperature in °F

Find the original starting temperature for a brass rod whose original length was 21'. The increase in length was 0.075" and the final temperature was 195°?

_____ Answer

13. Referring to problem 12, what is the final temperature for a 75' brass rod that increased $\frac{1}{2}$" if it started from a temperature of 68°?

_____ Answer

14. The perimeter of a rectangle can be determined by the equation $P = 2l + w$. What is the width of a rectangle whose perimeter is 66 m and length is 22 m?

_____ Answer

15. Referring to problem 14, determine the length of a rectangle with a perimeter of 480 cm and a width of 1500 mm.

_____ Answer

8-13
Describing Figures with Equations

Basic geometric figures can be described by use of equations. The area of a figure can be described by an equation as illustrated in Figs. 8-2 and 8-3.

Example

Total area of a geometric figure.

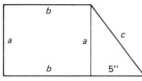

Fig. 8-2

Area of rectangle $= ab$

Area of triangle $= \dfrac{a(5)}{2}$

Total area of figure $= ab + \dfrac{a5}{2}$

$$A_T = ab + \frac{a(5)}{2}$$

Example

The area of the shaded portion.

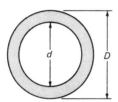

Fig. 8-3

Area of total figure $= 0.785D$

Area of the hole $= 0.785d$

Area of shaded portion $= 0.785D - 0.785d$ or $0.785(D - d)$

$$A_s = 0.785(D - d)$$

Exercises

Develop an equation that can be used to determine the areas of Figs. 8-4 to 8-8.

1.

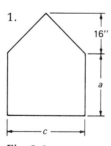

Fig. 8-4

$A =$ _____

2.

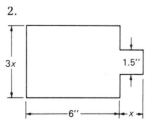

Fig. 8-5

$A =$ _____

3.

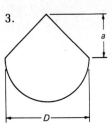

Fig. 8-6   A = _____

4.

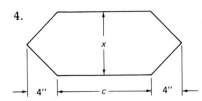

Fig. 8-7   A = _____

5.

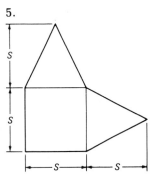

Fig. 8-8   A = _____

**8-14
Solving Trade Formulas
with Algebra**

When the volume is unknown in a standard equation like $V = lwh$, the solution is one involving arithmetic. The values for l, w, and h can be substituted in the equation, and V can be computed. However, if V, l, and w are known and h must be determined, principles of algebra must be applied.

Example 1 $V = lwh$

Find h if $V = 200$ in³, $l = 20''$, $w = 5''$.

$$200 = (20)\,(5)\,h$$

Multiply (5 × 20).

Divide by 100.

$$\frac{\overset{2}{\cancel{200}}}{\cancel{100}} = \frac{\cancel{100}h}{\cancel{100}}$$

$$h = 2''$$

Example 2

$$\text{Area of triangle} = \frac{ab}{2}$$

Find a if $b = 10$ cm and $A = 20$ cm³

Divide by 2.

$$20 = \frac{a(\overset{5}{\cancel{10}})}{\cancel{2}}$$

Divide by 5.

$$\frac{\overset{4}{\cancel{20}}}{\cancel{5}} = \frac{a\cancel{5}}{\cancel{5}}$$

$$a = 4 \text{ cm}$$

Exercises   The following problems are standard trade formulas and will require application of algebra to determine the solution.

1. The total piston displacement can be found by the use of the following formula

$$PD = 0.7854 \; d^2 ln$$

where d = diameter of bore of cylinder, in

l = length of stroke, in

n = number of cylinders

PD = piston displacement, in^3

a. Find the number of cylinders in an engine with a piston diameter of 3.125″ and a 4.5″ stroke, and a piston displacement of 310 in^3.

_____ Answer

b. Find the piston diameter of a 6-cylinder engine with a piston displacement of 220 in^3 and a 3.75″ stroke.

_____ Answer

2. A formula used by manufacturers and for purposes of taxation is called the S. A. E. horsepower formula. The formula is

$$hp = \frac{d^2n}{2.5}$$

where d^2 = cylinder-bore diameter squared

n = number of cylinders

a. How many cylinders would a car have if its horsepower rating is 25 and its bore is 3.95"?

_____ Answer

b. What would be the diameter of the bore if the horsepower rating of the car were 44 and it had 6 cylinders?

_____ Answer

3. The following formula can be used for finding the indicated horsepower of any type of engine: gasoline, steam, diesel, etc. The formula is

$$hp = \frac{PLAN}{33,000}$$

where P = average pressure (lb in²)

L = length of stroke (f)

A = area of piston (in²)

N = number of power strokes per minute

a. What is the area of the piston in a 30-hp gasoline engine with a stroke of 3", average pressure of 140 lb in², and 1200 power strokes per minute?

_____ Answer

b. In problem 3a, what is the diameter of the bore?

_____ Answer

c. What would be the length of the stroke in inches of a 75-hp engine with an average pressure of 120 lb, a piston area of 15 in², and 1600 power strokes per minute?

_____ Answer

4. The capacity in gallons of cylindrical tanks can be found readily by the use of the formula

$$g = \frac{0.7854 \, d^2 l}{231}$$

where g = capacity, gal

d = diameter of tank, in

l = length of tank, in

231 in² = 1 gal

a. A cylindrical-gasoline storage tank is limited in length 4.5′. If it is to hold 75 gal of fuel, what would be the diameter of the tank?

_____ Answer

b. A cylindrical water-storage tank has a diameter of 11′. What will the height of the tank be if it is to hold 22,000 gal?

_____ Answer

5. A formula used in determining the speed of a pulley is

$$D = \frac{ds}{S}$$

where D = diameter of the driving pulley

S = speed of the driving pulley

d = diameter of the driven pulley

s = speed of the driven pulley

a. A pulley 15″ in diameter is running at 240 rpm and is connected by a belt to a pulley 8″ in diameter. What is the speed of the smaller pulley?

_____ Answer

b. What is the diameter of a driving pulley if the speed is 40 rpm and the driven pulley is 3″ in diameter and has a speed of 180 rpm?

_____ Answer

c. Determine the speed of a ¾″ driven pulley if the driving pulley is 1.5″ in diameter and has a speed of 150 rpm.

_____ Answer

6. The velocity of a gear can be determined by the formula

$$V = \frac{nv}{N}$$

where V = velocity of the driving gear, rpm

N = number of teeth in the driving gear

v = velocity of the driven gear, rpm

n = number of teeth in the driven gear

a. A gear with 30 teeth meshes with a gear having 42 teeth. If the larger gear runs at 125 rpm, what will be the velocity of the smaller gear?

_____ Answer

b. How many teeth will a gear have if it has a velocity of 50 rpm and is driven by a gear with 22 teeth traveling 120 rpm?

_____ Answer

c. If a driving gear has 30 teeth and is moving at 80 rpm, how many teeth will the driven gear need if its speed is 240 rpm?

_____ Answer

7. Cutting speeds for lathe works can be approximately determined by the formula

$$CS = \frac{ds}{4}$$

where CS = cutting speed, f/min

d = diameter of the stock, in

s = rotational speed of the stock, rpm

a. Determine the rotational speed of a $\frac{7}{8}$"-diameter round stock cut in a lathe if the cutting speed is 42 f/min.

_____ Answer

b. What diameter stock can be cut if the cutting speed of the lathe is 90 f/min and the rotational speed is 916 rpm?

_____ Answer

8. An important factor in determining the shipping weight of wood is the percentage of moisture content. The percentage of moisture content can be determined by the equation

$$\text{Moisture content (\%)} = \frac{\text{weight of water in the board (lb)}}{\text{dry weight of the board (lb)}} \times 100$$

a. If the moisture content is $33\frac{1}{3}$ % and the dry weight of the board is 4 lb, how much will the wet board weigh?

_____ Answer

b. An oven-dried board weighs 7 lb and had a moisture content of 254%. What did the wet board weigh before drying?

_____ Answer

c. A board with 160% moisture contains 15 lb of water. What will the board weigh when oven-dried?

_____ Answer

REVIEW QUESTIONS

Standard equations for electrical circuits are

$$E = IR \qquad P = IE \qquad P = I^2R \qquad P = \frac{E^2}{R}$$

where E = voltage, V

I = current, A

R = resistance, Ω

P = power dissipated, W

The equation for the resistance of a series circuit is

$$R_T = R_1 + R_2 + R_3 + \cdots$$

The equation for the resistance of a parallel circuit is

$$R_T = \frac{1}{\dfrac{1}{R_1} + \dfrac{1}{R_2} + \dfrac{1}{R_3} + \cdots}$$

The equation for two resistors in parallel is

$$R_T = \frac{(R_1)\,(R_2)}{R_1 + R_2}$$

1. Find the current in an automobile headlamp that has a voltage of 12 V and a resistance of 3.5 Ω.

_____ Answer

2. A series circuit contains three resistances and has a total resistance of 850 Ω. One resistance is 50 Ω, and the second is 475 Ω. Find the third resistance.

_____ Answer

3. Find the total resistance of a parallel circuit if it contains three resistances: 50 Ω, 75 Ω, and 250 Ω.

_____ Answer

4. Find the total resistance of two resistances in parallel if one is 300 Ω and the other is 150 Ω.

_____ Answer

5. The total resistance of a parallel circuit containing two components is 80 Ω. If one of the resistances is 100 Ω, what is the other?

_____ Answer

6. In an automobile ignition system, the power dissipated by a voltage-dropping resistance in a series circuit is 25 W. If the voltage across the resistance is 6.2 V, what is the value of the resistance?

_____ Answer

7. Referring to problem 6, what is the current through the resistance?

_____ Answer

8. What voltage should be applied to an electric motor if it dissipates 200 W and has a current of 1.7 A?

_____ Answer

9. A 12-V automobile battery actually supplies 13.2 V. If this voltage is supplied to the starter of an automobile that consumes 237 W, what is the resistance of the starter?

_____ Answer

10. A diesel-oil storage tank in the shape of a cylinder is limited to a length of 12′. What is the diameter of the tank if the volume is 500 gal? (1 ft³ = 7.5 gal)

_____ Answer

11. The area of an ellipse is 380 cm² and its major diameter is 34 cm. What is the minor diameter?

_____ Answer

12. A water tank in the shape of an ellipse is to be built and mounted on a truck. The major diameter is limited to 225 cm and the length is to be 400 cm. What will be the length of the minor diameter if the tank holds 9000 L?

_____ Answer

13. The percent grade for roadway can be determined by the equation

$$G = \frac{100V}{H}$$

where G = percent of grade

V = vertical rise of roadway

H = horizontal distance of roadway

(V and H must be in the same units)

Find the vertical rise of a road for a horizontal distance of 3600′ if the percent grade is 4.5%.

_____ Answer

14. Referring to problem 13, what would be the horizontal distance for a 12% grade with a vertical rise of 250′?

_____ Answer

15. The Fahrenheit scale normally used to measure room temperature can be converted to Celsius (metric scale) by the equation

$$F = 1.8\ C + 32$$

where F = temperature, °F

C = temperature, °C

What is the temperature in Celsius of 195°F?

_____ Answer

CHAPTER NINE
POWERS OF TEN

Large numbers, such as the distance from the moon to the earth (250,000 mi) or the number of electrons in a coulomb (6,280,000,000,000,000,000) are awkward and cumbersome to work with. They are as much a part of our measurement vocabulary as 0.0000006 sec might be in a time measurement. The expression of these numbers can be simplified by using an *exponent* form of the number.

9-1
Expressing Even Multiples of Ten

$$100 = 10 \times 10 \quad\quad \text{or} \quad\quad 10^2$$
$$1000 = 10 \times 10 \times 10 \quad\quad \text{or} \quad\quad 10^3$$
$$10,000 = 10 \times 10 \times 10 \times 10 \quad\quad \text{or} \quad\quad 10^4$$

and so forth.

The number 258 could be expressed as

$$2.58 \times 10 \times 10 \quad\quad \text{or} \quad\quad 2.58 \times 10^2$$

The number 2580 could be expressed as

$$2.580 \times 10 \times 10 \times 10 \quad\quad \text{or} \quad\quad 2.58 \times 10^3$$

The number 25,800 could be expressed as

$$2.5800 \times 10 \times 10 \times 10 \times 10 \quad\quad \text{or} \quad\quad 2.58 \times 10^4$$

9-1a
Scientific Notation

As in the previous example, the number 2580 could be expressed as

$$2.58 \times 10^3 \quad \text{or} \quad 25.8 \times 10^2 \quad \text{or} \quad 258 \times 10^1 \quad \text{or} \quad 0.258 \times 10^4$$

All examples are numerically correct. To avoid the confusion over so many different forms, final technical data and final answers to math problems are usually expressed in a scientific notation.

The *scientific notation* is defined as an expression with one whole number to the left of the decimal point expressed to the proper power of ten.

Example

The known distance 93,000,000 mi to the sun could be expressed as

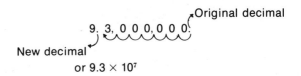

Proper power of ten

9.3×10^{7} mi

One whole number to left of decimal

The above scientific notation was accomplished by moving the original decimal point to the left and counting the number of places moved.

Original decimal

9.3,0 0 0,0 0 0.

New decimal

or 9.3×10^{7}

Exercises Express the following in scientific notation:

1. 126   **1.26×10^{2}**

2. 6520 _____

3. 435,000,000 _____

4. 890 _____

5. 67.56 _____

6. 7.75×10^{4} _____

7. 8657×10^{2} _____

8. 36978×10^{3} _____

9. 1597×10^{5} _____

10. 9306×10^{8} _____

9-2
Expressing Decimal Fractions in Scientific Notation

The decimal point is moved from its original position to the place where there will be one whole number to the left of the decimal point. The number of places moved will be counted and recorded as the proper power of ten by using a negative sign.

Example

$0.00272 = 2.72 \times 10^{-3}$

Scientific notation   Power of ten with negative sign

Exercises Express the following in scientific notation:

1. $0.00856 =$ **8.56×10^{-3}**

2. $0.742 =$ _____

3. $0.000418 =$ _____

4. $0.00314 =$ _____

5. $0.016 =$ _____

6. $0.015 \times 10^{-2} =$ _____

7. $0.18 \times 10^{3} =$ _____

8. $0.000648 \times 10^{4} =$ _____

9. $0.00794 \times 10^{-6} =$ _____

10. $0.008246 \times 10^{5} =$ _____

9-3
Multiplication of Powers of Ten

Quantities expressed in terms of powers of ten can be multiplied in any form. However, it may be easier to change the quantity into scientific notation before multiplication.

Example

$(4.24 \times 10^{3}) (3.2 \times 10^{2})$

First multiply the decimal quantities.

$4.24 \times 3.2 = 13.568$

Next, add the exponents.

$$3 + 2 = 5$$

Answer.

$$13.568 \times 10^5$$

Answer in scientific notation.

$$1.3568 \times 10^6$$

Example

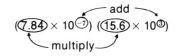

Answer.

$$122.304 \times 10^{-4}$$

Answer in scientific notation.

$$1.22304 \times 10^{-2}$$

Exercises Multiply the following, round answers to three significant figures, and leave in scientific notation.

1. $(746) (6.4 \times 10^3) =$ **$7.46 \times 10^2 \times 6.4 \times 10^3 = 4.77 \times 10^6$**

2. $(1.87 \times 10^2) (3.4 \times 10^4) =$ _____

3. $(2.5 \times 10^{-4}) (16 \times 10^{-3}) =$ _____

4. $(7.89 \times 10^{16}) (2.25 \times 10^8) =$ _____

5. $(92.4 \times 10^{-6}) (4.95 \times 10^2) (2.4 \times 10^{-2}) =$ _____

6. $(842) (79400) (3.6 \times 10^4) =$ _____

   _____

7. $(3.25 \times 10^{-10}) (64.8 \times 10^9) (200) =$ _____

8. $(1000) (10^6) (10^{-8}) =$ _____

9. $(178 \times 10^3) (645 \times 10^{-6}) (392 \times 10^2) =$ _____

10. $(900) (1600 \times 10^{-6}) (1000 \times 10^4) =$ _____

9-4
Division of Powers of Ten

In this process the whole numbers are divided as in regular division, and the exponents are subtracted.

Example

$$5 - 2 = 3$$
$$(9.4 \times 10^5) \div (3.5 \times 10^2)$$

$$9.4 \div 3.5 = 2.68 \times 10^3$$

$$6 - (-2) = 8$$
$$((6.4) \times 10^{\textcircled{6}}) \div ((2.5) \times 10^{\textcircled{-2}})$$
$$6.4 \div 2.5 = 2.56 \times 10^8$$

Exercises   Perform the following division, round answers to three significant figures, and leave in scientific notation.

1. $(9.82 \times 10^7) \div (6.3 \times 10^4) =$ _____**1.56 × 10³**_____

2. $(5.56 \times 10^{-2}) \div (3.9 \times 10^{-3}) =$ _____

3. $16{,}000 \div (8.4 \times 10^{-2}) =$ _____

4. $(7643 \times 10^2) \div (453 \times 10^2) =$ _____

5. $8.14 \div 0.00005 =$ _____

6. $16.7 \div (0.00018 \times 10^2) =$ _____

7. $0.0007 \div (3.5 \times 10^2) =$ _____

8. $(0.086 \times 10^3) \div (32 \times 10^{-4}) =$ _____

9. $77.9 \div (0.006 \times 10^{-2}) =$ _____

10. $10^6 \div (1.0 \times 10^{-2}) =$ _____

EVALUATION PROBLEMS

Perform the indicated operations using powers of ten:

1. $\dfrac{0.00186}{4365} =$ _____

2. $\dfrac{(4.2 \times 10^6)\,(180)}{(37.2 \times 10^{-3})\,(0.064 \times 10^{-2})} =$ _____

3. $\dfrac{8.4 \times 10^{16}}{0.0074\,(2.65 \times 10^{-5})} =$ _____

4. $\dfrac{(34.6 \times 10^2)\,(516 \times 10^6)}{(33 \times 10^6)\,(11.8 \times 10^2)} =$ _____

5. $\dfrac{180{,}000\ (0.00078)}{325{,}000\ (450{,}000)} =$ _____

6. $\dfrac{(456 \times 10^2)\ (700 \times 10^2)\ (38 \times 10^5)}{(0.0015 \times 10^{-2})\ (2.2 \times 10^{-4})} =$ _____

9-5
Applications of Powers of Ten

Powers of ten can be applied anywhere numbers are used, but especially where it can simplify the calculation. Scientific data and conversion tables are often listed in scientific notation.

Example

A table lists the conversion factor for converting cubic centimeters to cubic meters as 1.0×10^{-6}. Simply multiply the number of cubic centimeters by this factor.

Convert 8500 cm³ to m³ using power of ten

$$(8.5 \times 10^3) (1.0 \times 10^{-6})$$

$$8.5 \times 10^{-3} \text{ m}^3$$

Example

The voltage across a resistor can be determined by the formula $E = IR$. Often the current is measured in small values and the resistance in large values. If the current is 5.0×10^{-3} A and the resistance is 4.7×10^4 Ω, what is the voltage across the resistor.

$$E = IR$$

$$= (5 \times 10^{-3}) (4.7 \times 10^4)$$

$$= 2.35 \times 10^2 \text{ V}$$

Exercises
Application
Problems

Solve the following problems using powers of ten and leave final answers in scientific notation, rounded to three significant figures.

1. The population of the United States in 1750 was 1,200,000, and in 1960 the population had grown to 179,000,000. What percent increase does this represent?

_____ Answer

2. To convert cubic inches to cubic feet, multiply cubic inches by the conversion factor 5.787×10^{-4}. How many cubic feet are in 650,000,000 in³?

_____ Answer

3. Grams can be converted to ounces by multiplying grams by the conversion factor 3.527×10^{-2}. How many ounces are in 14,500?

_____ Answer

4. The area of the end of a tank is 9.56×10^4 cm². What is the volume of the tank in cubic centimeters if the length is 740 cm?

_____ Answer

5. The volume of a water-storage tank is 8.35×10 m³. How many gallons will it hold?

_____ Answer

6. A gasoline service station sells an average of 72,000 gal of gas per month. How many gallons would that amount to in $18\frac{1}{2}$ months?

_____ Answer

7. In problem 6, if the profit is 8.35 ¢/gal, how many dollars profit does this represent for $18\frac{1}{2}$ months?

_____ Answer

8. A swimming pool contains 125,000 gal of water. How many cubic feet of volume does this represent?

_____ Answer

9. A radio wave for communication travels through space at the speed of light (186,000 mi/sec.) How long would a voice transmission take to reach the moon? (The moon is approximately 250,000 mi from earth.)

_____ Answer

10. How many gallons of water in 300,000 acre feet? An *acre foot* is a square acre, 1′ deep, and is used to measure the volume of water behind a dam.

_____ Answer

9-6
Squaring Numbers Using Power of Ten

A number may be squared using powers of ten by first squaring the numerical value and then doubling the exponent.

Example

$$((1.5) \times 10^{\textcircled{3}})^2$$

square   double   Square 1.5. Double the exponent.

$$2.25 \times 10^6$$

Example

$$((1.2) \times 10^{\textcircled{-3}})^2$$

square   double   Square 1.2. Double the exponent.

$$1.44 \times 10^{-6}$$

Exercises Place the number in scientific notation, square the number, and double the exponent. Leave answer in scientific notation. (Round to three significant figures.)

		Scientific notation	Square	Answer
1.	12	1.2×10^1	1.44×10^2	1.44×10^2
2.	380,000			
3.	0.00131			
4.	1.21×10^2			
5.	0.0068			
6.	9.21×10^3			
7.	324,000,000			
8.	825×10^{-9}			
9.	64.7×10^8			
10.	0.0044×10^{-2}			

9-7
Extracting Square Root Using Scientific Notation with Powers of Ten

Convert the number into power-of-ten notation with an even exponent. The whole number may contain one or two digits to the left of the decimal point, whatever is required to obtain an even exponent.

Example

$$\sqrt{387 \times 10^7} = \sqrt{38.7 \times 10^\text{⑧}} \text{ even exponent}$$

The next step is to extract the square root of the whole number and divide the exponent by 2.

$$\underbrace{38.7}_{\text{Square root}} \times 10^{⑧} = \underbrace{6.22}_{} \times 10^{④} \quad (8 \div 2 =)$$

Example

$$0.000144 = \underbrace{1.44}_{\text{Square root}} \times 10^{④} = \underbrace{1.2}_{} \times 10^{②} \quad (4 \div 2 =)$$

Exercises Change each number to the correct powers of ten and extract the square roots. Leave answer in scientific notation. (Round to three significant figures.)

		Power of Ten	Square root
1.	126	1.26×10^2	1.12×10^1
2.	6520		
3.	0.000123		
4.	0.995		

5.   435,000,000   _____   _____

6.   0.00000678   _____   _____

7. 0.014×10^9 _____   _____

8. 6.2×10^{-7} _____   _____

9. 4367×10^4 _____   _____

10. 332×10^3 _____   _____

9-8 Addition and Subtraction of Powers of Ten

Keeping in mind that only like things can be added or subtracted, the exponent of ten is what makes one expression like another. The exponents must be expressed in like exponents to add or subtract.

Example

$$\text{Add} \qquad \begin{array}{r} 25.5 \times 10^4 = 25.5 \ \times 10^④ \\ 36.7 \times 10^3 = \ 3.67 \times 10^④ \\ \hline 29.17 \times 10^④ \end{array} \quad \text{Same exponents}$$

Example

$$\text{Subtract} \qquad \begin{array}{r} 18.5 \times 10^5 = 18.50 \times 10^⑤ \\ -22.3 \times 10^4 \quad\quad 2.23 \times 10^⑤ \\ \hline 16.27 \times 10^⑤ \end{array} \quad \text{Same exponents}$$

Exercises

Perform the addition or subtraction using power-of-ten notation and leave answer in scientific notation. (Round to three significant figures.)

1. $(8.98 \times 10^3) + (7.65 \times 10^1) = \underline{8.98 \times 10^3 + 0.0765 \times 10^3 = 9.06 \times 10^3}$

2. $(165 \times 10^3) + (1800 \times 10^2) + (1365 \times 10^1) = $ _____

3. $(0.0156 \times 10^{-2}) + (2.5 \times 10^2) + 0.00054 = $ _____

4. $(1650 \times 10^5) - (8.75 \times 10^7) = $ _____

5. $(0.0018 \times 10^{-2}) - (0.015 \times 10^{-3}) = $ _____

6. $(685 \times 10^{-9}) - (1365 \times 10^{-11}) = $ _____

REVIEW QUESTIONS

Solve the following using power-of-ten notation. The problems in this section are similar to those in previous sections with units expressed in powers of ten. Leave answers in scientific notation and round to three significant figures.

1. What is the diameter of a circle with an area of 13 million mm²?

_____ Answer

2. The cross-sectional area of a piece of L-shaped aluminum angle is 1.87×10^0 in². What is the weight of the angle stock if it is 1.85×10^1 ft long?

_____ Answer

3. A cylindrical tank has a storage capacity of 1.85×10^4 gal and a diameter of 1.75×10^1 ft. What is the height of the tank?

_____ Answer

4. A gear in a small servomechanism is traveling at a speed of 1.475×10^2 rpm, and it has a diameter of 0.015×10^3 cm. If the gear meshes with a gear having a diameter of 2.5×10^1 mm, how fast is the second gear traveling?

_____ Answer

5. Copper wire increases its resistance in direct proportion to increases in temperature. The new resistance can be determined by the equation

$$R_N = R_o(1 + \alpha t)$$

where R_N = new resistance, Ω

R_o = resistance of wire at 0°, Ω

α = temperature coefficient of copper

t = temperature, °C

If $R_o = 2.56 \times 10^{-2}$ Ω, $\alpha = 4.27 \times 10^{-3}$, what will be the resistance of the copper wire at 48°C?

_____ Answer

6. Using the equation from problem 5, determine the resistance of a piece of silver wire for a 20° increase in temperature if the temperature coefficient of silver is 4.12×10^{-3} and the resistance at 0° is 1.62×10^{-2}.

_____ Answer

7. The current in electrical circuit can be determined by the equation

$$I = \frac{E}{R}$$

where I = current, A

E = voltage, V

R = resistance, Ω

Determine the current in a circuit if the voltage is 1.2×10^2 V and the resistance is 3.30×10^5 Ω.

_____ Answer

8. Referring to problem 7, the equation for voltage is $E = IR$. What is the voltage in a circuit if the resistance is 1.2×10^3 Ω and the current is 1.4×10^{-2} A?

_____ Answer

9. Referring to problem 7, the equation for resistance is $R = E/I$. What is the resistance for a circuit whose voltage is 24 V and current is 1.5×10^{-6} A?

_____ Answer

10. The power in an electrical circuit can be determined by the equation

$$P = IE$$

where P = power, W

I = current, A

E = voltage, V

What is the power for a circuit with a current of 7.5×10^{-2} A and a voltage of 4.4×10^2 V?

_____ Answer

11. Referring to problem 10, power can also be determined by the equation $P = I^2R$ where R is resistance in ohms. Find the power in a circuit with a current of 3.5×10^{-4} A and a resistance of 2.2×10^2 Ω.

_____ Answer

12. Referring to problem 10, power can also be determined by the equation $P = E^2/R$. Find the power in a circuit with a voltage of 2.08×10^2 V and a resistance of 1.5×10^2 Ω.

_____ Answer

CHAPTER TEN
RIGHT-TRIANGLE
TRIGONOMETRY

Right triangles having corresponding acute angles equal are *similar figures* as discussed in Unit 7. The ratio of the corresponding sides of similar triangles are equal, regardless of their length, as shown in Fig. 10-1.

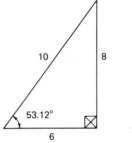

Fig. 10-1
Similar figures.

**10-1
Standard Right Triangle**

In defining right triangle trigonometry, a *standard right triangle* will be defined as shown in Fig. 10-2.

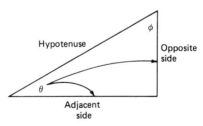

Fig. 10-2
Standard reference triangle for θ.

In relation to the angle defined as θ (theta), three ratios can be used and these ratios are called the *sine ratio* (sin), the *cosine ratio* (cos), and the *tangent ratio* (tan). Their ratios are defined as

$$\sin \theta = \frac{\text{opp}}{\text{hyp}} \qquad \cos \theta = \frac{\text{adj}}{\text{hyp}} \qquad \tan \theta = \frac{\text{opp}}{\text{adj}}$$

If these ratios are applied to the similar figures in Fig. 10-1, the following will result.

Large triangle	Small triangle
$\sin \theta = \dfrac{8}{10}$	$\sin \theta = \dfrac{4}{5}$
$\sin \theta = 0.8000$	$\sin \theta = 0.8000$

or

$\cos \theta = \dfrac{6}{10}$	$\cos \theta = \dfrac{3}{5}$
$\cos \theta = 0.6000$	$\cos \theta = 0.6000$

or

$\tan \theta = \dfrac{8}{6}$	$\tan \theta = \dfrac{4}{3}$
$\tan \theta = 1.3333$	$\tan \theta = 1.3333$

It can be seen that the ratios for each trigonometric function are equal. This is true for all similar right triangles. Table 6 indicates the angle θ for these ratios and is provided in the Appendix. Refer to these tables and find

Large triangle	Small triangle
$\sin \theta = 0.8000$	$\sin \theta = 0.8000$
$\theta = 53.12°$	$\theta = 53.12°$
$\cos \theta = 0.6000$	$\cos \theta = 0.6000$
$\theta = 53.12°$	$\theta = 53.12°$
$\tan \theta = 1.333$	$\tan \theta = 1.333$
$\theta = 53.12°$	$\theta = 53.12°$

Similar relationships could be illustrated for the angle ϕ (phi) using the triangle shown in Fig. 10-3. The opposite and adjacent sides reverse when referring to angle ϕ and the hypotenuse is always the longest side.

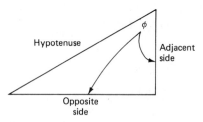

Fig. 10-3
Standard reference triangle for ϕ.

10-1a
Angles θ and ϕ

The sum of the angles of a triangle equal 180°. Since a right triangle has one 90° angle, the sum of θ and ϕ must equal 90° or

$$\theta = 90° - \phi$$
$$\phi = 90° - \theta$$

Angles can be expressed in degrees, minutes and seconds, or as decimal values as well as several other ways. This text will use the decimal system. (Round answers to three significant figures.)

1. Find the sin, cos, and tan of the following:

		sin	*cos*	*tan*
a.	62°	**0.8829**	**0.4695**	**1.881**
b.	43.8°			
c.	8.6°			
d.	87.9°			
e.	45°			

2. Find an angle whose sin is
   a. 0.7071 = **45°**
   b. 0.9291 = _____
   c. 0.7604 = _____
   d. 0.9792 = _____
   e. 0.2368 = _____

3. Find an angle whose cos is
   a. 0.7071 = _____
   b. 0.5707 = _____
   c. 0.9952 = _____
   d. 0.2706 = _____
   e. 0.9461 = _____

4. Find an angle whose tan is
   a. 0.7071 = _____
   b. 0.5774 = _____
   c. 16.35 = _____
   d. 1.477 = _____
   e. 0.0875 = _____

5. If ϕ = to 36.4°, find cos θ. _____ Answer

6. If θ = 72.4°, find tan ϕ. _____ Answer

7. If ϕ = 21.7°, find sin θ. _____ Answer

8. Find the angle θ if tan ϕ = 0.6346. _____ Answer

9. Find the angle ϕ if sin θ = 0.2181. _____ Answer

10. Find the angle θ if cos ϕ = 0.4258. _____ Answer

Example

Given the standard right triangle in Fig. 10-4 where $\theta = 42°$ and $a = 25$, find the angle ϕ and side c.

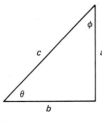

Fig. 10-4

$$\phi = 90° - \theta$$

$$\phi = 90° - 42° = 48°$$

$$\sin \theta = \frac{a}{c}$$

$$\sin 42° = \frac{25}{c}$$

$$c = \frac{25}{\sin 42°}$$

Taken from Table 6, sin 42° = 0.6991

$$= \frac{25}{0.6991}$$

$$= 37.36$$

Example

The $\frac{\text{opp}}{\text{hyp}}$ ratio for 30°, 45° and 60° angles are shown in Fig. 10-5.

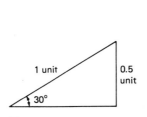
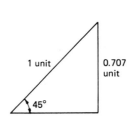
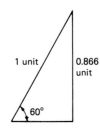

Fig. 10-5

These ratios can be very helpful in technical applications. For instance, if the plans for putting a roof on a barn called for 22′ rafters to be placed on a 45° angle, what would be the length of brace x in Fig. 10-6?

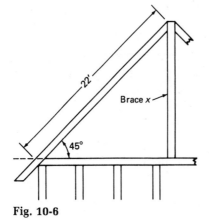

Fig. 10-6

$$\sin = \frac{\text{opp}}{\text{hyp}}$$

$$\sin 45° = \frac{x}{22}$$

$$x = \sin 45° \ (22)$$

$$= 0.707 \ (22)$$

$$= 15.55′$$

or $\qquad 15′\ 6\frac{5″}{8}$

1. The hypotenuse of a right triangle is 28.5″ and θ equals 63.7°. Find the altitude.

_____ Answer

2. In a right triangle, if the altitude is 13.65″ and $\theta = 36.5°$, find the hypotenuse.

_____ Answer

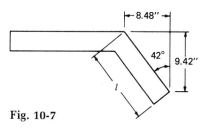

Fig. 10-7

3. Find the distance l in Fig. 10-7.

_____ Answer

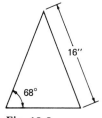

Fig. 10-8

4. Find the altitude of the isosceles triangle in Fig. 10-8.

_____ Answer

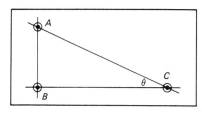

Fig. 10-9

5. In Fig. 10-9, the distance between the centers A and B is 3.75″ and $\theta = 35°$. What is the distance between A and C?

_____ Answer

Example

Given the standard right triangle in Fig. 10-10 where $\phi = 36°$ and $c = 30$, find the angle θ and side b.

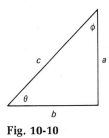

Fig. 10-10

$$\theta = 90° - \phi$$

$$\theta = 90° - 36° = 54°$$

$$\cos \theta = \frac{b}{c}$$

$$\cos 54° = \frac{b}{30}$$

$$b = \cos 54° \ (30)$$

Taken from Table 6, $\cos 54° = 0.5878$

$$= 0.5878 \ (30)$$

$$= 17.6$$

Exercises
Using Cosine Ratio

1. Find the base of a right triangle if the hypotenuse is 106 cm and $\theta = 12.6°$.

_____ Answer

2. The base of a right triangle is 640 mm and the angle $\phi = 72.8°$. What is the value of the hypotenuse?

_____ Answer

3. Find the missing side c in Fig. 10-11.

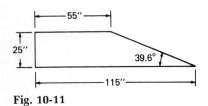

Fig. 10-11

_____ Answer

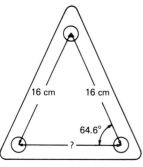

Fig. 10-12

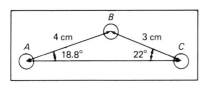

Fig. 10-13

4. Find the missing dimension in the hole layout shown in Fig. 10-12.

_____ Answer

5. In the hole layout shown in Fig. 10-13, find the distance between the centers A and C.

_____ Answer

10-4
Using the Tangent Ratio to Find the Side of a Right Triangle

Example

Given the standard right triangle in Fig. 10-14 where $\theta = 70°$ and $a = 45$, find the angle ϕ and side b.

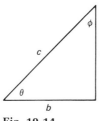

Fig. 10-14

$$\phi = 90° - \theta$$

$$\phi = 90° - 70° = 20°$$

$$\tan \theta = \frac{a}{b}$$

$$\tan 70° = \frac{45}{b}$$

$$b = \frac{45}{\tan 70°}$$

Taken from table 6, $\tan 70° = 2.74$

$$= \frac{45}{2.74}$$

$$= 16.42$$

Exercises
Using Tangent Ratio

1. The altitude of a right triangle is 128 m and the angle $\theta = 61.4°$. Find the base.

_____ Answer

2. Find the altitude of a right triangle if the base is 16.7 m and the angle $\phi = 27.3°$.

_____ Answer

3. The angle of inclination of a roadway is defined as the ratio of the vertical rise to the horizontal distance, which is also the tan ratio. What is the maximum vertical rise if the angle of inclination is 4.5°?

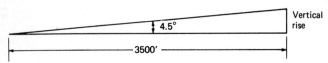
Fig. 10-15

_____ Answer

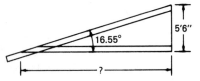
Fig. 10-16

4. A section of roof truss is shown in Fig. 10-16. Find the missing dimension.

_____ Answer

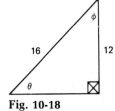
Fig. 10-17

5. Illustrated in Fig. 10-17 is a profile of a sharp V-thread. What is the depth of the thread?

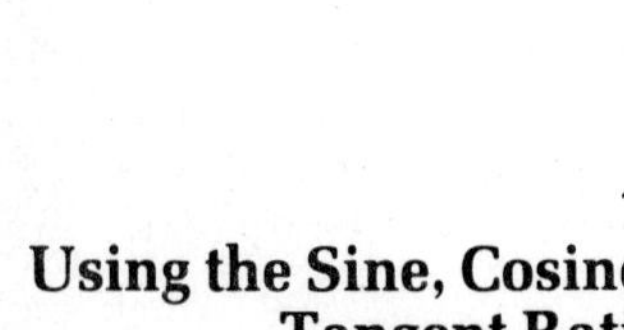

_____ Answer

10-5
Using the Sine, Cosine, or Tangent Ratio to Determine the Acute Angles of a Right Triangle

Example

Given the standard right triangle in Fig. 10-18, find the angle θ with sin ratio as shown.

$$\sin \theta = \frac{\text{opp}}{\text{hyp}}$$

$$= \frac{12}{16}$$

$$= 0.75$$

Fig. 10-18

From Table 6, find the closest angle whose sin = 0.75.

$$\theta = 48.6°$$

$$\phi = 90° - \theta$$

$$\phi = 90° - 48.6° = 41.4°$$

Example

Given the standard right triangle in Fig. 10-19, find the angle θ with cos ratio as shown.

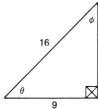

Fig. 10-19

$$\cos \theta = \frac{adj}{hyp}$$

$$= \frac{9}{16}$$

$$= 0.5625$$

From Table 6, find closest angle whose cos = 0.5625.

$$\theta = 55.8°$$

$$\phi = 90° - \theta$$

$$\phi = 90° - 55.8° = 34.2°$$

Example

Given the standard right triangle in Fig. 10-20, find the angle θ with tan ratio as shown.

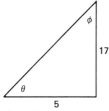

Fig. 10-20

$$\tan \theta = \frac{opp}{adj}$$

$$= \frac{17}{5}$$

$$= 3.4$$

From Table 6, find the closest angle whose tan = 3.4.

$$\theta = 73.6°$$

$$\theta = 90° - 73.6° = 16.4°$$

The same relationship can be shown for the angle ϕ.

Exercises
Trigonometry Problems

1. In the right triangle in Fig. 10-21, the altitude is equal to 92″ and the hypotenuse is 165″. Using the sin function, find the angle θ.

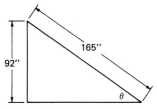

Fig. 10-21

_____ Answer

2. Find the angles θ and ϕ if the altitude is 16 cm and the base is 34 cm. Draw and label the right triangle as in Fig. 10-19.

$\theta =$ _____ Answer

$\phi =$ _____ Answer

3. The side adjacent to θ is equal to 14″, and the hypotenuse is equal to 28″. Find the angle θ. Draw and label the right triangle.

_____ Answer

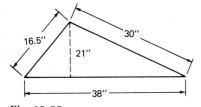

16.5″   30″

21″

38″

Fig. 10-22

4. Find the angle between the 38″ side and the 30″ side of the triangle shown in Fig. 10-22.

_____ Answer

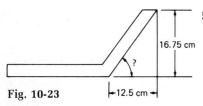

16.75 cm

?

Fig. 10-23   12.5 cm

5. On the brace illustrated in Fig. 10-23, determine the angle of bend indicated by the given dimensions.

_____ Answer

EVALUATION PROBLEMS

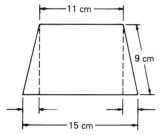

Fig. 10-24

1. Find the altitude of the trapezoid in Fig. 10-24 using trigonometric functions. Do not use the Pythagorean theorem.

_____ Answer

Fig. 10-25

2. In Fig. 10-25, find the angle between the two indicated radii if the diameter is equal to 10.5″.

_____ Answer

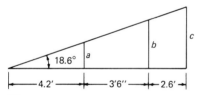

Fig. 10-26

3. Find the sides a, b, and c indicated in Fig. 10-26.

a = _____ Answer

b = _____ Answer

c = _____ Answer

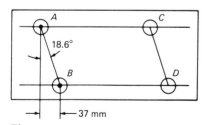

Fig. 10-27

4. In the mounting plate shown in Fig. 10-27, the hole labeled B is offset by 18.6°. Find the distance between the centers of the holes A and B.

_____ Answer

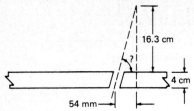

Fig. 10-28

16.3 cm

4 cm

54 mm

?

5. A 16 mm hole is drilled at an angle through the plate in Fig. 10-28. What will be the angle between the plate and the drill bit indicated in the drawing?

_____ Answer

10-6
Applications of Right-Angle Trigonometry

Example

Determine a method for laying out five equally spaced holes in a circle with a diameter of 16″. Find the angle indicated at the center of the circle (Fig. 10-29).

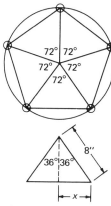

Angle $A = 360° \div 5 = 72°$

Fig. 10-29

This angle is part of an isosceles triangle that can be divided into two equal right triangles, where x can be determined by the sin function.

$$\sin 36° = \frac{x}{8}$$

$$x = \sin 36° \ (8)$$

Taken from Table 6, $\sin 36° = 0.5878$.

$$x = 0.5878 \ (8) = 4.70″$$

The distance between the centers of the hole is 2x or $2(4.7″) = 9.4″$ This method can be used for any number of holes layed out in a circle. The basic figure formed in Fig. 10-29 is a pentagon, and the distance between the centers of the holes is shown as the side of the pentagon. The same application of right-angle trigonometry can be applied to triangles, squares, hexagons, etc.

Exercises
Right-Angle Trigonometry

1. A circular cover plate is to be held in place with seven equally spaced holes. The diameter of the plate is 42 cm, and the centers of the holes will be placed 2 cm from the edge of the circle. Determine the straight-line distance between their centers.

_____ Answer

2. In problem 1, what would be the distance between the centers of the holes if they were placed 4 cm from the edge?

_____ Answer

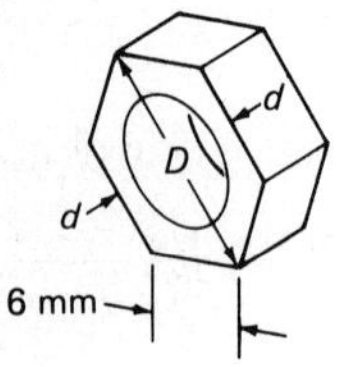

Fig. 10-30

3. Illustrated in Fig. 10-30 is the end view of a nut. Using right-angle trigonometric functions, what is the large diameter *D* if one side is 6 mm?

_____ Answer

4. In Fig. 10-30, what is the distance across the flats indicated on the drawing as *d*?

_____ Answer

Fig. 10-31

5. The holes in the cover plate of the transmission shown in Fig. 10-31 are equally spaced. What is the straight-line distance between their centers? The centers of the holes are $\frac{3}{8}''$ from the edge of the plate.

_____ Answer

6. In Fig. 10-31, what is the total length of the plate?

_____ Answer

REVIEW QUESTIONS

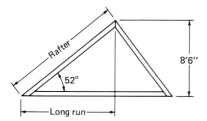

Fig. 10-32

1. A sketch of a roof truss is shown in Fig. 10-32. What will be the distance to the closest foot of the long run as illustrated?

_____ Answer

2. In Fig. 10-32, what will be the length of the rafter in feet and inches to the nearest inch.

_____ Answer

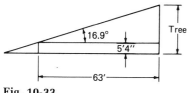

Fig. 10-33

3. The height of a tree is to be determined by using a transit. A sketch of the results is shown in Fig. 10-33. The height of the instrument from the ground is 5' 4". The angle measured by the transit is 16.9°, and the transit is 63' from the tree. Give answer to the closest inch.

_____ Answer

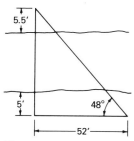

Fig. 10-34

4. The width of a small canyon is to be measured. A sketch of the surveyors layout is shown in Fig. 10-34. What is the approximate width of the canyon at the point indicated on the sketch?

_____ Answer

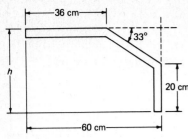

Fig. 10-35

5. A side or edge view of an aluminum panel is sketched in Fig. 10-35. Neglecting bend allowance, what will be the total width of the sheet of aluminum needed before bending if the completed panel is to be 60 cm wide?

_____ Answer

6. In Fig. 10-35, what is the height h of the completed panel, neglecting bend allowance?

_____ Answer

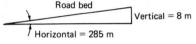

Fig. 10-36

7. Percent of grade on a road is the ratio of its vertical rise to the horizontal distance associated with the rise and is expressed as a percent for convenience. The principle is illustrated in Fig. 10-36. What is the percent of grade?

_____ Answer

8. In Fig. 10-36, the ratio of vertical distance to horizontal distance is the tan ratio. What is the angle between the horizontal distance and the roadbed?

_____ Answer

9. A road has a percent of grade indicated on a map to be 4.8%. What is the angle between the roadbed and the horizontal distance?

_____ Answer

10. If the road mentioned in problem 9 has the same percent of grade for a distance of 3.5 km, what is the vertical-rise distance?

_____ Answer

11. Five equally spaced holes are placed 8 mm from the edge of a circular plate. What is the straight line distance between their centers if the plate is 85 mm in diameter?

_____ Answer

Fig. 10-37

12. The reversing pulleys in Fig. 10-37 are the same diameter which is 12.5 cm. The distance between the centers of the pulleys is 45 cm. What is the circumference of the belt required?

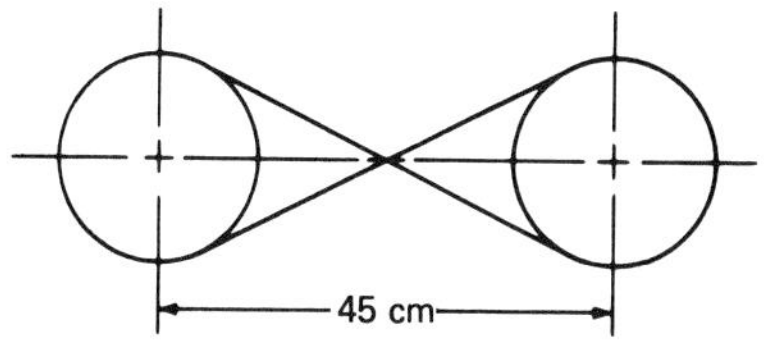

_____ Answer

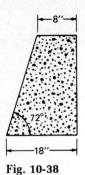

Fig. 10-38

13. How many yards of concrete would be required to pour a concrete retaining wall for a length of 18'? The cross section of the wall is shown in Fig. 10-38.

_____ Answer

14. A retaining wall similar to the one in Fig. 10-38 is to be built. The wall will remain 18″ wide on the bottom, but the top width will be reduced to 6½″. What angle will be formed by the bottom and non-vertical side of the form if the height is now 2′ 6″?

_____ Answer

APPENDIX

TABLE 1
CONVERSIONS

To change	To	Multiply by
Inches	Feet	0.0833
Inches	Millimeters	25.4
Feet	Inches	12
Feet	Yards	0.3333
Yards	Feet	3
Squares inches	Square feet	0.00694
Square feet	Square inches	144
Square feet	Square yards	0.11111
Square yards	Square feet	9
Cubic inches	Cubic feet	0.00058
Cubic feet	Cubic inches	1728
Cubic feet	Cubic yards	0.03703
Cubic yards	Cubic feet	27
Cubic inches	Gallons	0.00433
Cubic feet	Gallons	7.48
Gallons	Cubic inches	231
Gallons	Cubic feet	0.1337
Gallons	Pounds of water	8.33
Pounds of water	Gallons	0.12004
Ounces	Pounds	0.0625
Pounds	Ounces	16
Inches of water	Pounds per square inch	0.0361
Inches of water	Inches of mercury	0.0735
Inches of water	Ounces per square inch	0.578
Inches of water	Pounds per square foot	5.2
Inches of mercury	Inches of water	13.6
Inches of mercury	Feet of water	1.1333
Inches of mercury	Pounds per square inch	0.4914
Ounces per square inch	Inches of mercury	0.127
Ounces per square inch	Inches of water	1.733
Pounds per square inch	Inches of water	27.72
Pounds per square inch	Inches of mercury	2.04
Pounds per square inch	Atmospheres	0.0681
Feet of water	Pounds per square inch	0.434
Feet of water	Pounds per square foot	62.5
Feet of water	Inches of mercury	0.8824
Atmospheres	Pounds per square inch	14.696
Atmospheres	Inches of mercury	29.92
Atmospheres	Feet of water	34
Long tons	Pounds	2240
Short tons	Pounds	2000
Short tons	Long tons	0.89285

TABLE 2
EQUATIONS FOR GEOMETRIC FIGURES

Square

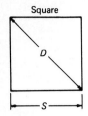

$A = \text{area} = s^2 = \frac{1}{2}D^2$
$D = 1.4142s = 1.4142\sqrt{A}$
$s = 0.70711 D = \sqrt{A}$

Equilateral triangle

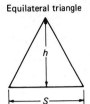

$A = \text{area} = 0.43301s^2$
$\quad = 0.57735h^2$
$h = 0.86603s$
$s = 1.1547h$

Circle

$A = \text{area} = \pi r^2 = 3.1416\ r^2$
$C = \text{circumference} = 2\ \pi r$
$r = 0.56419\ \sqrt{A}$
$d = 1.12838\ \sqrt{A}$

Fillet

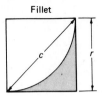

$A = \text{area}$
$\quad = r^2 - \frac{1}{4}\ \pi r^2$
$\quad = 0.2146\ r^2$
$\quad = 0.1073\ c^2$

Rectangle

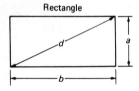

$A = \text{area} = ab$
$\quad = a\sqrt{d^2 - a^2} = b\sqrt{d^2 - b^2}$
$a = \sqrt{d^2 - b^2} = \dfrac{A}{b}$
$b = \sqrt{d^2 - a^2} = \dfrac{A}{a}$

Right-angle triangle

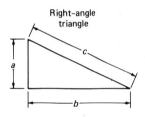

$A = \text{area} = \frac{1}{2}\ ab$
$a = \sqrt{c^2 - b^2}$
$b = \sqrt{c^2 - a^2}$
$c = \sqrt{a^2 + b^2}$

Annulus

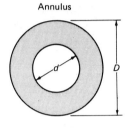

$\text{Area} = \dfrac{\pi}{4}\ (D^2 - d^2)$

Ellipse

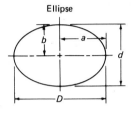

$\text{Area} = \pi ab = 0.7854\ D\ d$
$\text{Perimeter} = \pi\ \sqrt{2(a^2 + b^2)}$
$\quad\quad \text{approximately}$

Triangle

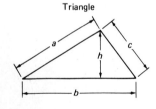

$A = \text{area} = \frac{1}{2}\ bh$
$A = \sqrt{s(s - a)(s - b)(s - c)}$
$s = \frac{1}{2}(a + b + c)$

Trapezoid

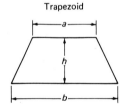

$A = \text{area} = \frac{1}{2}(a + b)h$

Hexagon

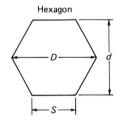

$d = 0.86603\ D = 1.73205\ s$
$D = 1.1547\ d = 2\ s$
$A = 0.64952\ D^2 = 0.86603\ d^2$
$\quad = 2.5981\ s^2$

Octagon

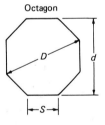

$d = 0.92388\ D = 2.4142\ s$
$D = 1.0824\ d = 2.6131\ s$
$A = 0.82842\ d^2 = 0.70711\ D^2$
$\quad = 4.8284\ s^2$

Sphere

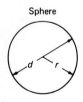

$V = \frac{3}{4}\ \pi r^3 = \frac{1}{6}\ \pi d^3 = 4.1888\ r^3$
$A = \text{area} = 4\ \pi r^2 = \pi d^2$
$\quad = 12.5664\ r^2$

Cylinder

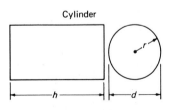

$V = \pi r^2 h = 0.7854\ d^2 h$
$s = \text{curved surface}$
$\quad = 2\ \pi rh = \pi dh$
$A = \text{total area}$
$\quad = 2\ \pi r(r + h)$

TABLE 3
WEIGHTS OF DIFFERENT MATERIALS

Material	lb/ft^3	lb/in^3
Aluminum	165	0.0955
Brass	524	0.3032
Brick	112	0.0648
Bronze	552	0.3195
Cement	94	0.0544
Concrete	137	0.0793
Copper	556	0.3218
Gasoline	43.7	0.0253
Gravel	109	0.0631
Ice	56	0.0324
Iron, cast	449	0.2600
Iron, wrought	490	0.2834
Lead	709	0.4105
Nickel	537	0.3108
Nitric acid	94	0.0544
Sand, dry	100	0.0579
Silver	657	0.3802
Steel	490	0.2833
Sulphuric acid	115	0.0664
Tin	455	0.2632
Water	62.4	0.0361
Wood, white pine	31.2	0.018
Wood, cherry	43.7	0.025
Zinc, cast	428	0.2476
Zinc, rolled	446	0.2581

TABLE 4
DECIMAL EQUIVALENTS: ENGLISH-METRIC

Inches	Decimal equivalent	Millimeters
$\frac{1}{64}$	0.015625	0.3969
$\frac{1}{32}$	0.03125	0.794
$\frac{3}{64}$	0.046875	1.190
$\frac{1}{16}$	0.0625	1.588
$\frac{5}{64}$	0.078125	1.984
$\frac{3}{32}$	0.09375	2.381
$\frac{7}{64}$	0.109375	2.778
$\frac{1}{8}$	0.125	3.175
$\frac{9}{64}$	0.140625	3.572
$\frac{5}{32}$	0.15625	3.969
$\frac{11}{64}$	0.171875	4.366
$\frac{3}{16}$	0.1875	4.763
$\frac{13}{64}$	0.203125	5.159
$\frac{7}{32}$	0.21875	5.556
$\frac{15}{64}$	0.234375	5.95
$\frac{1}{4}$	0.25	6.35
$\frac{17}{64}$	0.265625	6.747
$\frac{9}{32}$	0.28125	7.144
$\frac{19}{64}$	0.296875	7.541
$\frac{5}{16}$	0.3125	7.938
$\frac{21}{64}$	0.328125	8.334
$\frac{11}{32}$	0.34375	8.731
$\frac{23}{64}$	0.359375	9.128
$\frac{3}{8}$	0.375	9.525
$\frac{25}{64}$	0.390625	9.222
$\frac{13}{32}$	0.40625	10.32
$\frac{27}{64}$	0.421875	10.72
$\frac{7}{16}$	0.4375	11.11
$\frac{29}{64}$	0.453125	11.51
$\frac{15}{32}$	0.46875	11.91
$\frac{31}{64}$	0.484375	12.30
$\frac{1}{2}$	0.5	12.7
$\frac{33}{64}$	0.515625	13.097
$\frac{17}{32}$	0.53125	13.49
$\frac{35}{64}$	0.546875	13.89
$\frac{9}{16}$	0.5625	14.29
$\frac{37}{64}$	0.578125	14.68
$\frac{19}{32}$	0.59375	15.08
$\frac{39}{64}$	0.609375	15.48
$\frac{5}{8}$	0.625	15.88
$\frac{41}{64}$	0.640625	16.27
$\frac{21}{32}$	0.65625	16.67
$\frac{43}{64}$	0.671875	17.07
$\frac{11}{16}$	0.6875	17.46
$\frac{45}{64}$	0.703125	17.86

TABLE 4
DECIMAL EQUIVALENTS: ENGLISH-METRIC (cont.)

Inches	Decimal equivalent	Millimeters
$\frac{23}{32}$	0.71875	18.26
$\frac{47}{64}$	0.734375	18.65
$\frac{3}{4}$	0.75	19.05
$\frac{49}{64}$	0.765625	19.45
$\frac{25}{32}$	0.78125	19.84
$\frac{51}{64}$	0.796875	20.24
$\frac{13}{16}$	0.8125	20.63
$\frac{53}{64}$	0.828125	21.03
$\frac{27}{32}$	0.84375	21.43
$\frac{55}{64}$	0.859375	21.83
$\frac{7}{8}$	0.875	22.23
$\frac{57}{64}$	0.890625	22.62
$\frac{29}{32}$	0.90625	23.02
$\frac{59}{64}$	0.921875	23.42
$\frac{15}{16}$	0.9375	23.81
$\frac{61}{64}$	0.953125	24.21
$\frac{31}{32}$	0.96875	24.60
$\frac{63}{64}$	0.984375	25.00

TABLE 5
SQUARES AND SQUARE ROOTS

No.	Square	Square Root	No.	Square	Square Root	No.	Square	Square Root	No.	Square	Square Root
1	1	1.0000	50	2500	7.0711	100	10000	10.0000	150	22500	12.2474
2	4	1.4142	51	2601	7.1414	101	10201	10.0499	151	22801	12.2882
3	9	1.7321	52	2704	7.2111	102	10404	10.0995	152	23104	12.3288
4	16	2.0000	53	2809	7.2801	103	10609	10.1489	153	23409	12.3693
5	25	2.2361	54	2916	7.3485	104	10816	10.1980	154	23716	12.4097
6	36	2.4495	55	3025	7.4162	105	11025	10.2470	155	24025	12.4499
7	49	2.6458	56	3136	7.4833	106	11236	10.2956	156	24336	12.4900
8	64	2.8284	57	3249	7.5498	107	11449	10.3441	157	24649	12.5300
9	81	3.0000	58	3364	7.6158	108	11664	10.3923	158	24964	12.5698
			59	3481	7.6811	109	11881	10.4403	159	25281	12.6095
10	100	3.1623									
11	121	3.3166	60	3600	7.7460	110	12100	10.4881	160	25600	12.6491
12	144	3.4641	61	3721	7.8102	111	12321	10.5357	161	25921	12.6886
13	169	3.6056	62	3844	7.8740	112	12544	10.5830	162	26244	12.7279
14	196	3.7417	63	3969	7.9373	113	12769	10.6301	163	26569	12.7671
15	225	3.8730	64	4096	8.0000	114	12996	10.6771	164	26896	12.8062
16	256	4.0000	65	4225	8.0623	115	13225	10.7238	165	27225	12.8452
17	289	4.1231	66	4356	8.1240	116	13456	10.7703	166	27556	12.8841
18	324	4.2426	67	4489	8.1854	117	13689	10.8167	167	27889	12.9228
19	361	4.3589	68	4624	8.2462	118	13924	10.8682	168	28224	12.9615
			69	4761	8.3066	119	14161	10.9087	169	28561	13.0000
20	400	4.4721									
21	441	4.5826	70	4900	8.3666	120	14400	10.9545	170	28900	13.0384
22	484	4.6904	71	5041	8.4261	121	14641	11.0000	171	29241	13.0767
23	529	4.7958	72	5184	8.4853	122	14884	11.0454	172	29584	13.1149
24	576	4.8990	73	5329	8.5440	123	15129	11.0905	173	29929	13.1529
25	625	5.0000	74	5476	8.6023	124	15376	11.1355	174	30276	13.1909
26	676	5.0990	75	5625	8.6603	125	15625	11.1803	175	30625	13.2288
27	729	5.1962	76	5776	8.7178	126	15876	11.2250	176	30976	13.2665
28	784	5.2915	77	5929	8.7750	127	16129	11.2694	177	31329	13.3041
29	841	5.3852	78	6084	8.8318	128	16384	11.3137	178	31684	13.3417
			79	6241	8.8882	129	16641	11.3578	179	32041	13.3791
30	900	5.4772									
31	961	5.5678	80	6400	8.9443	130	16900	11.4018	180	32400	13.4164
32	1024	5.6569	81	6561	9.0000	131	17161	11.4455	181	32761	13.4536
33	1089	5.7446	82	6724	9.0554	132	17424	11.4891	182	33124	13.4907
34	1156	5.8310	83	6889	9.1104	133	17689	11.5326	183	33489	13.5277
35	1225	5.9161	84	7056	9.1652	134	17956	11.5758	184	33856	13.5647
36	1296	6.0000	85	7225	9.2195	135	18225	11.6190	185	34225	13.6015
37	1369	6.0828	86	7396	9.2736	136	18496	11.6619	186	34596	13.6382
38	1444	6.1644	87	7569	9.3274	137	18769	11.7047	187	34969	13.6748
39	1521	6.2450	88	7744	9.3808	138	19044	11.7473	188	35344	13.7113
			89	7921	9.4340	139	19321	11.7898	189	35721	13.7477
40	1600	6.3246									
41	1681	6.4031	90	8100	9.4868	140	19600	11.8322	190	36100	13.7840
42	1764	6.4807	91	8281	9.5394	141	19881	11.8743	191	36481	13.8203
43	1849	6.5574	92	8464	9.5917	142	20164	11.9164	192	36864	13.8564
44	1936	6.6332	93	8649	9.6437	143	20449	11.9583	193	37249	13.8924
45	2025	6.7082	94	8836	9.6954	144	20736	12.0000	194	37636	13.9284
46	2116	6.7823	95	9025	9.7468	145	21025	12.0416	195	38025	13.9642
47	2209	6.8557	96	9216	9.7980	146	21316	12.0830	196	38416	14.0000
48	2304	6.9282	97	9409	9.8489	147	21609	12.1244	197	38809	14.0357
49	2401	7.0000	98	9604	9.8995	148	21904	12.1655	198	39204	14.0712
			99	9801	9.9499	149	22201	12.2066	199	39601	14.1067

TABLE 5
SQUARES AND SQUARE ROOTS (continued)

No.	Square	Square Root	No.	Square	Square Root	No.	Square	Square Root	No.	Square	Square Root
200	40000	14.1421	250	62500	15.8114	300	90000	17.3205	350	122500	18.7083
201	40401	14.1774	251	63001	15.8430	301	90601	17.3494	351	123201	18.7350
202	40804	14.2127	252	63504	15.8745	302	91204	17.3781	352	123904	18.7617
203	41209	14.2478	253	64009	15.9060	303	91809	17.4069	353	124609	18.7883
204	41616	14.2829	254	64516	15.9374	304	92416	17.4356	354	125316	18.8149
205	42025	14.3178	255	65025	15.9687	305	93025	17.4642	355	126025	18.8414
206	42436	14.3527	256	65536	16.0000	306	93636	17.4929	356	126736	18.8680
207	42849	14.3875	257	66049	16.0312	307	94249	17.5214	357	127449	18.8944
208	43264	14.4222	258	66564	16.0624	308	94864	17.5499	358	128164	18.9209
209	43681	14.4568	259	67081	16.0935	309	95481	17.5784	359	128881	18.9473
210	44100	14.4914	260	67600	16.1245	310	96100	17.6068	360	129600	18.9737
211	44521	14.5258	261	68121	16.1555	311	96721	17.6352	361	130321	19.0000
212	44944	14.5602	262	68644	16.1864	312	97344	17.6635	362	131044	19.0263
213	45369	14.5945	263	69169	16.2173	313	97969	17.6918	363	131769	19.0526
214	45796	14.6287	264	69696	16.2481	314	98596	17.7200	364	132496	19.0788
215	46225	14.6629	265	70225	16.2788	315	99225	17.7482	365	133225	19.1050
216	46656	14.6969	266	70756	16.3095	316	99856	17.7764	366	133956	19.1311
217	47089	14.7309	267	71289	16.3401	317	100489	17.8045	367	134689	19.1572
218	47524	14.7648	268	71824	16.3707	318	101124	17.8326	368	135424	19.1833
219	47961	14.7986	269	72361	16.4012	319	101761	17.8606	369	136161	19.2094
220	48400	14.8324	270	72900	16.4317	320	102400	17.8885	370	136900	19.2354
221	48841	14.8661	271	73441	16.4621	321	103041	17.9165	371	137641	19.2614
222	49284	14.8997	272	73984	16.4924	322	103684	17.9444	372	138384	19.2873
223	49729	14.9332	273	74529	16.5227	323	104329	17.9722	373	139129	19.3132
224	50176	14.9666	274	75076	16.5529	324	104976	18.0000	374	139876	19.3391
225	50625	15.0000	275	75625	16.5831	325	105625	18.0278	375	140625	19.3649
226	51076	15.0333	276	76176	16.6132	326	106276	18.0555	376	141376	19.3907
227	51529	15.0665	277	76729	16.6433	327	106929	18.0831	377	142129	19.4165
228	51984	15.0997	278	77284	16.6733	328	107584	18.1108	378	142884	19.4422
229	52441	15.1327	279	77841	16.7033	329	108241	18.1384	379	143641	19.4679
230	52900	15.1658	280	78400	16.7332	330	108900	18.1659	380	144400	19.4936
231	53361	15.1987	281	78961	16.7631	331	109561	18.1934	381	145161	19.5192
232	53824	15.2315	282	79524	16.7929	332	110224	18.2209	382	145924	19.5448
233	54289	15.2643	283	80089	16.8226	333	110889	18.2483	383	146689	19.5704
234	54756	15.2971	284	80656	16.8523	334	111556	18.2757	384	147456	19.5959
235	55225	15.3297	285	81225	16.8819	335	112225	18.3030	385	148225	19.6214
236	55696	15.3623	286	81796	16.9115	336	112896	18.3303	386	148996	19.6469
237	56169	15.3948	287	82369	16.9411	337	113569	18.3576	387	149769	19.6723
238	56644	15.4272	288	82944	16.9706	338	114244	18.3848	388	150544	19.6977
239	57121	15.4596	289	83521	17.0000	339	114921	18.4120	389	151321	19.7231
240	57600	15.4919	290	84100	17.0294	340	115600	18.4391	390	152100	19.7484
241	58081	15.5242	291	84681	17.0587	341	116281	18.4662	391	152881	19.7737
242	58564	15.5563	292	85264	17.0880	342	116964	18.4932	392	153664	19.7990
243	59049	15.5885	293	85849	17.1172	343	117649	18.5203	393	154449	19.8242
244	59536	15.6205	294	86436	17.1464	344	118336	18.5472	394	155236	19.8494
245	60025	15.6525	295	87025	17.1756	345	119025	18.5742	395	156025	19.8746
246	60516	15.6844	296	87616	17.2047	346	119716	18.6011	396	156816	19.8997
247	61009	15.7162	297	88209	17.2337	347	120409	18.6279	397	157609	19.9249
248	61504	15.7480	298	88804	17.2627	348	121104	18.6548	398	158404	19.9499
249	62001	15.7797	299	89401	17.2916	349	121801	18.6815	399	159201	19.9750

TABLE 5
SQUARES AND SQUARE ROOTS (continued)

No.	Square	Square Root	No.	Square	Square Root	No.	Square	Square Root	No.	Square	Square Root
400	160000	20.0000	450	202500	21.2132	500	250000	22.3607	550	302500	23.4521
401	160801	20.0250	451	203401	21.2368	501	251001	22.3830	551	303601	23.4734
402	161604	20.0499	452	204304	21.2603	502	252004	22.4054	552	304704	23.4947
403	162409	20.0749	453	205209	21.2838	503	253009	22.4277	553	305809	23.5160
404	163216	20.0998	454	206116	21.3073	504	254016	22.4499	554	306916	23.5372
405	164025	20.1246	455	207025	21.3307	505	255025	22.4722	555	308025	23.5584
406	164836	20.1494	456	207936	21.3542	506	256036	22.4944	556	309136	23.5797
407	165649	20.1742	457	208849	21.3776	507	257049	22.5167	557	310249	23.6008
408	166464	20.1990	458	209764	21.4009	508	258064	22.5389	558	311364	23.6220
409	167281	20.2237	459	210681	21.4243	509	259081	22.5610	559	312481	23.6432
410	168100	20.2485	460	211600	21.4476	510	260100	22.5832	560	313600	23.6643
411	168921	20.2731	461	212521	21.4709	511	261121	22.6053	561	314721	23.6854
412	169744	20.2978	462	213444	21.4942	512	262144	22.6274	562	315844	23.7065
413	170569	20.3224	463	214369	21.5174	513	263169	22.6495	563	316969	23.7276
414	171396	20.3470	464	215296	21.5407	514	264196	22.6716	564	318096	23.7487
415	172225	20.3715	465	216225	21.5639	515	265225	22.6936	565	319225	23.7697
416	173056	20.3961	466	217156	21.5870	516	266256	22.7156	566	320356	23.7908
417	173889	20.4206	467	218089	21.6102	517	267289	22.7376	567	321489	23.8118
418	174724	20.4450	468	219024	21.6333	518	268324	22.7596	568	322624	23.8328
419	175561	20.4695	469	219961	21.6564	519	269361	22.7816	569	323761	23.8537
420	176400	20.4939	470	220900	21.6795	520	270400	22.8035	570	324900	23.8747
421	177241	20.5183	471	221841	21.7025	521	271441	22.8254	571	326041	23.8956
422	178084	20.5426	472	222784	21.7256	522	272484	22.8473	572	327184	23.9165
423	178929	20.5670	473	223729	21.7486	523	273529	22.8692	573	328329	23.9374
424	179776	20.5913	474	224676	21.7715	524	274576	22.8910	574	329476	23.9583
425	180625	20.6155	475	225625	21.7945	525	275625	22.9129	575	330625	23.9792
426	181476	20.6398	476	226576	21.8174	526	276676	22.9347	576	331776	24.0000
427	182329	20.6640	477	227529	21.8403	527	277729	22.9565	577	332929	24.0208
428	183184	20.6882	478	228484	21.8632	528	278784	22.9783	578	334084	24.0416
429	184041	20.7123	479	229441	21.8861	529	279841	23.0000	579	335241	24.0624
430	184900	20.7364	480	230400	21.9089	530	280900	23.0217	580	336400	24.0832
431	185761	20.7605	481	231361	21.9317	531	281961	23.0434	581	337561	24.1039
432	186624	20.7846	482	232324	21.9545	532	283024	23.0651	582	338724	24.1247
433	187489	20.8087	483	233289	21.9773	533	284089	23.0868	583	339889	24.1454
434	188356	20.8327	484	234256	22.0000	534	285156	23.1084	584	341056	24.1661
435	189225	20.8567	485	235225	22.0227	535	286225	23.1301	585	342225	24.1868
436	190096	20.8806	486	236196	22.0454	536	287296	23.1517	586	343396	24.2074
437	190969	20.9045	487	237169	22.0681	537	288369	23.1733	587	344569	24.2281
438	191844	20.9284	488	238144	22.0907	538	289444	23.1948	588	345744	24.2487
439	192721	20.9523	489	239121	22.1133	539	290521	23.2164	589	346921	24.2693
440	193600	20.9762	490	240100	22.1359	540	291600	23.2379	590	348100	24.2899
441	194481	21.0000	491	241081	22.1585	541	292681	23.2594	591	349281	24.3105
442	195364	21.0238	492	242064	22.1811	542	293764	23.2809	592	350464	24.3311
443	196249	21.0476	493	243049	22.2036	543	294849	23.3024	593	351649	24.3516
444	197136	21.0713	494	244036	22.2261	544	295936	23.3238	594	352836	24.3721
445	198025	21.0950	495	245025	22.2486	545	297025	23.3452	595	354025	24.3926
446	198916	21.1187	496	246016	22.2711	546	298116	23.3666	596	355216	24.4131
447	199809	21.1424	497	247009	22.2935	547	299209	23.3880	597	356409	24.4336
448	200704	21.1660	498	248004	22.3159	548	300304	23.4094	598	357604	24.4540
449	201601	21.1896	499	249001	22.3383	549	301401	23.4307	599	358801	24.4745

TABLE 5
SQUARES AND SQUARE ROOTS (continued)

No.	Square	Square Root	No.	Square	Square Root	No.	Square	Square Root	No.	Square	Square Root
600	360000	24.4949	650	422500	25.4951	700	490000	26.4575	750	562500	27.3861
601	361201	24.5153	651	423801	25.5147	701	491401	26.4764	751	564001	27.4044
602	362404	24.5357	652	425104	25.5343	702	492804	26.4953	752	565504	27.4226
603	363609	24.5561	653	426409	25.5539	703	494209	26.5141	753	567009	27.4408
604	364816	24.5764	654	427716	25.5734	704	495616	26.5330	754	568516	27.4591
605	366025	24.5967	655	429025	25.5930	705	497025	26.5518	755	570025	27.4773
606	367236	24.6171	656	430336	25.6125	706	498436	26.5707	756	571536	27.4955
607	368449	24.6374	657	431649	25.6320	707	499849	26.5895	757	573049	27.5136
608	369664	24.6577	658	432964	25.6515	708	501264	26.6083	758	574564	27.5318
609	370881	24.6779	659	434281	25.6710	709	502681	26.6271	759	576081	27.5500
610	372100	24.6982	660	435600	25.6905	710	504100	26.6458	760	577600	27.5681
611	373321	24.7184	661	436921	25.7099	711	505521	26.6646	761	579121	27.5862
612	374544	24.7386	662	438244	25.7294	712	506944	26.6833	762	580644	27.6043
613	375769	24.7588	663	439569	25.7488	713	508369	26.7021	763	582169	27.6225
614	376996	24.7790	664	440896	25.7682	714	509796	26.7208	764	583696	27.6405
615	378225	24.7992	665	442225	25.7876	715	511225	26.7395	765	585225	27.6586
616	379456	24.8193	666	443556	25.8070	716	512656	26.7582	766	586756	27.6767
617	380689	24.8395	667	444889	25.8263	717	514089	26.7769	767	588289	27.6948
618	381924	24.8596	668	446224	25.8457	718	515524	26.7955	768	589824	27.7128
619	383161	24.8797	669	447561	25.8650	719	516961	26.8142	769	591361	27.7308
620	384400	24.8998	670	448900	25.8844	720	518400	26.8328	770	592900	27.7489
621	385641	24.9199	671	450241	25.9037	721	519841	26.8514	771	594441	27.7669
622	386884	24.9399	672	451584	25.9230	722	521284	26.8701	772	595984	27.7849
623	388129	24.9600	673	452929	25.9422	723	522729	26.8887	773	597529	27.8029
624	389376	24.9800	674	454276	25.9615	724	524176	26.9072	774	599076	27.8209
625	390625	25.0000	675	455625	25.9808	725	525625	26.9258	775	600625	27.8388
626	391876	25.0200	676	456976	26.0000	726	527076	26.9444	776	602176	27.8568
627	393129	25.0400	677	458329	26.0192	727	528529	26.9629	777	603729	27.8747
628	394384	25.0599	678	459684	26.0384	728	529984	26.9815	778	605284	27.8927
629	395641	25.0799	679	461041	26.0576	729	531441	27.0000	779	606841	27.9106
630	396900	25.0998	680	462400	26.0768	730	532900	27.0185	780	608400	27.9285
631	398161	25.1197	681	463761	26.0960	731	534361	27.0370	781	609961	27.9464
632	399424	25.1396	682	465124	26.1151	732	535824	27.0555	782	611524	27.9643
633	400689	25.1595	683	466489	26.1343	733	537289	27.0740	783	613089	27.9821
634	401956	25.1794	684	467856	26.1534	734	538756	27.0924	784	614656	28.0000
635	403225	25.1992	685	469225	26.1725	735	540225	27.1109	785	616225	28.0179
636	404496	25.2190	686	470596	26.1916	736	541696	27.1293	786	617796	28.0357
637	405769	25.2389	687	471969	26.2107	737	543169	27.1477	787	619369	28.0535
638	407044	25.2587	688	473344	26.2298	738	544644	27.1662	788	620944	28.0713
639	408321	25.2784	689	474721	26.2488	739	546121	27.1846	789	622521	28.0891
640	409600	25.2982	690	476100	26.2679	740	547600	27.2029	790	624100	28.1069
641	410881	25.3180	691	477481	26.2869	741	549081	27.2213	791	625681	28.1247
642	412164	25.3377	692	478864	26.3059	742	550564	27.2397	792	627264	28.1425
643	413449	25.3574	693	480249	26.3249	743	552049	27.2580	793	628849	28.1603
644	414736	25.3772	694	481636	26.3439	744	553536	27.2764	794	630436	28.1780
645	416025	25.3969	695	483025	26.3629	745	555025	27.2947	795	632025	28.1957
646	417316	25.4165	696	484416	26.3818	746	556516	27.3130	796	633616	28.2135
647	418609	25.4362	697	485809	26.4008	747	558009	27.3313	797	635209	28.2312
648	419904	25.4558	698	487204	26.4197	748	559504	27.3496	798	636804	28.2489
649	421201	25.4755	699	488601	26.4386	749	561001	27.3679	799	638401	28.2666

TABLE 5
SQUARES AND SQUARE ROOTS (continued)

No.	Square	Square Root	No.	Square	Square Root	No.	Square	Square Root	No.	Square	Square Root
800	640000	28.2843	850	722500	29.1548	900	810000	30.0000	950	902500	30.8221
801	641601	28.3019	851	724201	29.1719	901	811801	30.0167	951	904401	30.8383
802	643204	28.3196	852	725904	29.1890	902	813604	30.0333	952	906304	30.8545
803	644809	28.3373	853	727609	29.2062	903	815409	30.0500	953	908209	30.8707
804	646416	28.3549	854	729316	29.2233	904	817216	30.0666	954	910116	30.8869
805	648025	28.3725	855	731025	29.2404	905	819025	30.0832	955	912025	30.9031
806	649636	28.3901	856	732736	29.2575	906	820836	30.0998	956	913936	30.9192
807	651249	28.4077	857	734449	29.2746	907	822649	30.1164	957	915849	30.9354
808	652864	28.4253	858	736164	29.2916	908	824464	30.1330	958	917764	30.9516
809	654481	28.4429	859	737881	29.3087	909	826281	30.1496	959	919681	30.9677
810	656100	28.4605	860	739600	29.3258	910	828100	30.1662	960	921600	30.9839
811	657721	28.4781	861	741321	29.3428	911	829921	30.1828	961	923521	31.0000
812	659344	28.4956	862	743044	29.3598	912	831744	30.1993	962	925444	31.0161
813	660969	28.5132	863	744769	29.3769	913	833569	30.2159	963	927369	31.0322
814	662596	28.5307	864	746496	29.3939	914	835396	30.2324	964	929296	31.0483
815	664225	28.5482	865	748225	29.4109	915	837225	30.2490	965	931225	31.0644
816	665856	28.5657	866	749956	29.4279	916	839056	30.2655	966	933156	31.0805
817	667489	28.5832	867	751689	29.4449	917	840889	30.2820	967	935089	31.0966
818	669124	28.6007	868	753424	29.4618	918	842724	30.2985	968	937024	31.1127
819	670761	28.6182	869	755161	29.4788	919	844561	30.3150	969	938961	31.1288
820	672400	28.6356	870	756900	29.4958	920	846400	30.3315	970	940900	31.1448
821	674041	28.6531	871	758641	29.5127	921	848241	30.3480	971	942841	31.1609
822	675684	28.6705	872	760384	29.5296	922	850084	30.3645	972	944784	31.1769
823	677329	28.6880	873	762129	29.5466	923	851929	30.3809	973	946729	31.1929
824	678976	28.7054	874	763876	29.5635	924	853776	30.3974	974	948676	31.2090
825	680625	28.7228	875	765625	29.5804	925	855625	30.4138	975	950625	31.2250
826	682276	28.7402	876	767376	29.5973	926	857476	30.4302	976	952576	31.2410
827	683929	28.7576	877	769129	29.6142	927	859329	30.4467	977	954529	31.2570
828	685584	28.7750	878	770884	29.6311	928	861184	30.4631	978	956484	31.2730
829	687241	28.7924	879	772641	29.6479	929	863041	30.4795	979	958441	31.2890
830	688900	28.8097	880	774400	29.6648	930	864900	30.4959	980	960400	31.3050
831	690561	28.8271	881	776161	29.6816	931	866761	30.5123	981	962361	31.3209
832	692224	28.8444	882	777924	29.6985	932	868624	30.5287	982	964324	31.3369
833	693889	28.8617	883	779689	29.7153	933	870489	30.5450	983	966289	31.3528
834	695556	28.8791	884	781456	29.7321	934	872356	30.5614	984	968256	31.3688
835	697225	28.8964	885	783225	29.7489	935	874225	30.5778	985	970225	31.3847
836	698896	28.9137	886	784996	29.7658	936	876096	30.5941	986	972196	31.4006
837	700569	28.9310	887	786769	29.7825	937	877969	30.6105	987	974169	31.4166
838	702244	28.9482	888	788544	29.7993	938	879844	30.6268	988	976144	31.4325
839	703921	28.9655	889	790321	29.8161	939	881721	30.6431	989	978121	31.4484
840	705600	28.9828	890	792100	29.8329	940	883600	30.6594	990	980100	31.4643
841	707281	29.0000	891	793881	29.8496	941	885481	30.6757	991	982081	31.4802
842	708964	29.0172	892	795664	29.8664	942	887364	30.6920	992	984064	31.4960
843	710649	29.0345	893	797449	29.8831	943	889249	30.7083	993	986049	31.5119
844	712336	29.0517	894	799236	29.8998	944	891136	30.7246	994	988036	31.5278
845	714025	29.0689	895	801025	29.9166	945	893025	30.7409	995	990025	31.5436
846	715716	29.0861	896	802816	29.9333	946	894916	30.7571	996	992016	31.5595
847	717409	29.1033	897	804609	29.9500	947	896809	30.7734	997	994009	31.5753
848	719104	29.1204	898	806404	29.9666	948	898704	30.7896	998	996004	31.5911
849	720801	29.1376	899	808201	29.9833	949	900601	30.8058	999	998001	31.6070

TABLE 6
NATURAL TRIGONOMETRIC FUNCTIONS

DEGREES	FUNCTION	0.0°	0.1°	0.2°	0.3°	0.4°	0.5°	0.6°	0.7°	0.8°	0.9°
0	sin	0.0000	0.0017	0.0035	0.0052	0.0070	0.0087	0.0105	0.0122	0.0140	0.0157
	cos	1.0000	1.0000	1.0000	1.0000	1.0000	1.0000	0.9999	0.9999	0.9999	0.9999
	tan	0.0000	0.0017	0.0035	0.0052	0.0070	0.0087	0.0105	0.0122	0.0140	0.0157
1	sin	0.0175	0.0192	0.0209	0.0227	0.0244	0.0262	0.0279	0.0297	0.0314	0.0332
	cos	0.9998	0.9998	0.9998	0.9997	0.9997	0.9997	0.9996	0.9996	0.9995	0.9995
	tan	0.0175	0.0192	0.0209	0.0227	0.0224	0.0262	0.0279	0.0297	0.0314	0.0332
2	sin	0.0349	0.0366	0.0384	0.0401	0.0419	0.0436	0.0454	0.0471	0.0488	0.0506
	cos	0.9994	0.9993	0.9993	0.9992	0.9991	0.9990	0.9990	0.9989	0.9988	0.9987
	tan	0.0349	0.0367	0.0384	0.0402	0.0419	0.0437	0.0454	0.0472	0.0489	0.0507
3	sin	0.0523	0.0541	0.0558	0.0576	0.0593	0.0610	0.0628	0.0645	0.0663	0.0680
	cos	0.9986	0.9985	0.9984	0.9983	0.9982	0.9981	0.9980	0.9979	0.9978	0.9977
	tan	0.0524	0.0542	0.0559	0.0577	0.0594	0.0612	0.0629	0.0647	0.0664	0.0682
4	sin	0.0698	0.0715	0.0732	0.0750	0.0767	0.0785	0.0802	0.0819	0.0837	0.0854
	cos	0.9976	0.9974	0.9973	0.9972	0.9971	0.9969	0.9968	0.9966	0.9965	0.9963
	tan	0.0699	0.0717	0.0734	0.0752	0.0769	0.0787	0.0805	0.0822	0.0840	0.0857
5	sin	0.0872	0.0889	0.0906	0.0924	0.0941	0.0958	0.0976	0.0993	0.1011	0.1028
	cos	0.9962	0.9960	0.9959	0.9957	0.9956	0.9954	0.9952	0.9951	0.9949	0.9947
	tan	0.0875	0.0892	0.0910	0.0928	0.0945	0.0963	0.0981	0.0998	0.1016	0.1033
6	sin	0.1045	0.1063	0.1080	0.1097	0.1115	0.1132	0.1149	0.1167	0.1184	0.1201
	cos	0.9945	0.9943	0.9942	0.9940	0.9938	0.9936	0.9934	0.9932	0.9930	0.9928
	tan	0.1051	0.1069	0.1086	0.1104	0.1122	0.1139	0.1157	0.1175	0.1192	0.1210
7	sin	0.1219	0.1236	0.1253	0.1271	0.1288	0.1305	0.1323	0.1340	0.1357	0.1374
	cos	0.9925	0.9923	0.9921	0.9919	0.9917	0.9914	0.9912	0.9910	0.9907	0.9905
	tan	0.1228	0.1246	0.1263	0.1281	0.1299	0.1317	0.1334	0.1352	0.1370	0.1388
8	sin	0.1392	0.1409	0.1426	0.1444	0.1461	0.1478	0.1495	0.1513	0.1530	0.1547
	cos	0.9903	0.9900	0.9898	0.9895	0.9893	0.9890	0.9888	0.9885	0.9882	0.9880
	tan	0.1405	0.1423	0.1441	0.1459	0.1477	0.1495	0.1512	0.1530	0.1548	0.1566
9	sin	0.1564	0.1582	0.1599	0.1616	0.1633	0.1650	0.1668	0.1685	0.1702	0.1719
	cos	0.9877	0.9874	0.9871	0.9869	0.9866	0.9863	0.9860	0.9857	0.9854	0.9851
	tan	0.1584	0.1602	0.1620	0.1638	0.1655	0.1673	0.1691	0.1709	0.1727	0.1745
10	sin	0.1736	0.1754	0.1771	0.1778	0.1805	0.1822	0.1840	0.1857	0.1874	0.1891
	cos	0.9848	0.9845	0.9842	0.9839	0.9836	0.9833	0.9829	0.9826	0.9823	0.9820
	tan	0.1763	0.1781	0.1799	0.1817	0.1835	0.1853	0.1871	0.1890	0.1908	0.1926
11	sin	0.1908	0.1925	0.1942	0.1959	0.1977	0.1994	0.2011	0.2028	0.2045	0.2062
	cos	0.9816	0.9813	0.9810	0.9806	0.9803	0.9799	0.9796	0.9792	0.9789	0.9785
	tan	0.1944	0.1962	0.1980	0.1998	0.2016	0.2035	0.2053	0.2071	0.2089	0.2107
12	sin	0.2079	0.2096	0.2113	0.2130	0.2147	0.2164	0.2181	0.2198	0.2215	0.2232
	cos	0.9781	0.9778	0.9774	0.9770	0.9767	0.9763	0.9759	0.9755	0.9751	0.9748
	tan	0.2126	0.2144	0.2162	0.2180	0.2199	0.2217	0.2235	0.2254	0.2272	0.2290
13	sin	0.2250	0.2267	0.2284	0.2300	0.2318	0.2334	0.2351	0.2368	0.2385	0.2402
	cos	0.9744	0.9740	0.9736	0.9732	0.9728	0.9724	0.9720	0.9715	0.9711	0.9707
	tan	0.2309	0.2327	0.2345	0.2364	0.2382	0.2401	0.2419	0.2438	0.2456	0.2475
14	sin	0.2419	0.2436	0.2453	0.2470	0.2487	0.2504	0.2521	0.2538	0.2554	0.2571
	cos	0.9703	0.9699	0.9694	0.9690	0.9686	0.9681	0.9677	0.9673	0.9668	0.9664
	tan	0.2493	0.2512	0.2530	0.2549	0.2568	0.2586	0.2605	0.2623	0.2642	0.2661
15	sin	0.2588	0.2605	0.2622	0.2639	0.2656	0.2672	0.2689	0.2706	0.2723	0.2740
	cos	0.9659	0.9655	0.9650	0.9646	0.9641	0.9636	0.9632	0.9627	0.9622	0.9617
	tan	0.2679	0.2698	0.2717	0.2736	0.2754	0.2773	0.2792	0.2811	0.2830	0.2849
16	sin	0.2756	0.2773	0.2790	0.2807	0.2823	0.2840	0.2857	0.2874	0.2890	0.2907
	cos	0.9613	0.9608	0.9603	0.9598	0.9593	0.9588	0.9583	0.9578	0.9573	0.9568
	tan	0.2867	0.2886	0.2905	0.2924	0.2943	0.2962	0.2981	0.3000	0.3019	0.3038
17	sin	0.2924	0.2940	0.2957	0.2974	0.2990	0.3007	0.3024	0.3040	0.3057	0.3074
	cos	0.9563	0.9558	0.9553	0.9548	0.9542	0.9537	0.9532	0.9527	0.9521	0.9516
	tan	0.3057	0.3076	0.3096	0.3115	0.3134	0.3153	0.3172	0.3191	0.3211	0.3230
18	sin	0.3090	0.3107	0.3123	0.3140	0.3156	0.3173	0.3190	0.3206	0.3223	0.3239
	cos	0.9511	0.9505	0.9500	0.9494	0.9489	0.9483	0.9478	0.9472	0.9466	0.9461
	tan	0.3249	0.3269	0.3288	0.3307	0.3327	0.3346	0.3365	0.3385	0.3404	0.3424
19	sin	0.3256	0.3272	0.3289	0.3305	0.3322	0.3338	0.3355	0.3371	0.3387	0.3404
	cos	0.9455	0.9449	0.9444	0.9438	0.9432	0.9426	0.9421	0.9415	0.9409	0.9403
	tan	0.3443	0.3463	0.3482	0.3502	0.3522	0.3541	0.3561	0.3581	0.3600	0.3620
DEGREES	FUNCTION	0'	6'	12'	18'	24'	30'	36'	42'	48'	54'

TABLE 6
NATURAL TRIGONOMETRIC FUNCTIONS (continued)

DEGREES	FUNCTION	0.0°	0.1°	0.2°	0.3°	0.4°	0.5°	0.6°	0.7°	0.8°	0.9°
20	sin	0.3420	0.3437	0.3453	0.3469	0.3486	0.3502	0.3518	0.3535	0.3551	0.3567
	cos	0.9397	0.9391	0.9385	0.9379	0.9373	0.9367	0.9361	0.9354	0.9348	0.9342
	tan	0.3640	0.3659	0.3679	0.3699	0.3719	0.3739	0.3759	0.3779	0.3799	0.3819
21	sin	0.3584	0.3600	0.3616	0.3633	0.3649	0.3665	0.3681	0.3697	0.3714	0.3730
	cos	0.9336	0.9330	0.9323	0.9317	0.9311	0.9304	0.9298	0.9291	0.9285	0.9278
	tan	0.3839	0.3859	0.3879	0.3899	0.3919	0.3939	0.3959	0.3979	0.4000	0.4020
22	sin	0.3746	0.3762	0.3778	0.3795	0.3811	0.3827	0.3843	0.3859	0.3875	0.3891
	cos	0.9272	0.9265	0.9259	0.9252	0.9245	0.9245	0.9239	0.9232	0.9225	0.9219
	tan	0.4040	0.4061	0.4081	0.4101	0.4122	0.4142	0.4263	0.4183	0.4204	0.4224
23	sin	0.3907	0.3923	0.3939	0.3955	0.3971	0.3987	0.4003	0.4019	0.4035	0.4051
	cos	0.9205	0.9198	0.9191	0.9184	0.9178	0.9171	0.9164	0.9157	0.9150	0.9143
	tan	0.4245	0.4265	0.4286	0.4307	0.4327	0.4348	0.4369	0.4390	0.4411	0.4431
24	sin	0.4067	0.4083	0.4099	0.4115	0.4131	0.4147	0.4163	0.4179	0.4195	0.4210
	cos	0.9135	0.9128	0.9121	0.9114	0.9107	0.9100	0.9092	0.9085	0.9078	0.9070
	tan	0.4452	0.4473	0.4494	0.4515	0.4536	0.4557	0.4578	0.4599	0.4621	0.4642
25	sin	0.4226	0.4242	0.4258	0.4274	0.4289	0.4305	0.4321	0.4337	0.4352	0.4368
	cos	0.9063	0.9056	0.9048	0.9041	0.9033	0.9026	0.9018	0.9011	0.9003	0.8996
	tan	0.4663	0.4684	0.4706	0.4727	0.4748	0.4770	0.4791	0.4813	0.4834	0.4856
26	sin	0.4384	0.4399	0.4415	0.4431	0.4446	0.4462	0.4478	0.4493	0.4509	0.4524
	cos	0.8988	0.8980	0.8973	0.8965	0.8957	0.8949	0.8942	0.8934	0.8926	0.8918
	tan	0.4877	0.4899	0.4921	0.4942	0.4964	0.4986	0.5008	0.5029	0.5051	0.5073
27	sin	0.4540	0.4555	0.4571	0.4586	0.4602	0.4617	0.4633	0.4648	0.4664	0.4679
	cos	0.8910	0.8902	0.8894	0.8886	0.8878	0.8870	0.8862	0.8854	0.8846	0.8838
	tan	0.5095	0.5117	0.5139	0.5161	0.5184	0.5206	0.5228	0.5250	0.5272	0.5295
28	sin	0.4695	0.4710	0.4726	0.4741	0.4756	0.4772	0.4787	0.4802	0.4818	0.4833
	cos	0.8829	0.8821	0.8813	0.8805	0.8796	0.8788	0.8780	0.8771	0.8763	0.8755
	tan	0.5317	0.5340	0.5362	0.5384	0.5407	0.5430	0.5452	0.5475	0.5498	0.5520
29	sin	0.4848	0.4863	0.4879	0.4894	0.4909	0.4924	0.4939	0.4955	0.4970	0.4985
	cos	0.8746	0.8738	0.8729	0.8721	0.8712	0.8704	0.8695	0.8686	0.8678	0.8669
	tan	0.5543	0.5566	0.5589	0.5612	0.5635	0.5658	0.5681	0.5704	0.5727	0.5750
30	sin	0.5000	0.5015	0.5030	0.5045	0.5060	0.5075	0.5090	0.5105	0.5120	0.5135
	cos	0.8660	0.8652	0.8643	0.8634	0.8625	0.8616	0.8607	0.8599	0.8590	0.8581
	tan	0.5774	0.5797	0.5820	0.5844	0.5967	0.5890	0.5914	0.5938	0.5961	0.5985
31	sin	0.5150	0.5165	0.5180	0.5195	0.5210	0.5225	0.5240	0.5255	0.5270	0.5284
	cos	0.8572	0.8563	0.8554	0.8545	0.8536	0.8526	0.8517	0.8508	0.8499	0.8490
	tan	0.6009	0.6032	0.6056	0.6080	0.6104	0.6128	0.6152	0.6176	0.6200	0.6224
32	sin	0.5299	0.5314	0.5329	0.5344	0.5358	0.5373	0.5388	0.5402	0.5417	0.5432
	cos	0.8480	0.8471	0.8462	0.8453	0.8443	0.8434	0.8425	0.8415	0.8406	0.8396
	tan	0.6249	0.6273	0.6297	0.6322	0.6346	0.6371	0.6395	0.6420	0.6445	0.6469
33	sin	0.5446	0.5461	0.5476	0.5490	0.5505	0.5519	0.5534	0.5548	0.5563	0.5577
	cos	0.8387	0.8377	0.8368	0.8358	0.8348	0.8339	0.8329	0.8320	0.8310	0.8300
	tan	0.6494	0.6519	0.6544	0.6569	0.6594	0.6619	0.6644	0.6669	0.6694	0.6720
34	sin	0.5592	0.5606	0.5621	0.5635	0.5650	0.5664	0.5678	0.5693	0.5707	0.5721
	cos	0.8290	0.8281	0.8271	0.8261	0.8251	0.8241	0.8231	0.8221	0.8211	0.8202
	tan	0.6745	0.6771	0.6796	0.6822	0.6847	0.6873	0.6899	0.6924	0.6950	0.6976
35	sin	0.5736	0.5750	0.5764	0.5779	0.5793	0.5807	0.5821	0.5835	0.5850	0.5864
	cos	0.8192	0.8181	0.8171	0.8161	0.8151	0.8141	0.8131	0.8121	0.8111	0.8100
	tan	0.7002	0.7028	0.7054	0.7080	0.7107	0.7133	0.7159	0.7186	0.7212	0.7239
36	sin	0.5878	0.5892	0.5906	0.5920	0.5934	0.5948	0.5962	0.5976	0.5990	0.6004
	cos	0.8090	0.8080	0.8070	0.8059	0.8049	0.8039	0.8028	0.8018	0.8007	0.7997
	tan	0.7265	0.7292	0.7319	0.7346	0.7373	0.7400	0.7427	0.7454	0.7481	0.7508
37	sin	0.6018	0.6032	0.6046	0.6060	0.6074	0.6088	0.6101	0.6115	0.6129	0.6143
	cos	0.7986	0.7976	0.7965	0.7955	0.7944	0.7934	0.7923	0.7912	0.7902	0.7891
	tan	0.7536	0.7563	0.7590	0.7618	0.7646	0.7673	0.7701	0.7729	0.7757	0.7785
38	sin	0.6157	0.6170	0.6184	0.6198	0.6211	0.6225	0.6239	0.6252	0.6266	0.6280
	cos	0.7880	0.7869	0.7859	0.7848	0.7837	0.7826	0.7815	0.7804	0.7793	0.7782
	tan	0.7813	0.7841	0.7869	0.7898	0.7926	0.7954	0.7983	0.8012	0.8040	0.8069
39	sin	0.6293	0.6307	0.6320	0.6334	0.6347	0.6361	0.6374	0.6388	0.6401	0.6414
	cos	0.7771	0.7760	0.7749	0.7738	0.7727	0.7716	0.7705	0.7694	0.7683	0.7672
	tan	0.8098	0.8127	0.8156	0.8185	0.8214	0.8243	0.8273	0.8302	0.8332	0.8361
40	sin	0.6428	0.6441	0.6455	0.6468	0.6481	0.6494	0.6508	0.6521	0.6534	0.6547
	cos	0.7660	0.76.49	0.7638	0.7627	0.7615	0.7604	0.7593	0.7581	0.7570	0.7559
	tan	0.8391	0.8421	0.8451	0.8481	0.8511	0.8541	0.8571	0.8601	0.8632	0.8662

DEGREES	FUNCTION	0'	6'	12'	18'	24'	30'	36'	42'	48'	54'

TABLE 6
NATURAL TRIGONOMETRIC FUNCTIONS (continued)

DEGREES	FUNCTION	0.0°	0.1°	0.2°	0.3°	0.4°	0.5°	0.6°	0.7°	0.8°	0.9°
41	sin	0.6561	0.6574	0.6587	0.6600	0.6613	0.6626	0.6639	0.6652	0.6665	0.6678
	cos	0.7547	0.7536	0.7524	0.7513	0.7501	0.7490	0.7478	0.7466	0.7455	0.7443
	tan	0.8693	0.8724	0.8754	0.8785	0.8816	0.8847	0.8878	0.8910	0.8941	0.8972
42	sin	0.6691	0.6704	0.6717	0.6730	0.6743	0.6756	0.6769	0.6782	0.6794	0.6807
	cos	0.7431	0.7420	0.7408	0.7396	0.7385	0.7373	0.7361	0.7349	0.7337	0.7325
	tan	0.9004	0.9036	0.9067	0.9099	0.9131	0.9163	0.9195	0.9228	0.9260	0.9293
43	sin	0.6820	0.6833	0.6845	0.6858	0.6871	0.6884	0.6896	0.6909	0.6921	0.6934
	cos	0.7314	0.7302	0.7290	0.7278	0.7266	0.7254	0.7242	0.7230	0.7218	0.7206
	tan	0.9325	0.9358	0.9391	0.9424	0.9457	0.9490	0.9523	0.9556	0.9590	0.9623
44	sin	0.6947	0.6959	0.6972	0.6984	0.6997	0.7009	0.7022	0.7034	0.7046	0.7059
	cos	0.7193	0.7181	0.7169	0.7157	0.7145	0.7133	0.7120	0.7108	0.7096	0.7083
	tan	0.9657	0.9691	0.9725	0.9759	0.9793	0.9827	0.9861	0.9896	0.9930	0.9965
45	sin	0.7071	0.7083	0.7096	0.7108	0.7120	0.7133	0.7145	0.7157	0.7169	0.7181
	cos	0.7071	0.7059	0.7046	0.7034	0.7022	0.7009	0.6997	0.6984	0.6972	0.6959
	tan	1.0000	1.0035	1.0070	1.0105	1.0141	1.0176	1.0212	1.0247	1.0283	1.0319
46	sin	0.7193	0.7206	0.7218	0.7230	0.7242	0.7254	0.7266	0.7278	0.7290	0.7302
	cos	0.6947	0.6934	0.6921	0.6909	0.6896	0.6884	0.6871	0.6858	0.6845	0.6833
	tan	1.0355	1.0392	1.0428	1.0464	1.0501	1.0538	1.0575	1.0612	1.0649	1.0686
47	sin	0.7314	0.7325	0.7337	0.7349	0.7361	0.7373	0.7385	0.7396	0.7408	0.7420
	cos	0.6820	0.6807	0.6794	0.6782	0.6769	0.6756	0.6743	0.6730	0.6717	0.6704
	tan	1.0724	1.0761	1.0799	1.0837	1.0875	1.0913	1.0951	1.0990	1.1028	1.1067
48	sin	0.7431	0.7443	0.7455	0.7466	0.7478	0.7490	0.7501	0.7513	0.7524	0.7536
	cos	0.6691	0.6678	0.6665	0.6652	0.6639	0.6626	0.6613	0.6600	0.6587	0.6574
	tan	1.1106	1.1145	1.1184	1.1224	1.1263	1.1303	1.1343	1.1383	1.1423	1.1463
49	sin	0.7547	0.7559	0.7570	0.7581	0.7593	0.7604	0.7615	0.7627	0.7638	0.7649
	cos	0.6561	0.6547	0.6534	0.6521	0.6508	0.6494	0.6481	0.6468	0.6455	0.6441
	tan	1.1504	1.1544	1.1585	1.1626	1.1667	1.1708	1.1750	1.1792	1.1833	1.1875
50	sin	0.7660	0.7672	0.7683	0.7694	0.7705	0.7716	0.7727	0.7738	0.7749	0.7760
	cos	0.6428	0.6414	0.6401	0.6388	0.6374	0.6361	0.6347	0.6334	0.6320	0.6307
	tan	1.1918	1.1960	1.2002	1.2045	1.2088	1.2131	1.2174	1.2218	1.2261	1.2305
51	sin	0.7771	0.7782	0.7793	0.7804	0.7815	0.7826	0.7837	0.7848	0.7859	0.7869
	cos	0.6293	0.6280	0.6266	0.6252	0.6239	0.6225	0.6211	0.6198	0.6184	0.6170
	tan	1.2349	1.2393	1.2437	1.2482	1.2527	1.2572	1.2617	1.2662	1.2708	1.2753
52	sin	0.7880	0.7891	0.7902	0.7912	0.7923	0.7934	0.7944	0.7955	0.7965	0.7976
	cos	0.6157	0.6143	0.6129	0.6115	0.6101	0.6088	0.6074	0.6060	0.6046	0.6032
	tan	1.2799	1.2846	1.2892	1.2938	1.2985	1.3032	1.3079	1.3127	1.3175	1.3222
53	sin	0.7986	0.7997	0.8007	0.8018	0.8028	0.8039	0.8049	0.8059	0.8070	0.8080
	cos	0.6018	0.6004	0.5990	0.5976	0.5962	0.5948	0.5934	0.5920	0.5906	0.5892
	tan	1.3270	1.3319	1.3367	1.3416	1.3465	1.3514	1.3564	1.3613	1.3663	1.3713
54	sin	0.8090	0.8100	0.8111	0.8121	0.8131	0.8141	0.8151	0.8161	0.8171	0.8181
	cos	0.5878	0.5864	0.5850	0.5835	0.5821	0.5807	0.5793	0.5779	0.5764	0.5750
	tan	1.3764	1.3814	1.3865	1.3916	1.3968	1.4019	1.4071	1.4124	1.4176	1.4229
55	sin	0.8192	0.8202	0.8211	0.8221	0.8231	0.8241	0.8251	0.8261	0.8271	0.8281
	cos	0.5736	0.5721	0.5707	0.5693	0.5678	0.5664	0.5650	0.5635	0.5621	0.5606
	tan	1.4281	1.4335	1.4388	1.4442	1.4496	1.4550	1.4605	1.4659	1.4715	1.4770
56	sin	0.8290	0.8300	0.8310	0.8320	0.8329	0.8339	0.8348	0.8358	0.8368	0.8377
	cos	0.5592	0.5577	0.5563	0.5548	0.5534	0.5519	0.5505	0.5490	0.5476	0.5461
	tan	1.4826	1.4882	1.4938	1.4994	1.5051	1.5108	1.5166	1.5224	1.5282	1.5340
57	sin	0.8387	0.8396	0.8406	0.8415	0.8425	0.8434	0.8443	0.8453	0.8462	0.8471
	cos	0.5446	0.5432	0.5417	0.5402	0.5388	0.5373	0.5358	0.5344	0.5329	0.5314
	tan	1.5399	1.5458	1.5517	1.5577	1.5637	1.5697	1.5757	1.5818	1.5880	1.5941
58	sin	0.8480	0.8490	0.8499	0.8508	0.8517	0.8526	0.8536	0.8545	0.8554	0.8563
	cos	0.5299	0.5284	0.5270	0.5255	0.5240	0.5225	0.5210	0.5195	0.5180	0.5165
	tan	1.6003	1.6066	1.6128	1.6191	1.6255	1.6319	1.6383	1.6447	1.6512	1.6577
59	sin	0.8572	0.8581	0.8590	0.8599	0.8607	0.8616	0.8625	0.8634	0.8643	0.8652
	cos	0.5150	0.5135	0.5120	0.5105	0.5090	0.5075	0.5060	0.5045	0.5030	0.5015
	tan	1.6643	1.6709	1.6775	1.6842	1.6909	1.6977	1.7045	1.7113	1.7182	1.7251
60	sin	0.8660	0.8669	0.8678	0.8686	0.8695	0.8704	0.8712	0.8721	0.8729	0.8738
	cos	0.5000	0.4985	0.4970	0.4955	0.4939	0.4924	0.4909	0.4894	0.4879	0.4863
	tan	1.7321	1.7391	1.7461	1.7532	1.7603	1.7675	1.7747	1.7820	1.7893	1.7966
61	sin	0.8746	0.8755	0.8763	0.8771	0.8780	0.8788	0.8796	0.8805	0.8813	0.8821
	cos	0.4848	0.4833	0.4818	0.4802	0.4787	0.4772	0.4756	0.4741	0.4726	0.4710
	tan	1.8040	1.8115	1.8190	1.8265	1.8341	1.8418	1.8495	1.8572	1.8650	1.8728

DEGREES	FUNCTION	0'	6'	12'	18'	24'	30'	36'	42'	48'	54'

TABLE 6
NATURAL TRIGONOMETRIC FUNCTIONS (continued)

DEGREES	FUNCTION	0.0°	0.1°	0.2°	0.3°	0.4°	0.5°	0.6°	0.7°	0.8°	0.9°
62	sin	0.8829	0.8838	0.8846	0.8854	0.8862	0.8870	0.8878	0.8886	0.8894	0.8902
	cos	0.4695	0.4679	0.4664	0.4648	0.4633	0.4617	0.4602	0.4586	0.4571	0.4555
	tan	1.8807	1.8887	1.8967	1.9047	1.9128	1.9210	1.9292	1.9375	1.9458	1.9542
63	sin	0.8910	0.8918	0.8926	0.8934	0.8942	0.8949	0.8957	0.8965	0.8973	0.8980
	cos	0.4540	0.4524	0.4509	0.4493	0.4478	0.4462	0.4446	0.4431	0.4415	0.4399
	tan	1.9626	1.9711	1.9797	1.9883	1.9970	2.0057	2.0145	2.0233	2.0323	2.0413
64	sin	0.8988	0.8996	0.9003	0.9011	0.9018	0.9026	0.9033	0.9041	0.9048	0.9056
	cos	0.4384	0.4368	0.4352	0.4337	0.4321	0.4305	0.4289	0.4274	0.4258	0.4242
	tan	2.0503	2.0594	2.0686	2.0778	2.0872	2.0965	2.1060	2.1155	2.1251	2.1348
65	sin	0.9063	0.9070	0.9078	0.9085	0.9092	0.9100	0.9107	0.9114	0.9121	0.9128
	cos	0.4226	0.4210	0.4195	0.4179	0.4163	0.4147	0.4131	0.4115	0.4099	0.4083
	tan	2.1445	2.1543	2.1642	2.1742	2.1842	2.1943	2.2045	2.2148	2.2251	2.2355
66	sin	0.9135	0.9143	0.9150	0.9157	0.9164	0.9171	0.9178	0.9184	0.9191	0.9198
	cos	0.4067	0.4051	0.4035	0.4019	0.4003	0.3987	0.3971	0.3955	0.3939	0.3923
	tan	2.2460	2.2566	2.2673	2.2781	2.2889	2.2998	2.3109	2.3220	2.3332	2.3445
67	sin	0.9205	0.9212	0.9219	0.9225	0.9232	0.9239	0.9245	0.9252	0.9259	0.9265
	cos	0.3907	0.3891	0.3875	0.3859	0.3843	0.3827	0.3811	0.3795	0.3778	0.3762
	tan	2.3559	2.3673	2.3789	2.3906	2.4023	2.4142	2.4262	2.4383	2.4504	2.4627
68	sin	0.9272	0.9278	0.9285	0.9291	0.9298	0.9304	0.9311	0.9317	0.9323	0.9330
	cos	0.3746	0.3730	0.3714	0.3697	0.3681	0.3665	0.3649	0.3633	0.3616	0.3600
	tan	2.4751	2.4876	2.5002	2.5129	2.5257	2.5386	2.5517	2.5649	2.5782	2.5916
69	sin	0.9336	0.9342	0.9348	0.9354	0.9361	0.9367	0.9373	0.9379	0.9385	0.9391
	cos	0.3584	0.3567	0.3551	0.3535	0.3518	0.3502	0.3486	0.3469	0.3453	0.3437
	tan	2.6051	2.6187	2.6325	2.6464	2.6605	2.6746	2.6889	2.7034	2.7179	2.7326
70	sin	0.9397	0.9403	0.9409	0.9415	0.9421	0.9426	0.9432	0.9438	0.9444	0.9449
	cos	0.3420	0.3404	0.3387	0.3371	0.3355	0.3338	0.3322	0.3305	0.3289	0.3272
	tan	2.7475	2.7625	2.7776	2.7929	2.8083	2.8239	2.8397	2.8556	2.8716	2.8878
71	sin	0.9455	0.9461	0.9466	0.9472	0.9478	0.9483	0.9489	0.9494	0.9500	0.9505
	cos	0.3256	0.3239	0.3223	0.3206	0.3190	0.3173	0.3156	0.3140	0.3123	0.3107
	tan	2.9042	2.9208	2.9375	2.9544	2.9714	2.9887	3.0061	3.0237	3.0415	3.0595
72	sin	0.9511	0.9516	0.9521	0.9527	0.9532	0.9537	0.9542	0.9548	0.9553	0.9558
	cos	0.3090	0.3074	0.3057	0.3040	0.3024	0.3007	0.2990	0.2974	0.2957	0.2940
	tan	3.0777	3.0961	3.1146	3.1334	3.1524	3.1716	3.1910	3.2106	3.2305	3.2506
73	sin	0.9563	0.9568	0.9573	0.9578	0.9583	0.9588	0.9593	0.9598	0.9603	0.9608
	cos	0.2924	0.2907	0.2890	0.2874	0.2857	0.2840	0.2823	0.2807	0.2790	0.2773
	tan	3.2709	3.2914	3.3122	3.3332	3.3544	3.3759	3.3977	3.4197	3.4420	3.4646
74	sin	0.9613	0.9617	0.9622	0.9627	0.9632	0.9636	0.9641	0.9646	0.9650	0.9655
	cos	0.2756	0.2740	0.2723	0.2706	0.2689	0.2672	0.2656	0.2639	0.2622	0.2605
	tan	3.4874	3.5105	3.5339	3.5576	3.5816	3.6059	3.6305	3.6554	3.6806	3.7062
75	sin	0.9659	0.9664	0.9668	0.9673	0.9677	0.9681	0.9686	0.9690	0.9694	0.9699
	cos	0.2588	0.2571	0.2554	0.2538	0.2521	0.2504	0.2487	0.2470	0.2453	0.2436
	tan	3.7321	3.7583	3.7848	3.8118	3.8391	3.8667	3.8947	3.9232	3.9520	3.9812
76	sin	0.9703	0.9707	0.9711	0.9715	0.9720	0.9724	0.9728	0.9732	0.9736	0.9740
	cos	0.2419	0.2402	0.2385	0.2368	0.2351	0.2334	0.2317	0.2300	0.2284	0.2267
	tan	4.0108	4.0408	4.0713	4.1022	4.1335	4.1653	4.1976	4.2303	4.2635	4.2972
77	sin	0.9744	0.9748	0.9751	0.9755	0.9759	0.9763	0.9767	0.9770	0.9774	0.9778
	cos	0.2250	0.2232	0.2215	0.2198	0.2181	0.2164	0.2147	0.2130	0.2113	0.2096
	tan	4.3315	4.3662	4.4015	4.4374	4.4737	4.5107	4.5483	4.5864	4.6252	4.6646
78	sin	0.9781	0.9785	0.9789	0.9792	0.9796	0.9799	0.9803	0.9806	0.9810	0.9813
	cos	0.2079	0.2062	0.2045	0.2028	0.2011	0.1994	0.1977	0.1959	0.1942	0.1925
	tan	4.7046	4.7453	4.7867	4.8288	4.8716	4.9152	4.9594	5.0045	5.0504	5.0970
79	sin	0.9816	0.9820	0.9823	0.9826	0.9829	0.9833	0.9836	0.9839	0.9842	0.9845
	cos	0.1908	0.1891	0.1874	0.1857	0.1840	0.1822	0.1805	0.1788	0.1771	0.1754
	tan	5.1446	5.1929	5.2422	5.2924	5.3435	5.3955	5.4486	5.5026	5.5578	5.6140
80	sin	0.9848	0.9851	0.9854	0.9857	0.9860	0.9863	0.9866	0.9869	0.9871	0.9874
	cos	0.1736	0.1719	0.1702	0.1685	0.1668	0.1650	0.1633	0.1616	0.1599	0.1582
	tan	5.6713	5.7297	5.7894	5.8502	5.9124	5.9758	6.0405	6.1066	6.1742	6.2432
81	sin	0.9877	0.9880	0.9882	0.9885	0.9888	0.9890	0.9893	0.9895	0.9898	0.9900
	cos	0.1564	0.1547	0.1530	0.1513	0.1495	0.1478	0.1461	0.1444	0.1426	0.1409
	tan	6.3138	6.3859	6.4596	6.5350	6.6122	6.6912	6.7720	6.8548	6.9395	7.0264
82	sin	0.9903	0.9905	0.9907	0.9910	0.9912	0.9914	0.9917	0.9919	0.9921	0.9923
	cos	0.1392	0.1374	0.1357	0.1340	0.1323	0.1305	0.1288	0.1271	0.1253	0.1236
	tan	7.1154	7.2066	7.3002	7.3962	7.4947	7.5958	7.6996	7.8062	7.9158	8.0285
DEGREES	FUNCTION	0'	6'	12'	18'	24'	30'	36'	42'	48'	54'

TABLE 6
NATURAL TRIGONOMETRIC FUNCTIONS (continued)

DEGREES	FUNCTION	0.0°	0.1°	0.2°	0.3°	0.4°	0.5°	0.6°	0.7°	0.8°	0.9°
83	sin	0.9925	0.9928	0.9930	0.9932	0.9934	0.9936	0.9938	0.9940	0.9942	0.9943
	cos	0.1219	0.1201	0.1184	0.1167	0.1149	0.1132	0.1115	0.1097	0.1080	0.1063
	tan	8.1443	8.2636	8.3863	8.5126	8.6427	8.7769	8.9152	9.0579	9.2052	9.3572
84	sin	0.9945	0.9947	0.9949	0.9951	0.9952	0.9954	0.9956	0.9957	0.9959	0.9960
	cos	0.1045	0.1028	0.1011	0.0993	0.0976	0.0958	0.0941	0.0924	0.0906	0.0889
	tan	9.5144	9.6768	9.8448	10.02	10.20	10.39	10.58	10.78	10.99	11.20
85	sin	0.9962	0.9963	0.9965	0.9966	0.9968	0.9969	0.9971	0.9972	0.9973	0.9974
	cos	0.0872	0.0854	0.0837	0.0819	0.0802	0.0785	0.0767	0.0750	0.0732	0.0715
	tan	11.43	11.66	11.91	12.16	12.43	12.71	13.00	13.30	13.62	13.95
86	sin	0.9976	0.9977	0.9978	0.9979	0.9980	0.9981	0.9982	0.9983	0.9984	0.9985
	cos	0.0698	0.0680	0.0663	0.0645	0.0628	0.0610	0.0593	0.0576	0.0558	0.0541
	tan	14.30	14.67	15.06	15.46	15.89	16.35	16.83	17.34	17.89	18.46
87	sin	0.9986	0.9987	0.9988	0.9989	0.9990	0.9990	0.9991	0.9992	0.9993	0.9993
	cos	0.0523	0.0506	0.0488	0.0471	0.0454	0.0436	0.0419	0.0401	0.0384	0.0366
	tan	19.08	19.74	20.45	21.20	22.02	22.90	23.86	24.90	26.03	27.27
88	sin	0.9994	0.9995	0.9995	0.9996	0.9996	0.9997	0.9997	0.9997	0.9998	0.9998
	cos	0.0349	0.0332	0.0314	0.0297	0.0279	0.0262	0.0244	0.0227	0.0209	0.0192
	tan	28.64	30.14	31.82	33.69	35.80	38.19	40.92	44.07	47.74	52.08
89	sin	0.9998	0.9999	0.9999	0.9999	0.9999	1.000	1.000	1.000	1.000	1.000
	cos	0.0175	0.0157	0.0140	0.0122	0.0105	0.0087	0.0070	0.0052	0.0035	0.0017
	tan	57.29	63.66	71.62	81.85	95.49	114.6	143.2	191.0	286.5	573.0
DEGREES	FUNCTION	0′	6′	12′	18′	24′	30′	36′	42′	48′	54′

ANSWERS TO ODD-NUMBERED EXERCISES

Chapter One
Fractions

Page 1

1. $\frac{8}{12}$ 3. $\frac{25}{40}$ 5. $\frac{21}{224}$
7. $\frac{45}{320}$ 9. $\frac{5}{16}$ 11. $\frac{1}{4}$
13. $\frac{3}{8}$ 15. $\frac{3}{8}$ 17. $\frac{1}{2}$
19. $\frac{7}{8}$ 21. $\frac{3}{4}$

Page 3

1. $\frac{8}{16}, \frac{12}{16}, \frac{5}{16}$ 3. $\frac{8}{12}, \frac{9}{12}, \frac{4}{12}$ 5. $\frac{9}{36}, \frac{24}{36}, \frac{16}{36}$

7. $\frac{14}{16}, \frac{12}{16}, \frac{3}{16}$ 9. $\frac{44}{64}, \frac{48}{64}, \frac{9}{64}$

Page 3

1. 4   3. 40   5. 12
7. 32   9. 90   11. 28
13. 15   15. 42   17. $\frac{6}{36}$
19. $\frac{30}{36}$ 21. $\frac{21}{36}$ 23. $\frac{26}{36}$
25. $\frac{33}{36}$ 27. $\frac{36}{36}$

Page 4

1. $2\frac{2}{3}$ 3. $13\frac{1}{3}$ 5. $26\frac{1}{5}$
7. $8\frac{3}{4}$ 9. $6\frac{5}{8}$

Page 4

1. $\frac{25}{4}$ 3. $\frac{37}{5}$ 5. $\frac{45}{2}$
7. $\frac{41}{4}$ 9. $\frac{1001}{2}$

Page 7

1. $13\frac{1}{8}$ 3. $10\frac{2}{3}$ 5. $13\frac{3}{4}$
7. 15

Page 8

1. $10\frac{1}{2}$ 3. $14\frac{5}{8}$ 5. $4\frac{1}{8}$
7. $2\frac{3}{4}$

Page 10

1. $\frac{9}{16}''$ 3. $2\frac{15}{16}''$ 5. $1\frac{5}{8}''$
7. $67\frac{1}{2}$ lb   9. $2''$

Page 12

1. $\frac{8}{21}$ 3. $\frac{5}{18}$ 5. $\frac{1}{2}$
7. $1\frac{1}{6}$ 9. $2\frac{2}{3}$ 11. $2\frac{1}{4}$

Page 13

1. $\frac{2}{5}$ 3. 6   5. 6
7. $\frac{4}{15}$ 9. $\frac{65}{72}$ 11. $\frac{8}{15}$

Page 14

1. 56   3. 12   5. $\frac{5}{8}$
7. 20   9. 36   11. $2\frac{1}{2}$
13. 5   15. 10

Page 17

1. $B = 31\frac{7}{8}''$ 3. $A = 39\frac{3}{8}''$
    $1 = 33\frac{1}{2}''$ $B = 14''$

Page 18

1. $15'1''$ 3. $35'5''$ 5. $31'4''$
7. $39'6\frac{1}{4}''$ 9. $36'4''$

Page 19

1. $4'2\frac{1}{4}''$ 3. $27'10\frac{1}{4}''$ 5. $109'1\frac{3}{4}''$

Page 20

1. $12'5''$ 3. $82'8\frac{1}{2}''$ 5. $65'3''$

Page 21

1. $1'2\frac{1}{2}''$ 3. $24\frac{2}{3}''$ 5. $25\frac{1}{8}''$

Page 21

1. 31   3. 90   5. $3''$
7. $A = 10\frac{1}{2}''$ 9. 232
    $B = 1\frac{3}{4}''$ 11. $54'$
    $C = 8\frac{3}{4}$ 13. $79,500.00
    $D = 3\frac{3}{4}''$
    $E = 6\frac{3}{4}''$

Chapter Two
Decimal Fractions

Page 30

1. 0.03   3. 400.082   5. 666.0666
7. 557,000   9. 0.0004

Page 30

1. 4.828   3. 852.025   5. 8.8088
7. 0.1111   9. 1.69

Page 31

1. 0.015   3. 12,900   5. 100.000
7. 38.373   9. 11.111

Page 32

1. 3   3. 3   5. 6
7. 5   9. 4   11. 4
13. 0.0422   15. 0.683   17. 18.6
19. 0.349

Page 33

1. 11.8	3. 96.5	5. 0.000350
7. 41.0	9. 82.4	

Page 34

1. 4120.000	3. 114.375	5. 396.000
7. 4.800	9. 8.000	

Page 35

1. 314.56	3. 268.2	5. 0.66
7. 1940.2	9. 1762.4	11. 0.0001
13. 0.1414		

Page 36

1. 0.125	3. 0.857	5. 0.312

Page 37

1. $\frac{13}{16}$	3. $\frac{4}{16}$	5. $\frac{25}{32}$
7. $\frac{4}{32}$	9. $\frac{27}{64}$	11. $\frac{7}{64}$

Page 38

1. 0.8806″	3. 0.900″	5. 1.635″
0.8826″	0.860″	1.615″
7. 2.363″	9. 81.5″	

Page 42

1. 0.8125″	3. 0.069″	5. 3.3525″
7. 0.815″	9. 1,100 lb	11. 0.7281″
13. 0.2844	15. 30	0.7231″
17. 20.44″	19. 6.53″	21. 2.374″
23. 1.4235″		
1.4290″		

Chapter Three
Percentage

Page 53

1. 32%	3. 30%	5. 4%
7. 3.3%	9. 300%	11. 100.8%
13. 10.9%	15. 159%	17. 50%
19. 37.5%	21. 7.5%	23. 133%
25. 0.25	27. 0.07	29. 0.62
31. 0.15	33. 0.03	35. 0.835

Page 54

1. 18	3. 4.48	5. 0.12
7. 23.5	9. 0.014	

Page 55

1. 50%	3. 11.8%	5. 2.4%
7. 2.6%	9. 37.5%	

Page 56

1. 20	3. 310	5. 35.88
7. 3.5067	9. 22.61	

Page 59

1. 47%
   53%
3. 978%
5. Medical $4.80. Before deductions $480.00.
   Take-home $355.20. Income tax $96.00.
7. 64%
9. 14.5%
11. 13.21%
13. $13.49
15. $709.80
17. 76.3%

Chapter Four
Metric System

Page 71

1. 2.2 kg
3. 1.28 km
5. 187 cm
7. 528 L
9. 0.084 kg
11. 87200 cm
13. 6.784 m

Page 71

1. 0.9525 cm to 9.525 mm
3. 1.27 cm to 12.7 mm
5. 1.5875 cm to 15.875 mm
7. 1.905 cm to 19.05 mm
9. 2.2225 cm to 22.2250 mm

Page 75

1. 0.635 mm
3. 0.05 mm; 0.1 mm; 0.15 mm;
   0.25 mm; 0.56 mm
5. 15 × 260 mm
7. 24 km/h; 40 km/h; 64 km/h;
   80 km/h; 88 km/h
9. 8.1 h
11. 8.23 km
13. 1.18″;
    59.84″
15. 2.5 mm
17. 306 cm
19. 1 cm
21. 26 mm; 80 mm
23. 34.9 cm
25. 26.7 kL
27. 12 mm

Chapter Five
Squares and Square
Roots

Page 86

1. 2.9
3. 1.3
5. 0.92
7. 94.3
9. 6.5
11. 1.2
13. 4.8
15. 0.79

Page 88

1. 180,625
3. 2,689,600
5. 0.0000792
7. 1050

Page 92

1. 9.2
3. 469
5. 0.80

Page 94

1. 49.6′
3. 41.6 cm
5. 9.18′
7. 45.8 cm

Chapter Six
Perimeters,
Areas, and
Volumes

Page 99

1. 14′
3. 0.23′
5. 2184 yd
7. 14.7″
9. 168″
11. 12300′

Page 100

1. 6.28′
3. 15.7″
5. 17.27 cm

Page 104

1.	40 in²	3.	880 in²	5.	64 in²
7.	42 cm²	9.	18 cm	11.	100 cm
			1018 cm²		7854 cm²

Page 110

1. 3.8025 in²   3. 4.03 in²

Page 112

1. 0.8459 in²   3. 0.8458 in²

Page 116

1. 58.4 in³   3. 67.5 in³   5. 359 in³

Page 117

1. V = 198 in³   W = 56 lb

Page 124

1. a = 2.85 yd³   3. 4.72 yd³
   b = 13.43 yd³
   c = $529.10
   d = 80 bags
   e = 60,220 lb

Chapter Seven
Ratio and
Proportion

Page 131

1. 600 kg to 20 kg, or 30 to 1   3. 180 cents to 30 cents, or 6 to 1
5. 600 rpm to 400 rpm, or 1.5 to 1   7. 60 kL to 0.1 kL, or 600 to 1
9. 8400 m to 12 m, or 700 to 1

Page 132

1. 7.84   3. 0.70
5. $3,655.27; $5,227.88; $6,686.48   7. 31; 49
9. 81.4%

Page 138

1.	1.2	3.	4.5	5.	26.875
7.	4	9.	250		

Page 139

1.	210 km	3.	770 kg	5.	195'
7.	Yes. 2.275 h	9.	5280 kg		

Page 142

1.	3500 rpm	3.	21.25 h	5.	843.75 rpm
7.	164 rpm				

Page 148

1. 1062 kg   3. 6827 lb   5. 2756 lb

Page 150

1.	10.2″	3.	172 lb	5.	113.2 m²
7.	480 kL	9.	490 gal		

Page 157

1. $x = 4a$
3. $3z = b - 4$
5. $p/3 = 45$
7. $2\frac{1}{2}p = b - 6$
9. $0.6x + 3x + 2.9x = xy$

Page 159

1. -6
3. -50
5. 34.21
7. -151
9. $1\frac{3}{4}$
11. -60
13. 136
15. -103
17. 0.041
19. $8\frac{7}{10}$
21. $a = 44°$ $b = 54°$ $c = 34°$
$d = 10°$ $e = 30°$

Page 161

1. -144
3. 12
5. -180
7. -4
9. 6
11. -2
13. -36

Page 163

1. 17
3. $-\frac{1}{5}$
5. 1
7. 0

Page 163

1. $-4a$
3. $12x$
5. $-103xy$
7. $4a + 25b$
9. $28z - 300$
11. $3xy$
13. $28y$
15. $-1.2cd$
17. $41ab$
19. $103a$

Page 164

1. $6a^2b$
3. $-125x^2y$
5. $-48a^2b^2$
7. a^2b
9. $-96a$

Page 165

1. 4
3. -5
5. -1
7. -4
9. $42b - 1$

Page 165

1. $18xy - 12x^2$
3. $-6x^2 + 24x$
5. $-5x - 5y + 5z$
7. $4b + 8$
9. $14b + x^2 - xy + 4x$

Page 166

1. 5
3. -14
5. -27
7. 25
9. 27
11. 9
13. $290\ \Omega$
15. $39\ V$
17. $12.5°$
19. 0

Page 170

1. 4
3. -3
5. 4.29
7. -0.3
9. 0.333
11. 11.78 cm
13. $360\ \Omega$
15. $4.33\ A$
17. $36''$

Page 173

1. 18
3. 1.5
5. 22.5
7. 27.5
9. 2
11. 5
13. $19,360$
15. 0.083
17. 8
19. 1344
21. $9.6''$
23. $8.125\ h$
25. 10.026 cm

Page 176

1. $\frac{23}{27}$
3. $8\frac{1}{3}$
5. 2
7. -3.5
9. 2.35 cm
11. $20°$
13. $121.3°$
15. 90 cm

Page 179

1. $A = 8b + ac$
3. $A = AD/2 + 0.78540^2$
5. $A = 2S^2$

Page 181

1. $a = 9$
   $b = 3.52$ in
3. $a = 23.5$ in^2
   $b = 5.48$ in
   $c = 0.859$ ft or 10.3 in
5. $a = 450$ rpm
   $b = 13.5$ in
   $c = 100$ rpm
7. $a = 91.4$ rpm
   $b = 0.393$ in

Chapter Nine
Powers of Ten

Page 192

1. 1.26×10^2
3. 4.35×10^8
5. 6.756×10^1
7. 8.657×10^5
9. 1.597×10^8

Page 192

1. 8.56×10^{-3}
3. 4.18×10^{-4}
5. 1.6×10^{-2}
7. 1.8×10^2
9. 7.94×10^{-9}

Page 193

1. 4.77×10^6
3. 4.00×10^{-6}
5. 1.10×10^{-3}
7. 4.21×10^3
9. 4.5×10^6

Page 194

1. 1.56×10^3
3. 1.90×10^5
5. 1.63×10^5
7. 2.00×10^{-6}
9. 1.30×10^6

Page 197

1. $1.40 \times 10^4\%$
3. 5.11×10^2 oz
5. 2.21×10^6 gal
7. \$111,055
9. 1.34 s

Page 200

1. 1.2×10^1 1.44×10^2 1.44×10^2
3. 1.31×10^{-3} 1.72×10^{-6} 1.72×10^{-6}
5. 6.8×10^{-3} 46.24×10^{-6} 4.62×10^{-5}
7. 3.24×10^8 10.49×10^{16} 1.05×10^{17}
9. 6.47×10^9 41.86×10^{18} 4.19×10^{19}

Page 200

1. 1.26×10^2 1.12×10^1
3. 1.23×10^{-4} 1.11×10^{-2}
5. 4.35×10^8 2.09×10^4
7. 14×10^6 3.74×10^3
9. 43.07×10^6 6.61×10^3

Page 201

1. 9.06×10^3
3. 2.57×10^{-2}
5. 3×10^{-6}

**Chapter Ten
Right Triangle
Trigonometry**

Page 209

	Sin	Cos	Tan
1.			
$a = 0.8829$		0.4695	1,881
$b = 0.6921$		0.7216	0.9589
$c = 0.1495$		0.9887	0.1512
$d = 0.993$		0.0366	27.27
$e = 0.7071$		0.7071	1.0

3. $a = 45°$ $b = 55.2°$ $c = 5.62°$
    $d = 74.3°$ $e = 18.9°$

5. 0.5934   7. 0.9291   9. 77.4°

Page 211

1. 25.5″   3. 12.6″   5. 6.54″

Page 212

1. 103 cm   3. 77.9 in   5. 6.56 cm

Page 213

1. 69.8 m   3. 275′   5. 0.043″

Page 215

1. 33.9°   3. 60°   5. 53.3°

Page 219

1. 16.4″   3. 12 mm   5. 2.2″

1255